A Spoilt Boy

A Spoilt Boy

Frederic Raphael

ORION

First published in Great Britain in 2003 by
Orion Books Ltd.
Orion House, 5 Upper St Martin's Lane,
London WC2H 9EA

A CIP catalogue record for this book is
available from the British Library

ISBN 0 75285 584 0

Typeset by Selwood Systems, Midsomer Norton

Printed and bound by Butler & Tanner Ltd,
Frome and London

For Beetle and our children,
and our grandchildren,
always.

ST LOUIS, MISSOURI, in the humid midsummer of 1933 or 1934. I am two or thee years old. I am being driven by my mother, Irene Rose Mauser Raphael, a slim, beautiful, page-boyed brunette in her early twenties, along a tree-lined street, typical of suburban St Louis, with houses high on each side, at the top of banks of sun-tanned grass. Stone steps go up in the middle of each block.

My mother parks the car (a two-door grey Plymouth) and tells me that we are going to visit a friend of hers. We climb the stone steps from the kerb to a narrow sidewalk at the level where flame trees have been planted. We go along a few yards and then up four wooden steps to the screened porch of a white clapboard house. My mother pushes the bell. A woman comes to greet us and invites us into the main room. I have been promised that this friend of my mother's has a little boy my own age for me to play with.

At first he does not appear. My mother and her friend chat and then, with a rush of naked feet on carpeted boards, a small blond child of my age runs into the living room, where there is a patterned carpet, with a tasselled fringe at each end. I am conscious that I am wearing shoes. The boy has blue eyes and curly whitish hair and he is happily naked from the waist down. He takes his stance in front of us, with his hips thrust out, and pisses without the smallest hesitation or shame. The yellow arc gushes and puddles and darkens the reddish brown of the carpet. It begins to splash. The boy's mother does not reproach or attempt to stop him. I sense that he is stronger than she is. His veined white penis tapers to a point. He goes on to the last drop. Then he looks at us and turns and runs out towards the back of the house.

My first memory of thinking anything at all is of that

moment. My thought was envious and explicit: 'I shall never, never be as bold and shameless as that, and I wish I could be.'

I have no memory of where we lived in St Louis. I know only that my father worked for Shell Oil and that one of my mother's aunts, Annette, I think, owned a wholesale bakery where I was left a few times while my mother was at her art class. Flour was stored in an annexe with blanched wooden partitions. The bakers wore white smocks and paper forage caps. Their faces were ghostly with flour.

When my mother came to collect me, we walked to the car, which was parked on an incline where there were rows of lock-up garages. She showed me her tools for working clay. Pouched in a canvas roll, like dentist's equipment, they were made of smooth wood. I looked at them without admiration. Though pleasant to the touch, they were what took her away from me.

I had by this age already been to England, but I had no memory of it. My father was British (Cedric's parents, Amy and Ellis Raphael, lived at 74 Cromwell Road) and Shell gave its British employees 'home leave' every three years. Cedric and Irene took me across the Atlantic on the SS *Scythia* when I was eighteen months old. The crossing was biliously rough. My father spent much of his time walking the deck, tight-lipped with the effort to keep down his sea-sickness. However, he almost certainly managed to play in the contract bridge games arranged by the purser. On nights when the storm allowed (the crossing took nine days), he no less certainly wanted to dance with his pretty young wife, even when the ballroom floor rolled its dinner-jacketed and evening-dressed occupants from one side to the other, while the tilted band played on. Their music stands were screwed to the floor of their dais.

Before Cedric met Irene, he had been world amateur

champion of the tango. His partner's name was Phyllis; she turned pro when Cedric left England. One of his closest friends in the world of ballroom dancing was Victor Silvester. 'Ginger' invited Cedric to be his manager when he formed a 'strict tempo' dance band. My father refused, partly because such an activity was ungentlemanly and partly because he saw no future in it. Victor Silvester's band became enormously successful; he sold millions of records. His slogan, 'slow-slow-quick-quick-slow', set the pace for correct tempo in an age of emulous rectitude. 'Ginger' was a regular broadcaster, though he never sounded easy in front of a microphone. It was as if his voice too wore a toupee. A little older than Cedric, he had been sent to Flanders as a young officer. His first duty had been to supervise the firing squad at the execution of a so-called coward.

During the roughest of Atlantic crossings, Irene ate her meals, often almost alone in the cabin-class dining room, appetite undiminished, if not enhanced, by the absence of other passengers. Thin wooden margins hinged upwards along the sides of the table to prevent dishes from sliding on to the floor or into the diners' laps; glasses were bunkered in shallow round sconces.

Cedric was used to shipboard life, though never to the sea. Since he had missed being transported to Flanders (he had just been commissioned as an officer in the Buffs when the Armistice was declared*), his first overseas trip was to India,

---

*When in Officers' Training Camp, on Wimbledon Common, Cedric found the breakfasts, of undercooked and often rancid bacon, particularly repulsive. His attitude to being a Jew was always eclectic: it would have seemed ignominious to him to conceal his 'religion', but he had no inclination to practise it. In the circumstances, however, he felt justified in going to his CO and explaining that it was against his religious principles to eat any form of pork. The next morning, he was the only officer cadet to receive a neatly fried egg for breakfast. After he explained the ruse he had adopted in order to be so privileged, a

with ICI. He joined the company soon after coming down from Oxford in the early twenties. A natural mathematician, he had been coerced into reading Greats and, partly on account of illness, he had not obtained a good degree. He still had his orange-bound Oxford texts with their neat interlinear annotations.

Cedric was a versatile athlete, who might have got his Oxford Blue for golf, had the final trials not taken place on a wet afternoon which so blurred his glasses that he could not keep his eye on the ball. In fine weather, he kept bespectacled wicket for Nomads, a touring club of slightly Bohemian provenance. Although not a big man, he had played rugger for St Paul's (and broken his collar bone).

Apart from dancing, Cedric's abiding passion was for bridge, which he passed on to his son. When I first showed signs of being a bad loser (which I remain), Cedric told me that I must learn to accept defeat with a smile. On the P&O liner on which he travelled to India, he had been mortified to overhear someone whom he had partnered at bridge refer to him as 'that sulky young man'. Thenceforth, by an effort of will, he eliminated all trace of emotion, whether triumphant or rueful, when playing games. In life itself, modesty became an expression of pride. The habit of eloquent reticence interdicted loud or prolonged speech. I knew my father both sentimental and sardonic, but I never heard him raise his voice, although in old age he did sometimes weep, silently.

number of his fellow officers-to-be (among them Charles Graves, whose poet brother Robert was to be up at St John's, Oxford, with my father) asked what you had to do to become a Jew. The requirements proved too surgical to provoke any mass apostasy. However, Cedric was more admired for his ingenuity than scorned for his alien piety. He seems rarely to have encountered anti-Semitism during his youth. He did once tell me, however, that when, aged six, he was first sent to boarding school, at Ascot House, in Brighton, a boy called him 'a name'. Sheenie? He 'knocked him over his tuck box', after which he had no further trouble.

As a young sahib, Cedric was instructed to walk along the Calcutta pavements brushing natives into the gutter in order to retain their respect. One day, he had a violent attack of renal colic in the street. The agony caused him to fall to the ground and contract himself into a foetal bean. Indians gathered round and watched his convulsions with unpitying and garrulous curiosity. Knowing that he must not lose face, he huddled there until the attack eased and then he hobbled to the club, from which, of course, all natives were banned.

After a shortened stay in India, he was invalided home, where he was operated on for kidney stones by a friend from his dancing days. Teddy Slesinger promised that it was a simple process. He later became a distinguished children's surgeon, but he was never an abdominal specialist. In his overconfidence, he severed Cedric's urethra during the operation, and repaired it ineptly. His patient suffered for the rest of his life from a stricture which, from time to time, prevented him, painfully, from urinating. It also led to a series of infections, and of quack cures, as agonising as they were useless.

Having left ICI, Cedric worked for a while in the City of London, at Japhet's, the merchant bankers. After an incident of which I should hear only when I was eighteen, Cedric decided to go to America and start a new life. Thanks to social connections in London, he was able to join the recently formed Royal Dutch Shell. His first job was as a salesman in Chicago, a city whose corrupt mayor, 'Big' Bill Thompson, later threatened to punch the king of England in the nose if he dared to pay a visit to his city. There were many Irishmen among Big Bill's electors.

Cedric went to the States on an immigrant visa which, in principle, authorised him to stay indefinitely. Despite his Oxford accent, and his Jewishness, he soon became a successful salesman. One of his best customers was a Fenian gas-station owner who embraced him warmly, thirty years later, when my father was on his retirement tour of the US.

Cedric relished the (dance) music and social life of Chicago. He wore seersucker suits in the summer, and ear flaps in the scathing winters. He met Irene on the blizzardy Christmas Eve of 1929, at the Edgewater Beach Hotel, on a blind date. A bright student, she had had to renounce all hope of going to college because of her father's bankruptcy. In the midst of the Depression, she had found a job as secretary to an architect and no difficulty in acquiring more or less urgent beaux in the artistic community. One of them smuggled a copy of James Joyce's *Ulysses* back from Paris. Irene carried it ostentatiously under her arm, though I doubt if she read as far as the adventures of Cunty Kate. Another arty admirer had a room lined entirely with silver paper. None had the remote magic of an Oxford graduate who danced like an angel and, no doubt, told her she was one.

Irene Rose Mauser was nineteen when she married Cedric Michael Raphael, in July 1930. He was thirty. He could not afford to buy a wedding ring, but another Irish friend, James Patrick Donovan, immediately wrote him a cheque for the necessary (very small) diamonds. Cedric's gratitude was mitigated when the cheque bounced; it took weeks to amortise Donovan's generosity. I was born, in the Grant Hospital, on 14 August 1931.

Irene kept a copy of the *Chicago Tribune* of the day. Gangland slayings (unless of the bloody scale of the St Valentine's Day massacre of 14 February 1929) were almost too banal to deserve the front page. The *Trib* did, however, carry the story of a driver who had been stopped, on Lakeshore Drive, and given a ticket for going at thirty-one miles an hour instead of the regulation thirty. He was quoted as having told the cops, 'Seems you can't get away with anything in Chicago these days, except murder.'

If I did not find my first trip to London memorable, Irene never forgot hers. It was a long way from Kansas City, where she had been born, to the cultural centre of the English-speaking world. Her plump baby was admired by Cedric's many aunts and uncles (neither he nor she had any brothers or sisters), but Americans were not to be encouraged. Youth made Irene vulnerable; beauty made her alarming. Cedric's mother, Amelia Sophia, was one of a quartet who had been known as 'the beautiful Benson sisters'. Cedric's very young bride reminded her of her age.

The sisters' family name, when they were born, had not been Benson, but Bebro. They had several brothers, with various talents. The oldest, Frederick Jessel, became a very rich financier. It was said that when a salesman came to his office to sell him life insurance, he left with a sheaf of shares in one of Jessel's companies. Frederic Michael Raphael was named in honour of Jessel, with whom Cedric had been quite a favourite, especially as a golf partner.

Another uncle, Lionel, was a bachelor barrister who – so I was later promised – once amused a judge (who presumably liked chestnuts) by saying in court, 'I deny the allegation and defy the alligator.' There is no evidence that he also won his case. Lionel was a man of forthright humour (when a man spat in the underground, Lionel called him a 'filthy beast'), but he did not live long enough to have a successful career at the bar.

Yet another brother, Harry, was the reason why his siblings elected to change their name in early adulthood. Harry was a charmer whose forte was coaxing old ladies out of their money. Like a malign but no less plausible Jessel, he sold shares in non-existent companies and invested the funds of credulous conquests in his own fugitive bank accounts. When the law caught up with him, though never with the money, 'FLASH HARRY'*, (as the cheaper prints headlined him)

---

*I had an American great-uncle who was also involved in a con trick, but as the mark not the villain. Mitchell was a poker player who won a was sentenced to ten years' penal servitude. He was not defended by Lionel.

The family met in urgent, shamed conclave. It was agreed that the name Bebro was tainted beyond reprieve. In any case, it had a distinctly foreign tinge. After some debate, it was almost unanimously decided to convert to Benson, which would not involve changing the initials on handkerchieves, tortoiseshell hairbrushes and other personal belongings. The only dissenter was one of the brothers, Godfrey, a stamp dealer (British Empire and Colonial) whom I later visited in his little house in Clapham. He declared that he saw no reason to cower behind a new, supposedly more Gentile name. Since the beautiful Benson sisters were indeed reluctant to be known to be Jewish, they were indignant at Godfrey's insolently accurate assessment of their motives. They informed him that they would not allow him to become a Benson; he would have to remain a Bebro. Godfrey was a mild man, and the least successful (as well as the longest-lived) of the siblings, but he was not without pride; rejecting his sisters' *diktat*, he neither became a Benson nor remained a Bebro. He changed his name simply to Godfrey, by which singular style he signed himself – like an abrupt English lord – for the rest of his long life.

The Benson sisters came originally from Manchester, as did many tough-minded English Jews, but they had their eyes on London (the West End, of course). I never discovered what kind of fortune my English great-grandparents might have had, nor yet its source, but the sisters seem to have followed their brothers into a comfortable level of metropolitan society without much difficulty. The most

lot of money in a game that was rigged to fleece him. Having got lucky quickly, he decided to have an early night, which did not amuse the mobsters who were setting him up before making a sucker out of him. They followed him into the alley and got their money back by shooting him dead.

striking of them was Minnie. Her violet eyes literally glowed in the dark, or gloom, of the Oakwood Court flat where she irregularly entertained Cedric's family to tea. It was wheeled in on a creaking trolley, with a silver teapot and a chafing dish for scones, by a maid in frilly cap and apron. At the time of Irene's first trip to England, Minnie was a *grande dame*, with a booming contralto voice on which, so she said, the Prince of Wales had congratulated her when she sang for him, and the troops, during the Great War.

Ethel too had a remarkable voice, and a stagey manner, though it was nothing compared to that of Cedric's paternal maiden aunt Polly, who had once been told that she looked like Marie Tempest. She thenceforth made every effort to match her expression, and profile, to the star's. Ethel also sang for the troops, while in the VADs, but she never married. Her sisters said that she considered no one to be good enough for her. Ethel lived in furnished rooms, first in Oxford and Cambridge Gardens and then in Chepstow Square. With age, she became more eccentric, but never less affable. She wore a green eye shade, like some provincial editor, and did elaborate, Balinesque, neck exercises in public.

At Christmas 1938, Ethel arrived at my grandparents' flat, white-bearded in a Santa Claus outfit, with a sack over her shoulder. She gave me a bus conductor's outfit, complete with ticket rack, and (since I had no other children with whom to play) she impersonated both a variety of passengers and a stern inspector. So far as I know, she never had a job and lived on a minuscule stipend bequeathed by her brother Jessel. Had there ever been a man in her life?

In the Edwardian age, Minnie and her sisters (Rosie was the fourth) were in the habit of taking holidays at the Grand Hotel, Eastbourne. Amy had married my grandfather, Ellis, a mild man who worked all his life for Raphael Tuck & Co. Tucks were renowned manufacturers of Christmas and

9

birthday cards (and three-ply jigsaw puzzles). Their fame, and fortune, lasted until after the Second World War. Reluctance to adopt more modern styles led to their decline and eclipse.

Ellis was a loyal servant of three generations: Gustave and Sir Adolphe were Raphael Tuck's heirs, Desmond his grandson. The walls of Adolphe's house, in Hamilton Terrace, were filled, from floor to ceiling, with the paintings from which greetings cards had been reproduced. My grandfather's fidelity was rewarded with a good salary, and with a four-door Austin saloon, which came with a peak-capped chauffeur called Theobald.

Marriage was endured, rather than enjoyed, by all my grandparents. Ellis was always in a hurry to get to 'business', which was his main pleasure. 'Can't stop,' was his customary, and unchallengeable, exit line. Amy had been the only one of the sisters to marry a Jew. This did not exempt her from distaste for the Chosen. On holiday, she and her sisters would sit in the palm court of the Grand Hotel and watch the revolving doors. When someone of Semitic appearance pushed into view, Minnie's voice would boom the single, denunciatory word 'Fish!'

The only other term which I know in the sisters' private language has no accessible etymology. When someone said something in their company that one of them suspected of being a lie, she would say, in a guileless tone, 'Have you seen anything of Mrs Hippum recently?' Who Mrs Hippum was, I cannot say; nor does cold print quite convey the guttural pronunciation of the 'h' (which was rasped out rather like the modern Greek *chi*). My father's use of this quizzical term was always enough to make his mother gasp and wince with uncontrollable and lachrymose giggles which not infrequently had to be treated with smelling salts.

Minnie's beauty had commanded a range of suitable suitors. She married money, twice, and was very happy with it; her second husband, who owned Cerebos salt, died and left her a large fortune. 'Mrs France' had by then converted to Christianity. She instructed Irene in the niceties of class. After being informed that Jews could never be ladies, Irene dared to say, 'But you're a lady, Min.' 'I was never a lady,' Minnie said, 'until I became a Christian.' Her charity began, and ended, at home. When her neighbour bought a Rolls-Royce, she went into her room, prayed, and then went and bought herself one.

Minnie had one daughter, Ivy, who was plump and plain. Embellished by her mother's money, Ivy was briefly married, to Maudie Doll, an England cricketer (amateur, of course) and mothered a son, Jimmy, who later flew thirty missions over Germany as observer – one wing only sewn over his breast pocket – in a Lancaster of Bomber Command. Ivy lived much of her divorced adult life in her mother's cavernous Oakwood Court flat. Despite thick white fingers, she was a pianist of almost professional competence. Required by her mother to play for the company on Sunday afternoons, she favoured Brahms, who caused her to sigh heavily, not least when she was being applauded: since she carried her musical gift like yet another undeserved burden, she did not solicit encores. Another Ivy, the novelist Ivy Compton-Burnett, lived in the same block of Victorian flats; she might have relished the sonorous domination which Mrs France exercised over her sadly cowed daughter.

When I was four years old, Shell transferred my father from St Louis to the American head office, in Rockefeller Center, New York City. If my mother's parents were no more happily married than my father's, they endured their unhappiness less resignedly, and took the opportunity to part. I had no notion of why my grandmother, Fanny, accompanied us to New York. She spent most of the trip in the 'rumble-seat' of the Plymouth. This ingenious, padded spare seat folded out from within the boot, or 'trunk' as we Americans called it. There was no cover from the rain, but its human luggage enjoyed a refreshing breeze as we headed north through the sweltering Midwest. Fanny was less privileged when we turned east, via Columbus, Ohio, and Aurora, Illinois, towards the Atlantic.

I remember being in the high-crowned car and pulling in at filling stations, Shell for preference, where the attendant had to pump the gas by hand into a pendant glass cylinder before discharging it into our tank. As we drove along the highway, my parents sang, to amuse me perhaps, a version of a current song, which went, 'The music goes round and round, aw-aw-aw Aurora.'

Men 'on relief' waited in kerbside lines in the small towns. In drab clothes and anonymising caps, they shared rumpled newspapers as they shuffled towards the steps of soup kitchens or employment agencies. Hermetically protected within the little car, we rolled past them as if they were scenery. My father's steady job and untroubled Englishness, no less than our metal shell, seemed to insulate us from any connection with their fate.

I have no memory of arriving in New York City, nor of where we lived before the film of memory grows bright and – on a cut as it were – we are already installed in an apartment at 30 W 70 St. Since the Depression was unabated, the landlord was eager to redecorate the empty rooms in whatever tones would secure him new tenants. My mother had the walls of the dining room painted egg-shell greeny-blue. Two pairs of lamp brackets with opaque, conical bulbs and imitation waxen drips on the mounts were also part of the inducement to sign the lease.

I cannot remember my room, but I recall mottled glass doors between the dining room and the living room. They could be slid wide open for festive occasions. The maid's room, where Irish and coloured helps later succeeded each other, was a small cell off the kitchen.

My grandmother Fanny was an unpretentious, fractious woman, of Lithuanian origin, at once sentimental and snappy. She had few social graces. When she did dress up, with a hat, she had the habit of saying, 'I look like a lady.' My father always replied, with untypical testiness, 'You *are* a lady, Fanny.' She used a number of catchphrases, which varied from the genial 'Sweet thing!' (accompanied by an open-handed caress of the hair) to the snappy 'Get away from me!', which shrugged off any attempt at apology or ingratiation. The latter phrase was applied, I suspect, in particular to her husband, Max.

Max Mauser had emigrated from Bad Kreuznach before the Great War. Having crossed the Atlantic, alone, when he was fourteen, he sought out an uncle in Missouri who was supposedly eager to welcome him. Having become – yes, sir! – One Hundred Per Cent American, Max was as amiable as his wife was tetchy. He was liked by most people, and trusted too many: scoundrelly buddies regularly relieved him of his money, of which there was little, and of his ideas for making a fortune, which were frequent. His best pal filched a patent which Max was guileless enough to share with him: it was for a detachable heel, which could be slid off a shoe when it was worn down, and replaced without the need for a cobbler. Folklore insists that Max's absconding partner made a fortune. There is, however, no evidence that the prosthetic heel ever went on the market. Perhaps the Shoemakers' Union bought and iced it.

Max and Fanny (who came from St Jo) lived in Kansas City both before their split and, eventually, after it. He was so blatantly honest that he was approached by one of the Prendergast mob, the gangsters who ran the city, and invited to become a health inspector. This would involve nothing more vigilant, or demanding, than going round the city's restaurants and awarding certificates of sanitary rectitude to those who had paid the right price to secure impartiality.

Only reluctant payers needed to have mouse droppings or roaches discovered in their kitchens and so be denied clearance. Max's honesty would alleviate all suspicion that the inspectorate was a racket. He declined the favour, politely, although the salary might have saved his marriage.

My first school was Ethical Culture. It was in a big building, only a block or two down from where W 70 St met Central Park West. There was a big upstairs room, with wide windows overlooking the park. We played with solid wooden building blocks, of different sizes. Each had holes drilled through it, which allowed them to be mounted on vertical metal rods. You had to reach way up to slot the next one into place. My teacher said that I was a very good little boy.

Many of my parents' friends sent their children to Ethical Culture. Central Park West was a catchment area inhabited mainly by middle-class Jews eager to assimilate with the America where they might be prospering but were not yet entirely at home. Ethical Culture was the duct through which Jewish kids were to be equipped with non-denominational morals, consistent with their origins, but not announcing them.

I walked to school every day past the surging Grecian colonnade of the Spanish and Portuguese synagogue. Iron railings between the columns deterred any curious visitors. I never saw anyone go in or out. My parents neither belonged to a New York 'temple' nor visited one, even on High Days and Holy Days. Christmas, on the other hand, was eagerly celebrated. The rite of decorating the tree (with a star at the top) was reserved for the grown-ups. I would get up on Christmas morning to find it all tinselled and lit up with conical coloured lights which were connected to a transformer to reduce the voltage.

Electricity was something to be very careful about. The

electric chair was the lurid symbol of what happened to murderers. The kidnapper of the Lindberghs' child was electrocuted when I was six. I made a false connection between this event and my grandfather's passion for Linberger cheese. Its smell, of unwashed feet, when it was disclosed in its heavy foil wrapper, caused Fanny to leave the room, if not the house.

Which Christmas did I get given my train set? It had broad rails, and a wind-up engine. The rails slotted together – male into female, though no one dreamed of putting it that way – to form a circle. The train went round and round, with the key turning slowly in its tin ribs. I was secretly disappointed that my new toy lacked the extension of the great freight trains which I had observed in the Midwest. We would wait at flashing level crossings while they clanked slowly past. Sometimes I could count up to ninety box-cars in a single clang-clanging, woo-wooing train. When did I first hear mention of 'riding the rails' and whispers about 'the Scottsboro boys' who were rail-roaded to an unjust death?

My parents' friends were never ideologically 'political', but 'anti-Fascism' was the natural attitude of Jews conscious of what was happening in Germany and of what (as a Sinclair Lewis best-seller warned) might yet happen in the US. The pro-Nazi German-American Bund was both strident and unnervingly popular in some districts of 'Jew York'. In general, however, anti-Semitism was banal. It was more with a smile than a wince that people spoke of the hotels in New England where, allegedly, there were signs 'No Dogs or Jews Allowed'. To avoid humiliation, many Jews took their holidays in hotels where only co-religionists would choose to go. There they were entertained by comedians with a repertoire of unabashed Yiddish and Jewish jokes of the kind which, when told by a Gentile, with whatever unprejudiced intentions, could cause my father to take terse offence. My parents never went near the 'Borscht belt' where shamelessly raucous establishments welcomed a clientele that revelled in unconcealed Jewishness.

My American grandparents, and their siblings, had a knowledge of Yiddish, and even my mother – in addition to calling my grandmother 'Fanschen', when in affectionate mode – sometimes made use of its sumptuous store of disparaging epithets. 'Shtuss' – meaning any kind of a mess – was particularly wide in its application, as was 'schtunk', meaning a fool. A schlump was something you did not want to look like; still less would you care to be taken for 'Itzig off the pickle boat'. Jews have rarely been slow to find ways of disparaging other Jews. The term 'kike', which was unforgivable on the lips of the goyim (a term my father never ever used), was first coined, it is said, by German American Jews to stigmatise those from eastern Europe, so many of whose names – before a good deal of Americanising truncation – ended in '-ski'. My father referred to Gentiles, if at all, as 'the Christians'. If he smiled at American Jewish humour, he rarely retailed it. However, I do recall his telling how one of my parents' friends, Seymour Wallace, was asked by his wife what was showing at a movie-house they were passing in the car, and replied, 'Sadie's tuchus, in two parts.'

There were not many books in our apartment, because my parents could rarely afford new ones. My mother read me Rudyard Kipling's Jungle Book, from an English edition with full-page colour pictures showing how the elephant got his trunk and the leopard its spots. I never warmed to Huck Finn and I was bored by Penrod (so, I suspect, was my mother: we preferred Heidi). I was, however, impressed when, on a visit to Linda and Sidney Scheuer, a textile manufacturer with a big apartment on Central Park West, I was shown a library which included pristine books from the Literary Guild (each with the dust jacket removed and folded within the pages). There was also a full set of Mortimer Adler and of Will Durant's The Story of Philosophy. My father epitomised the latter with the curtly prudent platitude, *meeden agan*. Aristotle's Golden Mean – advocating the avoidance of excess in any direction – was Cedric's careful idea of an appropriate philosophy for life. The wise middle way tempered pride with courtesy, enthusiasm with modesty, wit with self-deprecation. On the whole, he practised what Oxford had preached to him.

My father's office, in Rockefeller Center, was in one of New York's most famous, and most recent, skyscrapers. My mother and I sometimes went to meet him out of work at this cathedral of capitalism. We would wait for his descent in the side chapel where the express elevators could be heard humming. Single-handed clocks above each set of doors counted them down. As the brassy doors slid open, men waited for women to leave the car first. Then they put their hats on and came out themselves.

My father frequented a barber shop in the proto-mall of shops around the soaring lobby in which Diego Rivera had been commissioned to paint huge murals. My mother, who was well informed about art, pointed them out to me as my father had his trim and manicure. The manicurist, in a white coat, had a little trolley, with her tools on it, and sat on a low stool, silken knees to one side, holding her sheeted client's outstretched hand, in a hieratic pose. Although only in his middle thirties, my father was already losing his hair. He was persuaded to have curative sessions in which a rubber suction cap was fitted to his head. This purported to encourage skulking hair out of its cranial shell. It was the kind of thing that my grandfather Max might have invented, though he would probably have been too honest to market it.

Rivera had been impudent enough to include a heroic image of Karl Marx. His unamused plutocratic patrons had it painted out. There was a sort of fuzzy plaster cloud where the great man, and his tub-thumper's fist, had been erased.

The anti-Red significance of the resulting grey lacuna was not explained to me.

In the same mall was an art gallery where (at economic intervals) my parents bought two Hunter Wood water-colours of sailing clippers, the predecessors perhaps of the Cunarders on which we crossed the Atlantic. Opposite the entrance to Rockefeller Center, you could lean over the wall of the famous ice-rink where, all the year round it seemed, unfaltering glacial narcissists sailed and tacked on a scored mirror of ice. Most of the women seemed to have long white woollen legs and arched their backs in imitation of Sonya Henji. Their partners were usually Ramon Navarros or Ronald Colmans. Would Clark Gable *skate*?

I was convinced, and rightly, that I should never display such lissom aplomb. Unlike the dozens of kids who raced along the paths in the park with reckless zest and unchipped knees, I never even roller skated unhaltingly. My Christmas-present skates had adjustable metal footpieces (just the kind of idea that a successful Max might have thought of). I was not grateful to know that, however big my feet might grow, the machinery of my tottering embarrassment could expand with them.

My years in New York City return to me unsoured by a single remembered tear. Since I have always been something of a cry-baby, I am probably sentimentalising the lost par-adise of 1930s America. What is certain is that I knew no fear in those days. Although I felt the weight of parental expecta-tions, I was an unthreatened only child, never to be displaced or excelled by siblings: after my Caesarean birth, my mother was advised against having more children. Small families were, in any case, common during the Depression. Mary Jane Lehman, the freckled little girl I often played with in the park, was also an only child. Little Johnny Walker was adopted, but I must never, never say so.

My memories of blithe pre-war days are less selective than

partial: strips of disjoined film hang in the cutting room of my mind. There is no logic or drama in what survives for review; oblivion has edited my childhood with casually curt scissors. For example, I have not a single foot of images of Fanny Mauser in our apartment; I can see her, skinny in a one-piece black bathing suit, struggling in the under-tow at Jones beach, wearing a black rubber bathing cap, but never at home.

At some point, she and my grandfather changed places. Who knows what drama, if any, led to her displacement? With no explanation that I can recall, Fanny returned one day to Kansas City and Max came to live with us in W 70 St. Who proposed this, and with what courteous grace my father endured it, I cannot say. My grandfather's presence hardly registered, except on Sunday mornings, when he would invite me to get on his bed and read the 'funnies' which were unpacked from the fat, tightly strung, Sunday edition of *The New York Times*: Little Orphan Annie (not much fun), L'il Abner (ditto), Dagwood Bumstead (not bad), Popeye the Sailorman (whom Max could imitate quite well) and Dick Tracy (with his zippy profile and clever wrist-watch). I kept to myself what I always felt: the funnies were fun, but not funny. My grandfather, in striped flannel pyjamas and rimless glasses, laughed at them more than I did.

When we had finished with the paper, Max tried to teach me elementary German: *Bitteschoen, Dankeschoen, Brod und Butte, und so veiter*. One of his brothers, Wilhelm, had died fighting for the Kaiser, but he never alluded to Hitler; I did not think of my grandfather as being German, only as having left Germany. He was almost One Hundred Per Cent American: unlike me, he could never be President, because he had not been born in the US.

When I wrote a letter to him from England, years later, I typed it on a Royal Sovereign to which I had access when I accompanied my mother to WVS headquarters. Since I was not then, nor have yet become, an expert typist, I mistimed the shift key and typed 'germany'. Making capital from the lack of capital, I told Max that I had not written 'G' because germany didn't deserve to have a capital. Only recently, when I found a copy of the letter in my mother's keeping, did I wonder whether, or how much, I had hurt my grandfather's feelings.

Max was rarely around the apartment during the week. I would have lunch alone with my mother at the dining-room table, which had a leaf in it that – after the two ends of the table had been pulled apart – could be folded out, for company ('cump-ny' as they said in Missouri). There were six chairs, but only my father's had arms. I had no curiosity about where Max went or what he did during daylight hours. I assumed that, like my father, he had an office. In fact, he was an unqualified man in his mid-fifties with no prospect of employment. He spent his time walking the city streets, often as far as the Battery, at the extreme south end of Manhattan.

What he did on those walks, whether he talked to people or endured his solitude in silence or ever met or consorted with women, no one can now say. Did he even eat during those day-long absences? So far as I know, he had no source of income and was entirely dependent on Cedric. If my father had been given to Yiddish forthrightness – which was entirely alien to him – he might have been tempted to call Max a *schnorrer* (sponger), but he was never, so far as I know, expressly resentful.

Cedric's new job paid well enough for my mother never to have to consider working. He had graduated from being a salesman on the road to a promisingly sedentary executive position. If he had friends in the London office, who knew of his Oxford degree, and made sure that his abilities were not ignored, he was not without local enemies. His immediate superior was a man called Kittinger, whose admiration for the German-American Bund was unconcealed. 'Kit' could not entirely prevent Cedric's rise in the company, but he did his devious best to sour it.

When on the way to Saks Fifth Avenue or Bonwit Teller or I. Miller (where she bought her triple-A shoes), my mother and I would sometimes pass the entrance to the New York Racquet Club from which, I somehow soon learned, Jews were barred. There were whole sections of town where Jews were unofficially, but decisively, excluded from residence: somehow I heard that 'Sutton Place' (where Paul Getty and Greta Garbo lived) was 'restricted' in this way. Come to that, the whole of 'the Deep South' was somewhere that Jews were lucky never to have to visit: they might not be lynched, but they would certainly be abused. There was also a great number of magnolias and morning glories down there.

I remember a parade in which veterans of the Civil War marched, more or less side by side. It seems that we watched them from a balcony overlooking Central Park West. The Union soldiers wore blue uniforms and natty hats, slightly too reminiscent of the boy in the 'Call For Philip Morris' ad. The Confederates in their slouchy grey coats and broad-brimmed, cowboyish hats looked much more glamorous. For the first time in my life, I found myself furtively seduced by the Bad Guys. It was not the last: I was no less impressed by the wide-skirted overcoats and high-peaked caps (never mind the boots) of German officers during the war. Not the least of the stylistic mistakes of the Soviet Union was to have its generals look like A-number-one *Schlumps*.

It was an article of middle-class Jewish faith to advocate, and practise, tolerance; you did as you hoped to be done by. Although we did not know any coloured people personally (except the maids, whose names varied from Hilda to 'Phleggy'), their advancement was to be encouraged. A few, however, were apt for derision: Father Divine, the Harlem revivalist who headed 'the Holy Rollers', could be mocked for his rhetorical excesses. His parade of Packards – each with white wall tyres (red diamonds in the centre of each hubcap) and a spare tyre lodged next to the hood in a metal holster with a chromium clip – was paid for by the tribute of his credulous flock. A folk hero to his people, to us he exemplified the worst kind of Negro (no one referred to 'blacks', though my unreformed Missourian grandmother, like her girlfriends, spoke disdainfully, if mutedly, of '*Schwartzers*').

My father may have frowned, but he made no objection. His own admiration for black dancers and boxers was without nuance. If – until the advent of Mohammad Ali – he considered Fred Astaire to be 'the greatest man who ever lived', he liked little better than to go down to Harlem to dance and to watch the 'Bucks' trucking down the street on a Saturday night. His imitation of them deferred, with a champion's informed enthusiasm, to the 'natural rhythm' and spontaneity of Negroes (he said such things without condescension).

As for boxers, Joe Louis was so manifestly the best, the quickest, the hardest-punching, that there seemed no reason why, once he was champion, 'The Brown Bomber' would ever be dethroned. When he cut a swathe through his 1939 'bum-of-the-month' calendar of opponents ('Two-ton' Tony Galento among them), he seemed also to be on a mission to vindicate the dignity of his race. And then, by defeating Max Schmeling (whom people took, unfairly, to be the incarnation of Nazism), he seemed literally to be striking a blow for all of us. When the fatter, slower post-war Joe Louis was first knocked down, and stayed down, during his 1946 fight with Jersey Joe Walcott, it was as if my American childhood dream had at last been knocked conclusively on its ass.

Cedric was keen that I should learn to box (nobody wrestled until, like the poor old fat post-war Joe Louis, the noble art was beyond him) and tried to show me the elementary moves. One of our most famous neighbours on Central Park West was Jack Dempsey ('the Manassee Mauler', as *The Daily News* – never to be seen in our house – always called him). Dempsey was as well known for one of his defeats as he was for his many victories. In 1927, Gene Tunney had defended the heavyweight title against Dempsey (from whom he had taken it) in the fight which featured the 'Long Count': Dempsey had knocked the new champion down, but failed to go, as the referee required, to a neutral corner. Given time to recover his senses, his opponent went on, finally, to win on points. Tunney was a fighter of rare intelligence, who retired in time both to improve the fortune he had made (by the 1960s, he was the director of sixteen companies) and to excite the admiration of George Bernard Shaw, for whom strong men – including Mussolini, Stalin and, for a while, Hitler – had a muscular, if Platonic, attraction: dictators got things done.

Dempsey also retired from the ring without permanent damage, but his business activities were confined to opening a steak restaurant which Irene and I sometimes passed when walking home from the department stores. When there was a strike of elevator operators in the apartment block where Dempsey lived, the ex-champion was not disposed to solidarity. He walked up to one of the strikers circulating in the picket line and indicated that he wished to be taken in the elevator to his apartment on a high floor. When the man was properly reluctant, Dempsey pointed one finger at his chest and, when he failed to move, pressed the button, so to say. The striker was prodded backwards into the lobby of the apartment house and all the way into one of the elevators.

Did I have some feeling that Dempsey's performance was not wholly admirable? It was assumed that all Jews were liberals; none could ever vote Republican. The fact that no Southern red-neck ever voted Republican either seems not to have been significant. I went with my mother, in the winter

23

of 1936, when she voted for Franklin Roosevelt. Since the alternative was Alf Landon, there was no reason to hesitate. The voting machine resembled a one-armed bandit. We entered a curtained booth where my mother punched a long ticket before confirming her choices by pulling the lever. F.D.R. was naively assumed to be a philo-Semite: Rabbi Stephen Wise referred to him, a little too humbly, as 'the boss' when asking for help in admitting Europe's Jews to the US. It did him, and them, little good. The Jews had little choice but to support F.D.R. White Anglo-Saxon protestants dominated American society; the exclusiveness of the Republicans lacked even the hypocrisy of the democrats. Catholics were less openly despised than Jews, but had scant sympathy with them. Both Franco's 1936 Hitler-backed 'crusade' in Spain and the ranting anti-Semitic broadcasts of Father Coughlin – which attracted big audiences – made Catholicism alarming to middle-class Jews. Franco was the secular arm of a new Inquisition. What the 'Abraham Lincoln Brigade' actually did, I was unsure, but I gathered that it merited support.

How I knew this, and how soon, I cannot say. My profile of the world was created by joining up the dots of adult conversation. My parents never subscribed to anything more radical than *The New Yorker* (how old was I when I first dreamed of a place at the Algonquin round table, offering snappy comebacks to Robert Benchley and Dorothy Parker and the curmudgeonly Alexander Woolcott). I cannot recall that Cedric and Irene ever went to a political meeting, though I think that we did go a few times to hear the speakers in Union Square. My parents bought tickets for the Mercury Theatre, however, when Orson Welles directed (and, of course, starred in) his modern dress, Fascist armbanded version of *Julius Caesar*. I suspect they preferred Noël Coward's *Tonight at Eight Thirty* or the latest vehicle for Lynn Fontanne and Alfred Lunt, whose speciality was to find opportunities to turn his back, eloquently, on the audience. When did I first hear the story of how, during one of their long runs, there was a sudden, sustained and unrehearsed silence? The prompter, who was usually superfluous, realised with amazement that someone had 'dried'. He found the line and whispered it urgently. The silence continued. When the prompter offered the line again, more loudly, Mr Lunt was heard to say, 'We know the line, we just don't know which of us says it.'

Being an only child, I knew that the line was never likely to be mine. I was a silent listener who had to guess at meanings and kneaded crumbs of conversation into nuggets of unreliable knowledge. With no older brothers or sisters or cousins, I had no one with whom to check the impressions which grew weedily in the garden of my nervous fancies. Nothing bolder or braver was available to me than what my parents allowed me to hear or overhear. Their favourite radio programme was the Jack Benny half-hour, on which the character of Benny's factotum, Rochester, was to be distinguished from Step'n'Fetchit only by his Sam Wellerish repartee. There was nothing like a 'snappy comeback', Max taught me, if you wanted to get on in the US of A. It was the smart kid's equivalent of 'giving 'em a sock on the nose'.

For my father, Benny was the Fred Astaire of comedians. We would drive home, in our new Dodge, from Jones beach on summer Sunday afternoons in a hurry to catch his delayed-action wisecracks on the big, uncrackly Philco. The fluctuating radio in the car was all right for Guy Lombardo's band (which preceded Benny) but it garbled dialogue. Benny's programme was followed by that of Eddie Kantor, whom my parents regarded as vulgar. Kantor's suggestive rolling of his eyes might have been visible on our glowing Philco, so decisively was he extinguished. Yet I seem to remember my father singing Kantor's signature tune, 'If you knew Susie, oh oh oh what a girl'. Edgar Bergen and Charlie

McCarthy were not turned off; tuxedoed ventriloquism was assumed to be above my head. The only programme that was turned on especially for me was *Children's Hour* featuring 'Uncle Don', whom I detested. Legend promises that he was later evicted from the ether for being overheard to say, 'That'll keep the little bastards quiet,' at a moment when he presumed himself safely off the air. There was no panic at 30 W 70 St when the Martians invaded New Jersey during Orson Welles' radio dramatisation of *The War of the Worlds*; my parents failed to switched it on.

I never belonged to any group of neighbourhood kids. Warnings against 'strange company' converted timidity to virtue. I stayed near my mother when we went to the park (where there were still swarms of brown squirrels to be fed from a nickel's-worth of peanuts). The Good Humour man pedalled down the path, ringing his suspended bell, an ice-box at the front of his tricycle. His chocolate-covered ice-creams were mounted on sticks, a few of which, when licked clean, disclosed the magic lettering which entitled you to a free one next time around. The prospect of this divi-dend excited appetite, but abbreviated pleasure: once you realised that your stick was bare, good humour yielded to sulks.

My mother took me to my first movie, at the Museum of Modern Art: a biopic about Ludwig van Beethoven. Can it have been the version directed by Abel Gance? I remember only the scene in a garret where the tortured and misunder-stood artist played the piano, which he could not hear, in the midst of a clattering thunderstorm, which (though he could not hear it either) added electric zest to his playing. Light-ning scarified his face while his hair bounced up and down with energetic passion. In his creative agony, only the dream of immortal fame kept him, just, from suicide. Such aban-doned loneliness was clearly intended to be tragic, but I took it – and his leonine head, with its mane of dark hair – to be the symptom of rare talent. The result of this early exposure to the myth of a great genius was that I never wanted to go to the barber's again, even though, to encourage me, they put an elevating bench across the arms of the seat where my father was usually trimmed. When I looked in the mirror, I felt no complicity with the boy whom I saw in it.

Despite Irene's loving determination to expose me to art in as many forms as possible (she took me to children's concerts at Carnegie Hall and told me who Yehudi Menuhin was), my keenest memory of our excursions is of the shop window – on Broadway, north of Columbus Circle? – in which a broad hotplate was regularly dosed, in three or four places, with pancake mixture deposited from a circulating drum. Each dollop of wet white dough, with tiny bubbles in it, oozed out into a circle and then slowly browned from pasty sallowness into freckled temptation.

I also relished visits to the Automat, less for the quality of the food than for the pleasure of seeing the little windowed cells replenished, almost mysteriously, as soon as our nickels or dimes had sprung the doors at the front and allowed us to extract the lemon meringue pie or tuna sandwich ostentatiously imprisoned within. My mother's second cup of coffee was free.

Sometimes we would get in the car and drive downtown to the big market which adjoined the docks. Its permanently roofed stalls were said to cover a square mile. We left the car on a wharf where freight trains rolled slowly into position for loading from the ships moored beyond the crooked, swinging cranes (which also moved on wide rails). I was fascinated by a huge steam-powered pile-driver. The great tethered head of the hammer was hauled on a rope up a steel shaft until it reached a certain point, when – with a little steamy exhalation – it tripped free and fell flatly on to the black wooden pile it was butting into the Hudson River. This process was repeated with hypnotic deliberation. If its implacable, panting thrust excited some Freudian pre-pubescent ambition in me, I certainly had no idea of it.

Porters, usually coloured, carried our tall, double-brown-paper-bagged groceries, with ears of fresh corn on the cob pluming out at the top, from the food halls to the trunk of our new Dodge. My favourite dish was pot roast and mashed potatoes puddled with tomato-flavoured gravy (we said to-*may*-to, and Daddy said to-*mah*-to, but no one called the whole thing off).

When I had no appetite for a meal (usually if fish was involved), my mother would incite me to have a mouthful in honour of each of the Cunard fleet: the *Queen Mary*, the *Britannic*, the *Georgic* and so on. It was on the *Georgic* that we again sailed to England, on 'leave', in 1937.

Preparations for the journey began by getting the cabin trunks up from where the janitor stored them in the basement. They were like no trunks made today. Stood on their brass-studded ends, they hinged open to reveal curtained hanging space on one side and deep drawers on the other. The hangers were made of flat wood, so that everything could be compressed, without being wrinkled. Dresses and suits remained perpendicular throughout the journey. The drawers were made of canvas stretched over plywood frames; their leather handles could be pushed flush, again saving space. Cunard supplied oval sticky labels stipulating 'FIRST' or 'CABIN'. Luggage had to be designated as 'WANTED ON VOYAGE' or as 'NOT WANTED ON VOYAGE'. The latter category was stowed in the ship's hold and was not to be reclaimed until we reached Liverpool.

We were accompanied to the docks by some of my parents' friends. Others sent bowed and cellophaned flowers or candy (how I hated the sound of them being unwrapped!). The freshly minted passenger list told my parents which friends or celebrities were sailing with us. If senior members of Shell management were on board, there was the prospect, for my parents, of invitations to cocktails in their first-class 'staterooms', and perhaps to dinner in the dining room on the promenade deck. After the first night out, dinner jackets and long dresses were required.

Cabin class, however modest, seemed an eldorado of sumptuous lounges and dining rooms where, if your appetite survived the twin menaces of 'pitching' – when the ship rose at the prow and then fell forward – or 'rolling' (each Cunarder had its own propensity), there was no obligation ever to stop eating. The menus were long, staccato invitations to gluttony. Everything was free and copious. Did people tip the carver, in the English style?

As soon as we were on board, my father went down to the dining room to make sure that we were seated at a congenial table. The purser divined, with snobbish geniality, what kind of company would sit most happily together. My father's Oxford accent probably had some leverage, since the officers of the Cunard White Star line were all British. He sought a table neither too large, nor too centrally positioned (he had an abiding detestation of being bumped, however slightly, by passing waiters). A knowledge of shipboard etiquette was part of middle-class lore. Nothing was more gauche, for instance, than to make the mistake of dressing for dinner on the first night out.

Shortly before we were due to sail, a sailor walked around the deck ringing a brass bell of the same kind and with the same aggressive clangour, though I did not know it, as would one day wake me up at an English boarding school. 'All visitors ashore now, please.' The cabin emptied and I watched, through the port-hole (which could, in theory, be screwed open on fine days), as the dock slid away from us. We went on deck to wave goodbye to the Statue of Liberty and watch the white-numbered fireships throwing practice geysers into the sky. The long, lordly moan of the ship's hooter bayed over New York harbour as the squat and seething tugs cast us loose.

The next ritual act was to go on deck and secure chairs in a sheltered position. I never saw my father tip the allocating steward, but discreet massage was consistent with decorum, and necessary to favour: experienced passengers did not wait till the end of the voyage to show their appreciation of good service. Once chosen, the long wooden deck chairs had your name inscribed on a card slotted in a brass-framed 'window' screwed rustlessly to the back. Thick, precisely folded blankets were arranged on the slatted foot rest. As the ladies sat down, a steward would come and tuck a blanket around their feet and, respectfully, under and over their uplifted calves.

If people were sitting in your seats when you came on deck, you stopped and looked. There was no need to frown, or cough; you *stood at them*, politely, until they realised your priority, upon which, without shame or resentment, they would nod and depart, with their books and magazines. Halfway through the morning, the steward would enquire whether you wanted 'bouillon' (pronounced 'bullion') and water biscuits. The thin, hot drink was a beefy specific against chills. Although we never had four o'clock tea in New York, my father – now on British territory – reverted to his ancestral ways. In the afternoon, he often went to find a game of bridge, while my mother and I 'rested'.

The ship's newspaper was prolific with invitations to go to the movies, to take part in pingpong competitions, bingo sessions, deck-tennis games, 'horse-shoes', shuffle-board and other pastimes. You could also swim in the pool, situated on a very low deck indeed. Its shallow end vacillated according to the motion of the ship. Swimming could be uphill work.

There was a sweepstake to be won by the passenger who most accurately predicted the date and hour and minute of dropping anchor in English waters. In the early evening 'horse-races' were staged on the deck outside the saloon. The runners were large, numbered wooden horses, with jockeys in striped livery and coloured caps. The horses were moved down a long felt track, like a glorified hopscotch pitch, which had been unrolled by the purser's adjutant. Bets were placed and then they were off: the purser shook two large dice and the clerk of the course advanced, by a single space, the horses whose numbers had come up.

Before reaching Liverpool, the liner hove to outside Belfast docks, which were either too shallow to receive her or, more probably, too expensive for a brief stop, for such unprofitable passengers. A small boat, known as 'the tender', with wooden-benched uncovered seats – their huddled occupants liable to be drenched by soft pebbles of spray – came out and was tied up to a gangway which issued from a doorway almost at the waterline. We leaned over the rail to observe the few (doubtless steerage-class) passengers who were disembarking at such an unfavoured destination. The tender prompted my father, himself an implacable punster, to quotation from Thomas Hood, the only poet I remember him to have recited from memory: '"The tender-ship," said Nelly Gray. "What a hardship that must be!"' Nelly was lamenting her sweetheart who had been nabbed by a pressgang.

After Belfast, it was not many hours before we reached Liverpool. My first memory-footage of England derives from this trip. Nothing seemed less up-to-date than the soot-raddled, granite customs house, whose classically pilastered façade dominated the harbour. An LMS train took us south to London through a landscape which never spoke to me as had the clapboard houses, wide prairies and many-laned highways of the US with their voomf-voomf-voomfing automobiles (and motorcycle cops in ambush behind the billboards). The English train carriages were tight and stuffy.

There was a big leather strap which allowed you to haul, and then peg, the window shut, or drop it open, if you dared. My father seemed unexcited at being back in England; my mother was resigned. I watched and waited.

The approach to London, past rows of grim houses and drab suburbs, had nothing to match the glamour of the great bridges which took us across the Hudson River into towering, gleaming New York City. The London taxi (with a black leather roof, which could be folded down on sunny days) was a narrow-tyred box-on-wheels compared with the ritzy yellow cabs of Manhattan. Its only advantage was that the cabin trunk could stand upright next to the driver, who had neither door nor window to his left.

My grandparents still lived in their flat in the Cromwell Road, just around the corner from Stanhope Gardens, where we now spend much of the year. Theobald could park my grandfather's car outside the front door. Ellis's sisters, Nancy and Polly, had a small dressmaking business not far down the road, in a parade of unassuming shops which were shaken, with timetabled regularity, by the District Line which passed below them.

How soon was I told that I had the right to dual citizenship? Since Cedric was British, he had the imperial privilege of fathering British children, no matter where they happened to be born. By virtue of my American birth, and mother, I was no less entitled to be a Native Son. I had little sense of being connected with the English world to which I was now introduced. It was Daddy's old country, not mine. When they took me to Harrods, I said, 'Call this a department store? You should see Macy's.'

London's buildings were unimpressively stumpy, even if the red buses were cute. Some of the buses had open tops. I liked riding upstairs, in front. So, I learned, did my uncle Lionel, who had recently died. It had been one of his foibles to board a bus at Marble Arch as it headed down Oxford

32

Street and call out 'Marble Arch' as he scampered upstairs and took the front seat on top. The conductor would chase after him and explain, with panting politeness, that the bus was going *away* from Marble Arch. 'I know that,' Lionel said. 'I just like saying "Marble Arch" when I get on a bus.' The conductors chose to be amused by the gentleman's eccentricity. Lionel's humour was a function of vanities which neither he nor anyone else was disposed to question. Seeing a woman in a pinstripe suit, tie and trilby hat standing at a bus stop, he went up to her and slapped her robustly on the back with a cry of 'Jack, old man, haven't seen you in ages!'

My father had another uncle called Maurice, Ellis's brother. One day, he was accosted while crossing Hyde Park by a zealot who demanded whether he had found Jesus. Maurice replied, 'Why? Have you lost him again?' On his death bed, he observed, 'It's all worked out to beat you.'

Jessel too was now dead. I had been named for him in the polite hope of a bequest. My father's generation saw nothing ungentlemanly in having great expectations of rich relatives (nor yet did ancient Romans and Greeks, who often made a career of sycophancy). I am told that Jessel had indeed added a codicil to his will, leaving me five thousand pounds (no mean legacy in the 1930s), but he neglected to sign or have it witnessed. His heirs felt under no moral obligation to honour it. However, his oldest daughter, Thea, had been at Oxford with my father and, alone of her sisters, was hospitable to us. Like them, she had married a Gentile, with the uncomely name of Wadge. Thea never denied her Jewishness, but the others did. Many years later, their children discovered their origins and, in one notable case, embraced them. One of Jessel's grandsons is now a gay rabbi in New York.

Jessel had treated Thea with pitiless affection. One day, as a favour, he offered to take her for a ride down Park Lane in his new Rolls-Royce (when in London, he lived in a suite at the Connaught Hotel). As they approached Marble Arch, Thea thought it prudent to warn her father that the traffic was no longer allowed to circulate in both directions around that landmark. Unused to taking instruction, he continued on his usual route, which took him what had become the wrong way round. As buses and taxis bore down on them, squeezing their horns, even Jessel recognised that something beyond his control was happening. When he saw a bobby (as my mother always called English cops) starting to thread a dignified way through the stalled traffic, Jessel opened his door and got out of the car. As he hailed a cab, he said, 'You're driving, Thea.' By the time the policeman, and his notebook, had reached the Rolls, Jessel was already moving away from the scene. Since Thea was now alone in the car, her claim that she was not responsible for the infraction was difficult to sustain.

My father's hope of an inheritance may have been justified by the sentiment that it would be a just reward for services rendered. As a young man, he had often been conscripted to play golf with Jessel, who was not everyone's idea of agreeable company on the fairway, still less when in the rough. On one occasion, during the Oxford long vac, when he was supposed to have been studying Plato, Cedric was woken at six in the morning by a call from his uncle, who wanted to be on the tee at North Foreland in time for a round before lunch. My father's story was that he abandoned Plato's *Sophist*, and dressed hurriedly in a pair of mustard-coloured plus fours and co-respondent shoes and presented himself at the Connaught.

The chauffeur brought Jessel's bag and clubs to the Silver Cloud and they rolled sumptuously out of London and through the Kentish countryside. When they arrived at North Foreland, Jessel pushed to the front of those waiting for the first tee and said, 'Do you mind? My nephew is an Oxford

Blue and has to get back to his studies.' My father was obliged to drive off under angry eyes. Afterwards, as they went back into the clubhouse, Jessel said, 'We'll have a quick bite to eat and then we must be off.'

In the locker room, my father was surprised to see his uncle take a morning coat and striped trousers out of his bag. Asked the reason for so elaborate a costume, Jessel said, 'We're going to the races. I've got a horse running at Brighton. That's why we can't have much of a lunch.'

It was one thing to wear mustard-coloured plus fours at the golf club, another to sport them in the owner's enclosure. 'I can't possibly go to the races like this,' Cedric said.

Jessel looked at him as if for the first time. 'Don't worry about it,' he said. 'They'll think you're a bookie.'

Cedric endured what he could not avoid: having no funds for getting back to London alone, he went with Jessel to the races. His uncle's horse was running in the last race. Jessel had stayed with him in the public enclosure, but he now said that he had to go down to the paddock in order to speak to the trainer and, he hoped, electrify the jockey. Since Cedric's attire would be inappropriate, he told his nephew to wait for him to return.

The race was run and the winner, which was not Jessel's horse, was led in. The crowd thinned and departed. Cedric was finally quite alone in the public enclosure. Jessel did not return. Cedric ran to the car park, imagining that there had been a misunderstanding and that he would find that the Rolls was waiting for him. The only remaining form of transport parked on the cinders was a charabanc, which had yet to collect the last of its passengers. Cedric found a solitary florin in his pocket: enough to secure him an unoccupied seat to London.

My father was not often a person of imprudent passions, though he was, I was to discover, occasionally capable of them. Being both indignant and, maybe, ashamed of his unscholarly concession to Jessel's peremptory summons, he went, in a rage, to the Connaught and demanded admission to Mr Jessel Benson. The concierge made enquiries and then told the hot visitor that Mr Benson was in a business conference and not be disturbed. Cedric did not believe this unlikely story. He had been in the suite that morning and he knew the way, with or without an invitation.

When he threw open the door of the suite, he saw Jessel sitting with a number of soberly suited men looking at papers which they had taken from their briefcases. He was unquestionably in a business conference. He looked up and snapped his fingers, 'Good God, Cedric,' he said, 'I knew I'd forgotten something!'

The laughter of Jessel's associates found no echo in my father. He turned and slammed out. On returning to Kensington Park Gardens, where his parents then lived, he immediately wrote Jessel a very angry letter indeed. The study of Cicero's Philippics had armed him with a maquette for lapidary indignation. Was he also perhaps slightly affected by the radicalism of some of his Oxford contemporaries, with regard to hard-faced men who had done well out of the war?

Renouncing servility, Cedric wrote that he did not wish ever again to play golf with Jessel, who seemed to assume that his money gave him the right to interrupt a man's studies and behave like a cad and an *arriviste*. Prudence might have suggested sleeping on the letter before sending it, but vengeance trumped discretion. Cedric took the letter directly to the pillar box, where it was collected that same evening (there were five collections a day, and three deliveries).

The next morning, he had scarcely sat down to breakfast when the front doorbell rang. It was a post office messenger with a special delivery for Mr Cedric Raphael. Recognising the Connaught stationery, my father tore open the inner-lined envelope which looked to contain a lengthy, perhaps remorseful response to his righteous polemic. Inside were two letters, one of which was the one which he himself had sent the night before. It was crossed out with two slashes of red pencil. Appended to it was another, on the Connaught's embossed paper:

Dear Uncle Jessel,

Just a word to thank you for our delightful outing yesterday. How lucky I was to be privileged to play on such a magnificent course! Our delicious light lunch was just what one needed on a fine day. I am so sorry that my lurid choice of attire made me something of an embarrassment to you at the races. What a shame that you had no luck with your horse! I can well understand how disappointment, and the pressure of urgent business in London   do forgive my unwarranted intrusion on you and your important friends last evening! — led you to leave Brighton without remembering the presence of anyone so unimportant as . . .

Your affectionate nephew,
Cedric.

Jessel's premature death meant that, though my life was composted by tales of his financial genius, it was never literally enriched by it. Of my father's renowned uncles, only Godfrey ever actually gave me anything. It was an album — almost decadent in its pale blue, padded covers — designed specially to contain a complete set of mint stamps bearing the head of England's new, as yet uncrowned, king, Edward VIII. It came in a cardboard box which I discovered years later, with a whole sheet of each denomination, from halfpenny to sixpence, folded into it. The Stanley Gibbons catalogue promised that, in perfect mint condition, they had become quite valuable, even though (or because) the abdication had aborted the coronation which was billed in argent letters on the cover. In the interim, the gum had become sufficiently moist for them all to be glued inseparably, and worthlessly, together.

How much did Cedric change when he came back to England? His costume became sombrely British. He played golf with my grandfather at Sudbury, though not in plus fours. When in the States he had deferred, with enthusiasm, to American ways, and accepted that he had an American son; in London he was eager to instruct me in British habits and manners. He felt the pressure not to be 'different' and wished to spare me the humiliation of being a marked foreigner. He was to tell me later that one of the advantages of being in England was that I could grow up to be an English gentleman, not an American Jew.

I was taken to Buckingham Palace to see the changing of the guard. Christopher Robin went down with Alice; I went down with Winifred, my grandmother's long-serving maid, who provided better meals than my father's friends' cooks-general. The latter boiled their cod, their potatoes and their cabbage into unpalatable sogginess. Winifred mashed Brussel sprouts, with butter and pepper, into a pulpy treat. Accompanied by crisply fatty roast potatoes, they garnished the roast chicken with clove-spiked bread sauce, the one thing my father admitted to wishing that my mother could make. Winifred's chicken was addictive. When I refused to eat anything else, I had to be told that the roast lamb was 'chicken-lamb'. Chicken itself was advertised as 'chicken-chicken'. The parson's nose was an arcane, frequently mentioned English delicacy whose obscure anatomical location amused my grandmother. 'Bubble and squeak' was another un-American dish.

Winifred Stanley was a Seventh Day Adventist who, almost accusingly, regularly sent me a Jewish New Year card once I had married and settled in England. In my grandmother's service, she wore a white lace apron and bib with a big bow at the back. I was licensed to imitate my father's habit and undo Winifred's bow when she turned her back. How dutifully she giggled!

My father himself took me to Madame Tussaud's, where

we met his great-aunt Sophie, a childless widow of great wealth, probably the dividend of an advantageous marriage. Cedric was no more ashamed of hoping for a legacy from her than from Jessel. Sophie was renowned for reluctance to part with money, but my father hoped that his charm and my artless presence would have some leverage. On the way to the tea room, his great-aunt said, 'The boy should have an ice-cream.' Taking this to imply unbuttoned generosity, Cedric ordered me a large one.

During the course of the conversation which followed, he expressed surprise at some wild assertion on his great-aunt's part: 'Can that really be true?' he said. 'It's certain,' she said. 'As certain as you're paying for that boy's ice-cream.'

It never occurred to me in 1937 that I should ever live permanently anywhere but in New York. My father's antique family seemed incurably alien; they were all immeasurably older, and graver, than anyone I could possibly meet in America. Their homes were dark brown with cumbrous mahogany furniture and staffed by intimidating servants who winced whenever my hands touched a polished surface. The servants' main activity seemed to be opening doors, dusting, and bringing, and removing, dishes.

We sailed for home on the MV (motor vessel) *Britannic*. The packing was done by Winifred. My grandmother had shown my mother little kindness, but she must have given her (or my father) some of the 'family silver'. We had to have something 'hallmarked' to prove our class. Winifred – who was in every respect a law-abiding, God-fearing citizen – concealed the silver by rolling the napkin rings into my father's socks and distributing larger objects in recondite places where any customs' officer of the smallest competence would be sure to look. Fortunately, her predictable ingenuity was superfluous: antiques were not subject to duty.

I returned to Ethical Culture. Life resumed its New York routine, but the montage of memory fails to recapture many of its details. We must have been back in New York by the time the Hindenburg made its transatlantic flight, because I can still see it stitching the blue sky above Manhattan like a thick silver needle. It was on the way to Lakehurst, New Jersey, where it caught fire as it docked with its mooring mast. A radio commentator famously burst into unprofessional tears as the great envelope of hydrogen exploded and subsided into a blackened skeleton. Was there a secret feeling of pleasure that another symbol of the New Germany had, like Max Schmeling, hit the deck? I think not; the world was less hard-hearted then, at least if the victims were white.

When exactly did I get frostbite, struggling home from school along a trench of snow dug along the sidewalk by the wide shovels of 'unemployed men'? My mother and I had to hold on to the railings of the Spanish and Portuguese synagogue, in a scorching wind, as we turned the corner into W 70 St. I was frostbitten under my chin. It was painless but it attracted a great deal of attentive sympathy: the ideal misfortune.

In the early summer of 1938, we drove to Canada for a week's holiday in a lakeside resort called St Jovite. In the evening, we crossed a long bridge, with double globes of white light along it, into Montreal. Once in the mountains, we hit a storm so torrential that the Dodge's windshield wipers were useless. My father pulled in at the side of the road. I sat behind my parents and rejoiced in the lightning-slashed possibility that we were marooned for ever.

On an earlier occasion, also in the car, we were on our way to visit some friends who had, or had rented, a little house on Long Island. There was no storm, but we got lost as night came on. Tall trees were flashed by our nervous head-lamps. There were no markers or street names. It was way past my bedtime and I was exhilarated by what alarmed my parents. Again and again in life, I have found myself indifferent to situations in which I was myself involved, as if I were less a participant than a bemused spectator. In fact, we soon found the right address on Long Island, just as the Canadian storm abated quickly enough for us to reach Lake Champlain without even missing a meal.

My parents had rented a cabin on the lake. The water was very cold, but my father swam every day. He was resolutely British about taking painful pleasures. At night, he hung his bathing costume – a black woollen garment, with a yoke of shoulder straps – over the porch railing. One morning, he put it on as usual and immediately gave an uncharacteristic yell of pain. He had been stung on the belly by an accidentally compressed wasp. The pain was so fiery that he ran straight into the cold, anaesthetic water of the lake.

My mother hurried to the office for help, but found difficulty in explaining to the French-Canadian staff what exactly had happened. The word 'wasp' meant nothing to them. They kept saying 'Wops? Wops?' Finally, someone supplied the word '*guêpe*'. No remedy other than an ice-pack could be supplied. However, the wasps' nest was discovered under our eaves and was attacked, witlessly, with a broom.

I observed my father's pain with interest, as if his misfortune were a stranger's. The wooden cabin and the black lake reminded me of a film in which Charlie Chaplin had dived from his holiday porch, also in a one-piece bathing suit, and landed on his head in five inches of water.

Cedric and Irene were determined that my childhood should not resemble theirs. Since they had both been victims of their parents' loud unhappiness, they vowed never to have rows in front of me. Their resolve was honoured with unmitigated determination. I experienced whatever stresses there were between them, and between them and the wide world, only in what remained unsaid; their silences spoke anxiously to me. Guessing what I was not told, I imagined that more depended on me than it did. Thinking that, by being 'good', I could reduce the occasional, only-too-human tensions between them, I moralised my place in my parents' life. Because they so wanted my happiness, I felt that theirs was dependent on it. I had responsibility without power, the only child's burden. I never went out of the apartment without one or other of them, unless it was to walk to the corner with my grandfather to buy a ten-cent cigar or *The New York Times*.

Confident of my parents' love and protection, I believed that the world was a nice place if you were nice to it. New York cops would always take care of you if you got lost. I was unfrightened by doctors or dentists. When I was diagnosed as having acute appendicitis, I was not at all alarmed to be driven to the hospital across town at night. My brief memory is of a close-up of the handle which wound the window up and down in an unfamiliar car in which we are travelling. The door is upholstered in soft beige material. Sickness and luxury seem to go together.

Later, I am lying on a gurney while someone puts a mask over my raised face and drips a burning, pungent liquid on to it. As the ether puts me down, my blurred mother is standing there, promising to see me when I wake up.

When I did wake, I said that my parents would be coming to see me soon. The nurse warned me not to be upset if they didn't arrive. 'They will,' I said. 'They promised.' They did.

Not many months later, I discovered that having your tonsils and adenoids removed was more painful. It was compensated by unlimited quantities of strawberry ice-cream. They gave me my adenoids to take home in a jar. I should not, we were assured, have wanted to see my tonsils.

The proposal that my father spend a year in London, at Shell head office, before returning to take up a new, and better, job at Rockefeller Center, was the result at once of how well he was regarded and of the tension between him and the anti-Semitic Kittinger. The prospect of a long absence from New York had a consequence of which I was unaware: my grandfather would have to return to Kansas City. My father never disclosed to me whether he had been relieved to have good reason to say a definitive goodbye to Max. A side effect of our transfer to London was that it repaired my grandparents' marriage, at least superficially: they opened a delicatessen in Kansas City which, unlike Max's other enterprises (perhaps because Fanny had some control over it), became quite successful.

At one point, they were menaced by a new generation of Kansas City mobsters, who tried to unload large quantities of inferior soda pop on them, at an inflated price. Max's amiable connections with what was left of Prendergast's old guard seem to have been enough to procure some immunity from such hassles. They continued to stock only the best soda pop.

We sailed for London in the summer of 1938, once again on the MV *Britannic*. Stewards greeted us with flattering recognition. In the hold was our brand-new 1938 Buick which I was never to see with its wheels on the ground. My only vision of it was in mid-air as it was being hoisted aboard. It was bright yellow, which might have been all right in America but was too brash to be paraded in London. It was garaged, in pristine condition, when we arrived. Sometime during the war, it was sold – with the infallible bad timing which dignified all my father's business dealings – for seventy pounds. Petrol rationing had made it a liability. Who knows what such a classic car, with double-figure mileage, would fetch at auction today?

This time, the *Britannic* went via Cherbourg and to Southampton. We had so recently been in London, and were now to be there for so long, that my father's family paid us less attention than before. Things had changed, and not changed. My grandparents had quit the Cromwell Road and were living in a new flat in Dorset House, in Gloucester Place, adjacent to Baker Street, but Winifred was still with them; Theobald still waited at the recessed kerb in the Austin until my grandfather was able to say 'Can't stop' and hurry off to Tuck's in the City.

My parents were determined to avoid 'north London'. It was full of 'the kind of people' (Jews) with whom they did not wish to be identified. When my grandmother asked where they were house-hunting, my mother replied, 'We think we've found a flat in Putney.' Amy said, 'I shouldn't say Putney, my dear, if I were you. I should say ... Roehampton.'

Amy had taken to spending most of her time in bed, on account of what had been diagnosed, Winifred whispered loudly, to be '*angina pectoris*, the most painful affliction known to medical science'. This had not been the view of my grand-mother's until recently regular doctor, who was an ex-England rugger player. He advised her to take more exercise and eat fewer fatty foods and chocolates (Maison Lyons' 'violets' were her, and my father's, favourites). His self-denying prescription was not to her taste. Displeased at having her condition downgraded to indigestion, she called a new doctor who, for three guineas, seconded Amy's more dramatic diagnosis. The new man had more tact than preci-sion. On one occasion, he asked Amy whether she had had anything like this – whatever it was – before. When she said yes, he looked at her over the top of his spectacles and said, 'Well, I very much fear that you've got it again.'

Selective, but chronic, valetudinarianism became her way of life. It was suspended, valiantly, at the weekends for family bridge games: Amy and Ellis played against Cedric and Irene, while I watched for hours, without hope of reprieve, still less of entertainment. A silver dish of violet chocolates was at Amy's right hand, adjacent to her smelling salts in their opaque green bottle. A very small-printed, round label gave the polysyllabic details of its contents, and recommended careful use. The teardrop stopper lent a perfumier's touch of rarity and value. A lace handkerchief was ready to filter the resuscitating fumes which, even when screened, brought tears to the sniffer's eyes.

I neither resented nor relished the hours of nicely behaved tedium. They resulted in my learning how to play bridge, before I had so much as held a card in my hand. Boredom was cumulatively instructive: as Sunday succeeded to Sunday, I began to guess where errors were being committed or bids misconceived. The seeds of lifelong addiction were sown among yawns.

My parents found a first-floor flat (on what my American self would have called the second floor) in a new block called Highlands Heath, on the Portsmouth Road. There was a green metal fence around the grounds, which abutted on to Putney Heath, where highwaymen had once threatened travellers with 'your money or your life?'. Part of the comic persona of Jack Benny was that he was very, very tight with a dollar. In one of his most famous sketches, he failed to respond to a highwayman's traditional challenge. When the highwayman repeated his question, more aggressively, Benny said, 'I'm thinking about it.' We no longer heard him, or Rochester. English radio was generally nicely spoken, though people were heard doing the Lambeth Walk, oy!

Highlands Heath sported lawns and flower beds and lock-up garages. It was the first time I had lived anywhere where I could go out and play. My father resumed his Englishness more thoroughly, since we were here for a long stay: he joined the Wimbledon Park Golf Club (Royal Wimbledon and Roehampton barred Jews) and he played bridge at The Hamilton with his Oxford friend, Guy Ramsey. I saw him for the first time in a bowler hat, and carrying a rolled umbrella. His office was in St Helen's Court, in the City of London, where taller-than-usual 'bobbies' had red instead of blue on their wristlets; their helmets were more elaborately crested than a routine bobby's. My father had to go in something called 'the drainpipe' to travel from Waterloo to the Bank.

Irene now took me shopping to Harrods or else to Derry and Tom's, and sometimes to Barker's, where she had accounts (she never had a chequebook until well after the war). We seldom went into Ponting's, which was part of the same trinity of companies as Derry and Tom's and Barker's, but of inferior class. I liked it for the pneumatic tubes through which money was whisked to some unseen treasury. In order to reach Harrods from Putney, we had to drive through the slums of Fulham. It was rude to stare at the threadbare urchins. To go to High Street Kensington, we crossed Hammersmith Bridge (until the IRA did something dangerous to it) through streets redeemed from slum status by the proximity of St Paul's School, where I now might one day go. Rounding Shepherd's Bush (no shepherds, few bushes), we drove up past Olympia, which had housed not only Chipperfield's circus but also Oswald Mosley's most notorious rally.

My father's reminiscences of St Paul's seemed unclouded by misfortune. Did he edit them in order to entertain and to reconcile me to the prospect of an English education? He had been in the Eighth in the great era of eccentric masters whom Compton Mackenzie portrayed in Sinister Street (the young Cyril Connolly's spiteful italicising of redundant words in Mackenzie's Edwardian narrative appeared at just about this time, in Enemies of Promise, the sort of arty book that my parents were certain never to read). Old Elam, for legendary instance, was renowned for crying out, when 'the boy Raphael', or any other, failed to construe his Virgil correctly, 'My boys, my dearest wish is to die before you.' He also had a less resigned astringency: Cedric recalled being in a tea room with him in Hammersmith, adjacent to some obstreperous people. As they left, Elam called out, 'Excuse me, but you've left something behind.' 'Have we? I don't see anything. What?' 'An extremely bad impression.'

While the Buick stood 'on blocks' in some garage, my parents temporised by buying a modest black Standard Eight (EYR 332). The patriotic chromium device on the bonnet incorporated an enamel, three-colour Union Jack. My mother made no effort to lose her American accent (she still has it), but there was a new wariness in her tone. In that summer of Munich, when the talk of war, or at least of having to 'do something' about Hitler, came even to my ears, I was sprung from the insulation in which I had been coddled in New York. On fine days, I was taken to play on the 'Common' outside the gates of our fenced enclave. Other mothers brought their children and I was urged to mix with them. There were bushes (into which we were forbidden to stray) and silver birches. On one occasion, a man with field glasses was detected watching us covertly from behind the brambles. Such a man was more alarming even than a tramp. Mothers literally pulled their prams into a circle and called a policeman.

At the weekend, men in white clothes played cricket on 'the square'. My father insisted that it was a very exciting game when you understood it. It was watched in silence broken by a patter of applause when something undetectably exciting had happened. This usually prompted a man to hang new metal numbers on a sort of gallows near the pavilion. The only time I was impressed was when a burly batsman struck a ball which flew over our heads and bounced on the roof of a parked car. 'Home run?' I said. My father explained that the man was a 'slogger' who would soon be out.

Despite my One Hundred Per Cent Americanism, I had never become a fan of baseball. I had, of course, heard of Babe Ruth and of Lou Gehrig and sided with the New York

47

Yankees against the Brooklyn Dodgers (people from Brooklyn had funny accents, though not as funny as those of people from the Bronx). 'The bleachers' and 'left field', 'three strikes and you're out', 'bunts' and 'the bottom of the ninth' were terms I had heard in undulating commentaries on the radio, but the game itself never appealed. When life in England became unavoidable, I took to cricket with innate zeal.

No games were played at my first English school. Leinster House was lodged in a big red-brick house on Putney Hill. The headmaster was called Mr Moyles, a name with a Dickensian ring. My father sought to acclimatise me to English culture by reading The Pickwick Papers to me. I tried to share his amusement at the antics of Mr Tracy Tupman and the other Pickwickian clubmen, but – as with my grandfather Max, when he read me the funnies – I was conscious of doing him a tactful favour. Whether the complete set of his works – bound in grey leatherette with red lettering – came with us from New York or was the fruit of some Northcliffian special offer, I was advised of the immeasurable kudos attached, in England, to 'knowing one's Dickens'. Over the years, I did my best to be touched by A Christmas Carol, engrossed by David Copperfield and exhilarated by Great Expectations, but Dickens never genuinely delighted me. I cannot warm to his warmth or smile at his humour. Oliver Twist leaves me unmoved; I am no more indignant about Fagin than grateful for the unmemorable nice Jew – can anyone remember his name? – whom Dickens introduced, in a later book, to compensate for him. My father also incited me to read Ivanhoe, surely the most tedious of all the ineffably tedious novels of Sir Walter Scott. One of its characters was a beautiful Jewess; the female of the species was ripe for rescue.

England in 1938 made me conscious of being Jewish in a way which I never knew in New York. My parents made no

48

pretence of passing for what my father called 'Christians', but they wanted to move freely in Gentile society. Like not a few English Jews, they watched what was happening in Germany with outraged ambivalence. Refugees excited both pity and apprehension: their maltreatment was a scandal, but the possibility of their unlimited arrival, and of a hostile reaction to it, was a threat. In fact, immigration was rigorously limited, especially for the 'unqualified', who – it was alleged – would work for lower wages than the many native unemployed. As for the elite, the academic world could be hospitable, but the British Medical Association almost entirely embargoed Continental doctors whose competition would be 'unfair'. English practitioners, it declared, had nothing to learn from foreigners.

My father, like the Jewish Board of Guardians, feared that newcomers would revive dormant prejudice. What insulated us from anti-Semitism was nothing more reliable than good manners and a reputation for personal integrity. What would refugees know, or care, about the rules of the British game? Their lack of scruple would license unhappy conclusions about Jews in general. 'Decent opinion' as typified by readers of *The Daily Mail* – which we took because my father's old friend, Guy Ramsey, was one of its leader writers – scarcely embraced the Jews, though it deplored their persecution in Germany. G. Ward Price, the *Mail*'s crack foreign correspondent (author of *I Know These Dictators*), was a scarcely veiled admirer of 'many of the things' which Hitler and Mussolini were doing. He was not alone.

Although an avowed philo-Semite, Guy Ramsey confessed that it was Hitler's spiteful achievement to have made even those who disliked him all too aware of who was Jewish and who was not: sweaty brows were a giveaway, if you looked hard enough. Guy's admiration for my cool father went back to their days as fellow lounge lizards at the Empress Rooms in Hammersmith. 'Cedric was a dago when he danced the

49

tango,' he told once me, 'and a Hapsburg dandy when he did the waltz.' My father's ability to change his manner as the occasion required was never blatant, and rarely advertised. Though nothing like an impostor, he acted the Englishman with the same understated stylishness with which he played the rake or the dago on the dance floor.

Guy Ramsey was later to be my sole access to the literary world. Married to a minor novelist, he was an uxorious Hampstead Bohemian whose lack of funds never inhibited him from taking a taxi, even to cross a wide, wet street. When I decided that I wanted to be a writer, he volunteered to play 'Flaubert to your Guy de Maupassant'. He never wrote his *Madame Bovary* (his only novel, *On the Spike*, was a detective story about Fleet Street), but he was an informed reviewer (one of the last to use the word 'limn'), a tactful tutor, a fluent journalist and a bridge writer of modest genius. In his classic *Aces All*, he pays unguarded tribute to his idol, S.J. Simon, whom everyone called 'Skid' in abbreviated allusion to his original name, Skidelski.

Skid was chosen to play for England in the bridge Olympiad of 1936. Since his chest was usually covered with cigarette ash ('Give tube' was one of the master's slogans) and his unshaven profile would have needed little exaggeration to be suitable for caricature in the Jew-baiting Nazi magazine *Der Sturmer*, it was bold of the selectors to include him against the straight-nosed Germans. Skid combined ruthless competitiveness with scrupulous sportsmanship. At the end of the match, which the Englishmen won, the German captain said, 'If the Führer could only meet Mr Simon, all this absurd anti-Semitism would come to an end.'

It may not have been very noble of my parents to distance themselves from 'the Jewish community', but I should be a humbug if I crimed them for it; when I hear the word community, I reach for my passport. There has always been a certain vindictiveness in the way some Jews wish to oblige others to their exclusive company, quite as if it were pretentious or disloyal to seek, or enjoy, any other. My father had no use for this prophylactic, self-ordained ghettoisation. If he made little of his St Paul's and Oxford education, he regarded himself as at least as English as he agreed to be Jewish. He taught me almost nothing about Judaism; he probably did not know much, though he could read, if not understand, Hebrew. Jewishness might have been a characteristic as inescapable, and slightly limiting, as left-handedness. If it was nothing to apologise for, nor yet need it be trumpeted. Since Jews were always going to be a minority, how could it be ignominious to defer to the ways and manners of the majority?

When the great thirteenth-century Spanish rabbi Nahmanides was compelled by Jaime I, king of Aragon, to defend his faith against a Dominican friar called Dolin (who happened to be a *marrano*, a converted Jew), he was warned that while he might defend Judaism, he would risk his life if he went so far as to attack or seek to refute or ridicule Christianity. The best result that Nahmanides could contrive was a draw. When he succeeded, it still required all the king's geniality to protect him from the Holy Inquisition. Any dispassionate reader of the minutes of the debate can perceive that Nahmanides practised a kind of ironic reticence. My father's observation of the niceties of English social usage had something of the same punctilious disrespect for Christian *force majeure*: his unostentatious rectitude hinted at how withering he might have been, had prudence not inhibited him. In private, he could be less guarded; my childhood was mined with sudden explosions of candour in which he would advise me of the pettiness and malice of at least some of our betters. More often, he turned his acidity on me; my mother was often distressed by what he insisted were our 'discussions'. As I became more British, and articulate, I began to catch, and match, his caustic irony. He held the resulting testy dialogue to be 'Socratic'.

Jews in pre-war England were abruptly divided between those who arrived before and after What's-Happening-in-Germany. My father's forebears were attested residents as far back as the late eighteenth century, where they appear in the register of the West End synagogue. Family myth insisted that the Raphaels had been among the first families 'invited back' by Oliver Cromwell ('reluctantly readmitted' would be nearer the truth). I have never verified this claim, but if it is true, their early start did them little good in the race for fame and fortune. They may have become respectable, but the Raphaels were distinguished neither for riches nor for scholarship. It is plausible, however, to assume them to be of Sephardic origin; eighteenth-century Jewish immigrants generally came from the Low Countries.

In 1939, the refugees whose heavily accentuated presence was now so marked in north London were nearly all *Ashkenazim*. Their eastern European, non-Iberian provenance offered a small, fatuous reason to regard them as members of a different tribe. My mother's family had all been *Ashkenazim*, but that was less significant in 1938 Putney than her Americanism: Franklin Roosevelt's politic reluctance to take sides in Europe smacked of Mercutio, if not of Pontius Pilate. Irene became doubly vulnerable to cruel or tactless remarks. Since she was beautiful as well as female, she was subjected only to inadvertent anti-Semitism: Jews were always male, as well as hook-nosed, in the polite imagination.

Oswald Mosley was the strutting incarnation of Fascism *à l'anglaise*. 'Tom' (as in tomcat?) belonged to the Establishment and affected to have no quarrel with Jews who were not Reds or plutocrats. William Joyce (later 'Lord Haw-Haw') accused him of being 'kosher'. The boxer Ted 'Kid' Berg had been one of Mosley's early bodyguards. Nevertheless, he led marches through the East End, while his supporters chanted 'We've got to get rid of the Yids'. He claimed that his Blackshirts limited their violence to the 'good old British straight left' and that the Communists provoked them into it. Mosley's marches never came near anyone we knew, but All Decent People applauded government measures to limit his appeal by banning the use of 'military-style' uniforms. It was never mentioned in print that part of Mosley's hold over a certain stratum of high society was his renown as a lover at whose feet many beautiful women, and not a few men (Harold Nicolson in particular), were eager to throw themselves.

Fascism impinged directly on SW15 only by post. On arriving in London, my parents had seen a seductive advertisement for 'The Right Book Club'. Assuming it to have some affinity with the Literary Guild in New York, they agreed to subscribe. A succession of furiously fascistic books (in nice tweedy covers) began to arrive. Among them, I recall only *The Spanish Arena*, whose author, Alastair Reed, proclaimed General Franco to be a Christian gentleman engaged on a righteous crusade against Reds, Masons and (of course) Jews. It took some time for my parents to realise that the lesser dexterity of The Right Book Club lay in duping middle-class readers into subsidising propaganda. They then switched to The Reprint Society, which had no hidden agenda; it supplied the basis of what became an eclectic, if unadventurous, library (Charles Morgan, Monica Dickens, Eric Linklater, Angela Thirkell, James Hilton, but also John Steinbeck).

At some point during those pre-war months, my parents hired a Viennese refugee called Gertrud as cook and housekeeper. She was a small dark woman, hunched with reticent tragedy. When she arrived, and why she departed, I cannot be sure.

Work at Leinster House School was divided, in the standard English fashion, into forty-five-minute periods of writing, arithmetic and geography (ah those proud maps, with a quarter of the earth's surface coloured imperial red!). I sometimes walked down the hill to school and back up, in my green and red cap, with a boy called Martin. We became sufficiently friendly for me to go to play with him 'on the Common' after lessons.

When did I first sense that our year in England might be stretched indefinitely? What prompted me to start homogenising my American origins, as Max Mauser had his German, with the dominant, drawling culture? The first evidence of metamorphosis was my mimicking of Martin's accent: I began to drop my aitches. As a result, I learned a new application of the un-American word 'common': it applied, pejoratively, to Martin. He was no other sort of a bad influence, but I was advised to find a new friend.

The flight from Americanism was not halted. I heard correctly spoken models in the voices on the radio (Uncle Mac displaced Uncle Don, and Toytown's Larry the Lamb bleated endearing servilities to 'Mr Mayor, sir'). My ear for the varieties of English speech became as acute as my fear of saying the wrong thing in the wrong way. Conceit and deference procured accuracy. It was not long before I could pass for one of the natives, while knowing very well that I was and was not of their number. No one could deny that I was British, but I was never sure how British I was. My genuine falseness made me at once proud and cautious; the impostor has always to be on his guard. His most revealing error is to speak the local dialect a little too correctly: such was the mistake of Shaw's Hungarian elocutionist in *Pygmalion*, which I saw, in black and white, with Leslie Howard and Wendy Hiller.

An illustrative clip from the pre-war past is projected in my secret cinema. I am in the car, on the way to school with my mother. At a crossroads on Putney Heath, we pull up at a traffic light (no longer called a 'stop light') outside Wildcroft

Manor – another block of recently built middle-class flats, with Tudoresque plaster and black-stained wood cladding – and find ourselves halted next to a straight-backed limousine in which sits the straight-backed figure of Queen Mary, the Queen Mother, the recently widowed wife of the late King Emperor George V.

She is doubly impressive because she bears the same name as the latest Cunarder (on which we have yet to 'cross'). Alert to British proprieties, my mother continues to look to her front – it's rude to stare, worse to point – and whispers, 'Take off your cap to the lady.' I do so, with something of a flourish (if toadying, you might as well go all the way) and am rewarded by a regal inclination of the head and a Windsor (gloved) hand signal. I had qualified as a nice little English boy.

I received the first form prize from Mr Moyles at the end of the school year: a child's edition of Nathaniel Hawthorne's *Tanglewood Tales*, with pen-and-ink illustrations. In his edifying recension of Greek myths, Hawthorne pasteurised into a pitcher of milk the jug of inexhaustible wine with which Baucis and Philemon were rewarded for entertaining Zeus and Hermes, when the gods were travelling incognito. The tale's xenophile moral remained intact: receive strangers with generosity; you never know how divinely important they might turn out to be.

The prize introduced me to the Graeco-Roman world in which I was to be immersed for the next decade and in which I have never ceased to continue to take regular holidays. In his report, Mr Moyles said that he looked forward to welcoming me back to Leinster House for the September term of 1939; it was to begin on the twenty-first, my mother's twenty-ninth birthday.

That summer, my parents decided to take a week's holiday at Knokke-le-Zoute in Belgium. What disposed them to choose this crowded and unglamorous resort? Perhaps its proximity to England. We took the ferry from Dover to Zeebrugge (where, during the Great War, an heroic British captain had rammed the 'mole' with an old destroyer packed with dynamite). I had never set Barker's-shod foot on the Continent before and – fortunately for me – would not be called on to do so again until well after the war. Europe's lease on peace was shortening like a fuse.

I stock only three brief memory-clips of our holiday. In one we are playing 'miniature golf' on a course not far from the beach; there are the usual obstacles, hoops and tunnels through which the ball has to be driven. My father advises me of the magic formula for success at whatever form of golf I might attempt: 'Keep your head down'. It was the same advice that Jews were constantly being given if they wanted to avoid attracting attention. The alternative was to 'look for trouble' the result of which would be that, being 'their own worst enemies', they would have only themselves to blame.

In another clip, spliced neatly into the first, we are walking along the front when we notice that everyone is sitting up on his or her white-slatted beach bed looking out to sea. Two grey ships are passing from left to right. 'Destroyers,' my father says. They are close enough inshore for the White Ensigns to be visible at their sterns. We had to hope that German tourists, if any, would be prompted to warn Hitler to think again before tweaking the lion's tail.

Finally, we took a tour of the Great War battlefield at Dixmude, which my father had escaped by being just too young to challenge the grim actuary who gave subalterns on the Western Front an expectation of life of about two weeks. Under a transparent roof, we walked along an antique trench, where tin hats and abandoned equipment lay half-buried, and into a 'dug-out' where there were bunks and a 'storm-lantern'. Later we went to Ypres and admired the half-ruined Cloth Hall and the church spire which had ('miraculously' said the guide) escaped bombardment. Was it from him that I learnt the terrible word 'minenwerfer'? The name for the huge, whirling landmines which flattened most of Ypres had not figured in Max Mauser's German vocabulary.

From Dixmude, we drove on to the Menin Gate and gazed at the thousands of names incised in its minatory white marble. The eternal flame was a reminder of the war to end all wars and of why we always had to take our hats or caps off when passing the Cenotaph.

By the time we returned to England, trenches were being dug in Hyde Park. As we drove up Park Lane to Dorset House, to see my grandparents, again, I could see the black ramparts and the flash of the spades. On the way back, we went into the park, where the speed limit was twenty miles an hour. My father must have accelerated to a reckless twenty-five or thirty. Suddenly we were being 'gonged' by a police Wolesley, whose sole distinction was to have the maker's logo on the radiator illuminated in metropolitan blue. The only indication that we should pull over was a mild bong on the silver bell above the police car's front bumper. It was enough, of course, to cause my father to pull up at once. The Prime Minister, Neville Chamberlain, was still hoping that Hitler could be brought similarly, discreetly, to observe the rules of the diplomatic road.

My parents soon volunteered for Civil Defence. As part of their initiation, we went to a centre in Wandsworth where novices were instructed in how to get into and out of burning buildings. A concrete hut billowed dense smoke and we had to crawl through and out the other side. Provided you kept as flat as possible there was, we were promised, no danger whatsoever of suffocation. The instructor had an accent very like Martin's, but everyone listened respectfully as they were taught the right and wrong way (too full) to fill a sandbag. Wartime classlessness made its embryonic appearance as toffs, businessmen and the real-life equivalents of 'Me and My Girl' lined up for the common crawl. Once the *rite de passage* had been accomplished to the instructor's satisfaction, my parents were, it seemed, qualified to sign on as air raid wardens, *should they be required*.

When my father's expertise in the distribution of oil products was deemed essential to the imminent war effort, patriotism required that he not return to New York. There was a long discussion between my parents over whether, like Max Mauser all those years ago, I should be sent alone across the Atlantic, to the safety of Kansas City. Whatever the clinching reason, it was concluded that we should all stay together, in England. Perhaps Cedric was slightly relieved: no more Kittinger.

In late August, when the first trainloads of evacuees began to leave the least-favoured parts of London, we were invited by Gladys and Teddy Slesinger (the surgeon whose ineptitude had blighted Cedric's life) to come and stay with them in their country house near East Grinstead. The generosity of the invitation was tainted by the fact that, although I did not know it, we were to be treated as what used to be called 'panel (or charity) patients'. Our presence exempted our hosts from having what Byron once called 'cockneys'* billeted on them. It was a *donnée* to be given prompt use by Evelyn Waugh in *Put Out More Flags*.

As usual, I was a docile little boy. The Slesingers had a son called John (by no means the same John Schlesinger as the film director) who drove around the gravelled paths of their garden in a model electric Daimler. I was suffered to

---

*Byron referred to Leigh Hunt's children by this unflattering term when Hunt and his 'common' wife came to stay with him in Pisa. The visit was intended to consolidate the joint editorship of a new liberal magazine which would advocate progressive principles and, no doubt, deplore snobbery. Byron's egalitarianism never inhibited him from being more equal than other people.

admire, but not to ride in it. John had a boiled egg for breakfast; I did not. I cannot remember resenting (or noticing) my small humiliations. Was I already sufficiently inured to England to be unsurprised by minute gradations of social status and their demeaning consequences? Or was I still enough of a Yank beneath the skin to regard the habits of the natives with unamazed, unaffronted curiosity? While my father commuted to London from Three Bridges station, my mother and I were limited to Certain Rooms in the house. I had to take my meals in the kitchen with John and mam'selle. We were somewhere between cabin class and steerage.

To know people who lived in a house, and not a flat, was unusual. The Slesingers' place was probably not as large as memory reconstructs it, but it was ample enough to have a chintzy 'morning room' and a conservatory and a garage for more than one car. It sported a grass tennis court, on which I cannot remember anyone playing, and an orchard. The hoop of drive at the front had an exit and an entrance. Mam'selle was supposed to teach John to speak French; there was also a cook and a housekeeper; gardeners manned the Atco mower and trimmed the edges and hedges.

Sunday, 3 September 1939, is a fine day. The sun glints on the dew which beads the wire surrounding the tennis court. Towards eleven o'clock in the morning everyone – family, guests and whatever staff are working at the weekend – assembles on the tennis court. A brown portable radio is put in the middle of the lawn, near the drooping net. We wait for the bongs of Big Ben to finish striking eleven, the very hour at which the Great War ended less than twenty-one years earlier. Everyone knows what Neville Chamberlain is about to say, but it will not be true until he says it: Germany has not withdrawn from Poland and 'accordingly' a state of war exists between Germany and Great Britain. No one smiles; no one sighs.

Chamberlain's voice sounded as if it had a bad back. It went on, and on, to say more than anyone cared to hear about the 'evil thing' which 'we shall now be fighting'. Was any declaration of war ever made in more civilian tones? How old Chamberlain sounded, how exhausted by the futility of his long accommodation with what he now denounced! He took it as a personal affront that Herr Hitler had not taken weakness for strength. I listened as a stranger: interested but not affected. The solemnity of the adults had to be respected, but I saw no clouds in my sky.

They were not slow in gathering. That afternoon, we heard the first air raid sirens. It was somehow known that it was a 'practice', but the undulant wailing introduced us to a school of apprehension. We went for a drive in the long evening shadows. There was an anti-aircraft emplacement on Crawley Down, lagged with properly filled sandbags. The thin Bofors barrels pointed upwards, and could be rotated by urgent hands. I had Dinky toys very like them. The clouds in my sky began to blacken only when it was decided that it would be unwise to return me to school in London. Sussex was not a target; the capital might well be. The bomber, it had been frequently said, 'will always get through'.

A few days later I was taken to see John Slesinger's preparatory school. It was called Copthorne, after a neighbouring village. Large brick buildings, with a gravel drive in front, looked out over the heathered downs. The school resembled an enlarged, institutional version of where we were staying. My parents spoke at length with the Headmaster, Mr Workman, and with his substantial wife.

Being the cossetted pawn of whatever moves seemed best to my parents, I knew neither dread nor hope. When they remarked on the fine grounds and the nice, big airy classrooms (the pupils were still on holiday) and on how lucky people were to be able to go to such a place, I sensed purpose in their enthusiasm but not yet its menacing relevance. In the car, they spoke, with rehearsed envy, as if I were not there, of how wonderful it would be if they could afford to send me to 'a place like that'.

Mr Moyles had made no provision for the outbreak of war. His school did not even have an air raid shelter. When the autumn term began, only a few pupils returned to Leinster House. I was not among them. I suspect that, until the last moment, I averted my attention, like a condemned man, from what was in store. The war had always been 'inevitable', but even now we were reassured by Chamberlain's advertised confidence that Hitler had 'missed the bus'. After that first false alarm, we heard no more wailing sirens. John continued to drive his electric Daimler along the crumbling, weedless gravel paths. I walked after him like an unmounted footman. Plump with money and easy expectations, he had a sleekness of body and social bearing. Neither kind nor unkind, he was of another species.

Towards the end of September, my parents went alone to Copthorne School and returned with what they promised was thrilling news: Mr Workman was making a special concession in taking me, at short notice and on generous terms, into what was recognised as 'one of the seven best prep schools in England'. Offering me this privilege was, it seemed, part of his war effort. Despite being taken 'up to town' to be fitted for the school uniform and other items on the long list of required clothing (including elastic-sided 'house shoes'), I had little idea of what boarding school entailed until the day came when, with my trunk packed (F.M.R. stencilled on the front) and my attaché case ready with 'overnight things', I was told that The Time Had Come. EYR 332 was waiting at the door, flying its metal flag.

As an inducement to be grateful, I was given a large wooden box containing a 'compendium of games'. It would be a collector's item today, so ingeniously was it fitted with bevelled partitions and of such well-turned quality were the chess- and draughtsmen. There was Halma, and Snakes and Ladders, on two sides of the same hinged board, and coloured discs to be advanced (or retreated) as the throw of the fat dice dictated. There were packs of cards, spillikins and other innocent pleasures which I might share with my new friends. Was I ready?

In New York, I had gone to hospital without fear or doubt about my parents' loving intentions. When I had to get into the Standard and drive the short way to Copthorne School, I lost both trust and dignity. I clung to the bannisters of the Slesingers' stairs and screamed until I was, literally, sick. As vomit puddled the patterned carpet, a look of disgust crossed the housekeeper's face. *Mam'selle* turned away. I was a long way from resembling the little boy whom I had observed peeing so impudently, and so smugly on his mother's carpet in St Louis. My parents were ashamed of me; I was ashamed of myself, but I yelled for a reprieve and would not be placated. Until that moment, I had never shown serious reluctance to do anything that I was told. That previous docility rendered my present behaviour all the more embarrassing (the Slesingers' servants were waiting to clear my room) and disloyal. It was very nearly unpatriotic.

My dread of leaving my mother was, no doubt, cowardly and selfish. I was an eight-year-old only child who did not want to be abandoned in a school where I would know nobody and sleep in a dormitory. Urged to 'think of the poor Poles', I did not feel the vocation; told that John would be my protector and friend, I knew better: I cannot remember ever even seeing him at Copthorne. It may be that he never went back there. For all I know, he was shipped off to safety in Canada.

My pale fingers had to be prised from the white paintwork of the nice clean bannisters. I doubt if anyone ever wanted to see me again as we left the Slesingers' house. My mother's face was clenched and thick with blood. She blushed for me and, I suspect, for herself: what was less likely for an

American (Jewish) mother than to have to say goodbye to her only child at the age of just eight? Irene's inability to save me from an English fate was something like a betrayal; we were never again to be quite the friends that we were before.

The oval driveway in front of the school was mournful with black cars. My father must have discussed the matter of my Jewishness with Mr Workman, because I was introduced to a slightly older boy called Henriques, in whose dorm I was to sleep.

For how many hours, or days, did I weep, and sniff? The Headmaster's wife was a wide, grey-haired woman and she called me 'Ra-file' with rasping tenderness. I had never been called anything but Freddie before. The nasal shrillness of her diction required me to answer to a name alien to my true self: little Freddie was someone 'Ra-file' now had not to be. Once we put on the uniforms of our surnames, our first (Christian) names might have been handed in, like our pocket money, for safe keeping. Only fools disclosed what their middle initials stood for: it was contemptible to have a 'funny' middle name. Although my 'M.' stood for nothing more improbable than Michael, I kept it to myself as if it were Montmorency or (heaven forbid) Mordecai. Nobody seemed amused by any of the last names of my fellow pupils. Brasier-Creagh, for instance, was never greeted with derision. It was apparently an honour to be 'hyphenated', perhaps because Americans never were.

Poor Mr Moyles, who now faced ruin, had prepared me well for Copthorne. I was put in form six(a) and settled, tearfully, to do whatever was asked of me. I added and subtracted; I spelt and I read aloud, in my Britished accent. I got up and folded my tartan blanket, had a cold bath and ate lumpy porridge. I ran about on the asphalt, skinned my knees, and learned a game called 'French and English'. In the afternoons, we played soccer.

63

When it rained, we went and changed from house shoes to outdoor shoes, put on our (blue) mackintoshes and went for a 'walk down the lane'. The masters had umbrellas. You could cadge shelter by asking them interesting questions. Mr McGaw, who had private means and arrived from his own house on a motor bicycle, sported a golfing umbrella with a wide span and panels of different colours. If he had not had private means, his umbrella might have been a bit off, but he was rumoured to run to a grapevine in his Horsham glass-house. Such a luxury was almost un-English, but it proved how hells rich he was. Mr McGaw taught maths with the genial authority which went with his heartlessly accurate nickname: 'Fatty Magaloon', as in 'Fatty Magaloon went up too soon/They thought he was a barrage balloon'. He called me 'Blackie', on account of my very black hair. Mr Woodward, Mr Crowe and a few of their other colleagues were quartered in 'the masters' cottage'. Only twenty yards from the main buildings, they remained within easy range of Mrs Workman's undeniable summons.

The school had its own raspberry-coloured chapel, with a square tower and a gilded cross on the top. On Sundays, Mr Workman, in a surplice, read the lesson from a gilt lectern. How soon was it before, in the line of Christian duty, he uttered the word 'Jew'? By what instinct of covert refusal did I refrain from bowing my head in the Creed, for which we all turned towards Jerusalem, in ritual orientation? Did Henriques bow? Were there other Jews who practised a similar furtive recusance? I never looked, and hoped they never looked at me. Two boys were said to be 'RC'. They went off on Sunday mornings to some unmentionable desti-nation. Catholicism was not despicable, like Jewishness; it was more like a sort of spiritual boss-eyedness.

I entered on a long decade of dissident conformity. It was made easier by not clashing with any deeply held belief or expected practice. My mother had assured me that we all

64

worshipped the same God, but that Jews did not believe that the Messiah had yet put in an appearance, whereas Christians did. Despite the squeamishness of my parents, and of a culture in which the word penis was proscribed, I was aware that being circumcised was a mark of Jewishness. However, I soon realised, with relief, that it was not unique to Jews: the cold baths in the morning were taken in a row of tubs which denied privacy to their shivering users. The prepubertal size of our genitals was further shrivelled by instinctive retraction from the cold water, but enough was visible to confirm that 'roundheads' and 'cavaliers' were quite evenly distributed.

I discovered at Copthorne that English society proceeded on what I lacked the vocabulary to call a binary notation. In almost all aspects of life, the English were divided into two camps, one of which assumed the high ground. Not only was Oxford better than Cambridge, but the Navy trumped the Army (the RAF came nowhere, yet); chess outranked draughts; amateurs professionals; cricket rounders; soccer rugger; Rolls-Royces Jaguars; boys girls (obviously); Englishmen foreigners; the titled the untitled; the AA the RAC (RAC men didn't salute); trams trolley-buses. The cars of richer parents paraded silver affiliations to all kinds of associations. Their front bumpers were surmounted by a rack of badges, which could be lethal to pedestrians. To avert such accidents, England had been newly furnished with 'Belisha beacons'. Their orange globes flashed adjacent to silver-studded crossings where motorists were required to defer to those on foot. The beacons had been invented by, or at least named after, Leslie Hore-Belisha, the Transport Minister, whose fame had been enhanced by their proliferation. Whether or not he himself had given the beacons their still current prefix, Hore-Belisha had undoubtedly *drawn attention to himself* on account of them. That he was a Jew was widely known and became a matter for sour comment when he was promoted to Minister of War. The Nazis and their local supporters in the British Union of Fascists drew sneering attention to the 'alien' provenance of the man in charge of the War Office; so did a number of obsolete generals whose competence he questioned or whose tactics he sought to modernise.

The *Evening Standard* cartoonist David Low had invented a character called Colonel Blimp, whose reactionary pronouncements were preceded by 'Gad, sir...'. Low favoured Hore-Belisha's renovation of the War Office and so, probably, did Winston Churchill, whose return to the government, as First Lord of the Admiralty, was as popular now as his 'trouble-making' had been reprehensible in the long years of Chamberlain's ascendancy. A signal had been flashed to the fleet 'WINSTON IS BACK', which – Lord Beaverbrook's *Daily Express* promised – had hugely raised morale. It had certainly raised Beaverbrook's, if not that of the majority of Tory MPs, whose hero was still Neville Chamberlain. They had cheered when he announced 'PEACE IN OUR TIME' and hoped that even now he might retrieve it. The datedness of his personal wardrobe – the wing collar, the droopy cravat, the umbrella, the homburg hat – seemed to certify his honesty. The evidence that, like the undertaker he resembled, he took no pleasure in his office proved his aptitude for it, at least until men were called upon to die.

Hore-Belisha was given little time to reform the backward-looking Army. The Brass regarded him as a menace without the pedigree to excuse his impudence. He was encouraged to urgency, and tactlessness, by colleagues, perhaps including Chamberlain, who failed to stand by him when he ran up against more Blimps than he could resist single-handed. The Jew's unlamented eviction was a symptom of something which I, as a small boy, could not articulate, but of which I was anxiously conscious. I associated Hore-Belisha with my shiny-faced fellow-Copthornian Henriques who, rather like the minister, figured only briefly,

66

and marginally, in my life. Henriques left without our ever having acknowledged the affinity which supposedly bound us. I was not sorry. Hore-Belisha was unembittered and became a long-lived Lord.

I had my first sexual experience when sitting at one of the desks in Big School. Three places long and made of solid wood, they were mounted on cast-iron hinges which allowed the portion on which we usually rested our books to be rotated so as to form the back of a bench from which to watch plays or magic lantern shows. My experience in no way declared itself as sexual. Involuntary pleasure preceded knowledge, or desire. No precocious erotic fancies accompanied what happened until I reached puberty and matched appetite to performance. What happened was an involuntary response to the pressure to write answers in good time for a test. I found it a comfort to sit forward on the bench and fret myself, inside my shorts, by rubbing my behind against the bench in such a way that I became excited. It would be sweet to claim that I discovered this form of obtaining relief from anxiety while conjugating the Latin verb *amo, amas, amat* (I love, thou lovest, he loves); it may even be true. I never found myself in a state of excited apprehension except towards the end of a lesson: the need to finish caused a general acceleration. Only when I was twelve or thirteen, and discovered myself wet after this secret indulgence, did I guess its source, or make it a consciously contrived pleasure. Lacking a suitable gutter in which to fish, I was not a precocious or well-informed child.

When, years later, I read that Byron had been introduced to sex by May Gray, a Scottish nurse, at the age of nine, I saw no reason to share his biographers' questioning of wee Georgie's veracity. Am I alone in associating solitary sex with work rather than with pleasure? I doubt it; writing, in particular, can be a somewhat furtive act, and close to an erotic one: a scene is often certified by the degree to which it excites its author. Why else does he so often crave privacy and a closed door? Few writers, however grandiose their affectations, would choose to compose in a room where they could easily be observed. The penis mightier than the sword is a misprint that needs no Freud.

My parents must have come to see me that first term at Copthorne, but I remember neither their visits nor the Christmas of 1939. Since it seemed safe to return to London, I took the school train from Horley to Waterloo and was met by my mother. Had I had a good term? My report said so. Had I enjoyed myself? Perhaps I said so. Where was my compendium of games in its fine wooden box with the plywood partitions? It had been too ostentatious, and I too powerless to protect it from the experienced pirates among the older boys. They 'borrowed' its contents and 'forgot' to give them back. I was wise, or intimidated, enough not to report them (nothing was worse than a sneak). Thenceforth I tried to limit my personal possessions to what could be kept in my pockets.

My parents were now air raid wardens. They had been kitted with blue uniforms and greyish tin hats for when they went on duty in the sandbagged brick ARP Post. The 'tin' of their hats was, in fact, some kind of composition. A lace threaded around the brim deprived them of martial aspect. The wardens' duties were to patrol, with muted torches, and to be on hand if there was an Incident. Their equipment included a stirrup pump for dealing with incendiaries which – official posters warned – *were to be expected*.

The stirrup pump was designed to straddle a bucket of water, so that the end of the pipe was under the surface and the metal footpiece on the ground. You put your foot on the stirrup to keep the apparatus steady and then pumped hard while directing the hose at the conflagration. There were also buckets of sand with which to douse the flames. The ARP Post was a social centre, important with a baize noticeboard and a red telephone *for authorised use only*. My mother's prompt enrolment, and charming presence, somewhat alleviated the acid disappointment which American aloofness excited. 'No one's blaming *you*, Irene,' was the preamble to the usual reproaches.

The grassy grounds of the flats were soon divided into allotments. Only the lawns not visible from the main road were dug up. Our neighbour was Brigadier Morgan, who had a gammy leg from the First Show. In the daytime, he obeyed the injunction to Dig for Victory; in the evenings, he sometimes partnered his wife at bridge against my parents. The Brigadier was an immoderate version of Colonel Blimp. His wife's bidding – or her understandable hesitations before doing so – caused his face to become engorged. When she bid, whatever she bid, his monocle (of course he had one) dropped, like a hanged man, to the limit of its black ribbon. On more than one occasion, he rushed from the room and slammed more doors than the flat was known to contain. When he returned, he said, 'I have just taken two aspirin tablets to avoid having an apoplectic fit.'

The Brigadier was not usually given to apoplexy during daylight hours. The cultivation of patriotic cabbages was his pride and, it seemed, his sedative. One morning, however, he was heard exploding with rage. The United Dairies' horse had profited from the milkman's absence up the back stairs of our block to enjoy the maturing cabbages which were just within reach when he stretched his neck over the Brigadier's fence. The horse should have been courtmartialled, and shot, in any properly run country. Since my mother always had the Express Dairy (shapelier bottles with foil, not cardboard, caps), no blame could be imputed to us.

The air raid shelters were strengthened compartments, with bunks and chairs and tables, built in the half-underground garages of the flats. Good women made cocoa and offered biscuits. If the sirens went at the right moment, instead of having to go to bed, I could stay up, waiting for the All Clear, till past midnight, listening to adult conversation and being admired for my stoicism. It was so enjoyable that I became quite resentful if the Germans refrained from provoking the undulating moan of the sirens. Can those unfrightening early alerts date from as early as the winter of 1939–40? How soon was rationing introduced? When I went to Cullen's with my mother, I was amazed that as well as taking your coupons (clipped out by officiously sharp scissors) the shop still expected to be paid. I had had the naive expectation of a communist society in which everyone would be handed equal shares of everything.

The *Daily Express*, always in the patriotic vanguard – as its helmeted talisman, the Beaverbrookian Crusader, insisted – had a special offer: you could send for a detailed map of France, where it was assumed that the war would again be sited, and sheets of gum-backed swastikas, Union Jacks and tricolours. You cut the flags out and folded them over a pin before licking the gum. One such map was stuck on the wall in Big School. Activity on the Western Front could then be pinpointed according to the latest communiqués. During the first months of the war, there was small detectable movement of any kind.

Occasionally, we would see khaki lorries crossing Crawley Down and the odd aeroplane made us all look up, but the biggest military excitement for us was when Mr Woodward went into the Army. Delamain was knowledgeable about the Air Force; he could even recognise a Bolton-Paul defiant: its four machine-guns were mounted in a bubble behind the pilot and rotated to pursue enemy aircraft. In the event, the machine proved too unmanoeuvrable and its turret too ill-sited to stay in production. Spitfires and Hurricanes were faster and better designed, and just as well, considering how good the Messerschmitt 109 and 110s were.

While the BEF and the French faced the Germans along the Maginot Line, and Bud Flanagan – my father's favourite English comedian – sang about 'hanging out the washing on the Siegfried Line', I was sentenced to become an English schoolboy. Ethical Culture forgotten, *mensa, mensa, mensam* supplanted progressive education. Latin had a labyrinthine grammar which would keep me busy, and memorising, for years. No sooner had one conjugation or declension been mastered than another took its place, more terrible yet in the multiplicity of its unpredictable formations. What American kid called 'Quis?' when he wanted to get rid of something, or '*ego!*' if he craved it? Or had heard of *amabimini* at the age of eight? As the war proceeded outside, the panoply of Latin grammar marched through my classroom in unstoppable, endless force. The active voice was succeeded by the passive, the passive by the middle. The first conjugation, with its heavy equipment for all possible temporal contingencies (the future perfect had a utopian ring), was succeeded by a second and a third and a fourth. Even then, there were – like some exotic colonial volunteers – the irregular verbs, with their shaggy eccentricities. Behind the two-faced deponent brigade (*hortor* and co.) came a file of gallantly verbose 'defective' verbs. Like legless veterans (such as Douglas Bader) who still wanted to do their bit, *accidit* and *convenit*, as it happened, performed limited duties: *oportet** (it behoves) set a good example.

Diligence in learning whatever was set before me became a kind of war work. I was eager to shine, and to stay unreproached and, if possible, unremarked. My Jewishness was the secret which might, at any moment, make me the target of schoolboys who – however genial individually – were

---

* 'Impersonal' forms often ordained what should done. Copthorne's library contained a Winchester glossary: '*Non licet*' ('it is not lawful') Gate denoted an entrance not licensed for boys' use.

united by a compendium of jeers ('Don't be a Jew', 'Don't let him Jew you') which they brought with them from home, along with their sponge bags, toothbrushes, Cash's name-taped wardrobe and recondite middle ('family') names. There was no personal animus in their malice; it was the fruit of a presumption of superiority warranted by Britannia's ruling of the waves, and of the Empire. If you didn't like it, you could go back where you came from; if they'd have you.

One of the boys I liked best was called Richardson; he was large and protective and unmistakably fair. At the beginning of 1940, I was briefly shocked to hear that he had left the school at Christmas: he was going to be evacuated to America. I was already sufficiently indoctrinated to share the view that my friend was being a bit unpatriotic, not to say yellow. The same was being said of Auden and Isherwood, but not by anyone whom I or my parents knew. What was Auden or Isherwood to them?

A week or two later, Richardson's photograph was on the front page of the skimpy newspapers. He was depicted, white-toothed but oil-darkened, being picked up from the lifeboat where, so the other survivors said, he had kept everybody cheerful after the ship in which they were heading for Canada had been torpedoed in the North Atlantic. I could not help thinking that, given the chance, I should be very happy to keep people cheerful if it meant getting my picture in the newspaper. The only time I had ever seen my name in the headlines was when my mother took me to the New York World's Fair. She paid for a single copy of that day's The New York Times to carry a special headline, 'LITTLE FREDDIE RAPHAEL VISITS WORLD'S FAIR', in place of the regular one.

Nothing specific flickers on the screen of memory until the beginning of the summer term of 1940. Each of us was given a small plot of ground in which to plant Carter's Tested

Seeds, whose factory I had seen adjacent to the (three-lane) Kingston bypass. The plots were squared off by intersecting concrete paths along which we carried our watering cans. Like Brigadier Morgan, we were vigilant for any malevolent or envious intruder who might muck about with our mustard or crush our cress.

The goalposts had now been removed and cricket pitches mown and rolled. The mower, towed behind the groundsman's tractor, was several yards wide. It threw up coils of green shards in its gnashing wake. There was a terraced pavilion for the top game, which was controlled by Mr McGaw in his Nomads club sweater. His Nomads had nothing to do with those for whom my father had kept wicket; the former played for a school called Charterhouse, where Mr McGaw had been. The noblest ambition for Copthorne boys was to go to Winchester; Eton was all right, if your father had been there. Even day schools such as St Paul's were not quite proper public schools. Grammar schools were the utter end.

Beginners were sent to the smaller pavilion, at the bottom of the long, sloping field, to learn cricket under Mr Crowe. Our Pav. was a thatched shed. The benches inside had slatted seats that lifted up for bats and pads to be stored inside. Unpopular boys were put in there too, and the bench sat on until they 'lobbed' (wept) to be let out, and then a little longer.

It was more fun to play cricket than to watch it on Putney Heath. We started with only one leg padded. Narrowmouthed Mr Crowe threw the hard ball with sardonic accuracy, just a little harder than he need, in order to teach us the rudiments of stroke play. I was discovered to require radical correction: my instinct was to play 'the wrong way round'. There might be people who succeeded in batting in this sinister fashion (Maurice Leyland played for England), but it would not do for schoolboys. Mr Crowe took me by the shoulders and reversed my stance. That was much better, wasn't it? I endured what I was powerless to resist. Was conforming any more unnatural than to 'pitch' the ball without bending one's arm? English life was full of aberrations which were said to be the only way to do things, and therefore *were*, if you didn't want to be an outsider.

English lessons were dominated by a chunky green textbook in which the rules of grammar, and acceptable clichés, were set out. Things might be 'as easy as falling off a log', but 'easy as pie' was 'slang'. Grammar included not only the proper spelling of singulars and plurals but also something called 'Correct Forms of Address'. Implicit in a middle-class education was learning how to speak to one's betters, or to those on whom one hoped to make a good impression, such as mayors or magistrates ('Your Worship'), bishops or judges ('My Lord'). The younger sons of major peers were referred to in one way ('Lord Edward Horsham') and mere peers ('Lord Horsham') in another. To make a mistake in such matters was not as socially damning as dropping an aitch, but it was nearly as bad as saying 'Pardon?' or wiping your nose on your sleeve. Our laundry was done once a week, and one handkerchief was meant to last that long. When you had a cold, it became stiff and stinking, but you still had to wait to have it replaced. You could wipe your nose on 'Bronco', but the lavatory paper was quite stiff, and slick, and unabsorbent.*

In English, we also learned the proper way of speaking to,

---

*I was surprised to be conscripted to go to the lavatory immediately after breakfast. Mr Howard had a chart, on a clipboard, with a square for each boy and each day. As he despatched us to a vacated stall, he put a slanted pencil mark against our names. An only child, I was unaccustomed to the smell of used toilets and, as an American, to scratchy 'bog paper'. I often did not do my duty when Mr Howard sent me to a smelly 'bog'. I held my breath, and waited and pulled the chain and went back later.

or about, ambassadors, colonial governors and, of course, members of the royal family and the peerage all the way down to those who were merely 'honourable'. It was unlikely that we should soon be called upon to greet a prince of the blood, but it was important to be equipped to do so at a moment's notice. The expression 'Mr President' never figured in our preparations for social ascent. 'Mr Chairman' was more useful: England flourished with committees. 'Mr Mayor' was, of course, familiar to us: Larry the Lamb often addressed him in Children's Hour. How many of us were now prepared to admit to anything so wet as having listened to it?

In May 1940, Things Started Moving on the Western Front. The Allied flags, which had stood stiffly immobile on the Daily Express war maps, ever since we inserted them, had to retreat and 're-group' according to the latest news in Mr Howard's copy of The Times, the only newspaper he trusted. Mr Howard taught French to the First and Second Forms. He was Mr Workman's partner, though he did not dispute 'Skete''s primacy. Mr Workman had to be called 'Sir' to his face but his steely-eyed wife called him 'Skete', sharply, and unconcealedly, whenever she needed him. The boys used this name, behind his back, with a frisson of impudence. Mr Howard had no nickname that I can remember. On walks, he carried an ash stick, with a knuckled top. His and Mr Workman's dyarchy was most evident in the fact that they alone could cane delinquent pupils. If it was not unknown for small American boys to be threatened with being 'spanked', did any American school to which my parents would have dreamed of sending me make a ritual of whipping small boys on their bare behinds?

I was neither shocked nor surprised to hear that this happened. I listened, or overheard, with interest that while Mr Workman was known to give you more strokes (a pretty instance of what I would learn, before I left the school, was to be termed *meiosis*), Mr Howard was feared for the skill with which he landed all his, in stingingly rapid succession, on the same spot. To be punished in this way required some signal act of 'impertinence' or wilful mischief. The school slang for having been caned was to have been 'sponged', which rhymed with 'longed'. Who knows the origins of this term? I never saw it used in any schoolboy tales (*The Fifth Form at St Dominic's* was to be one of my favourites). 'Skete' and 'spong' were, so to say, *hapax legomena*, one-offs limited to Copthorne School, Sussex. Part of the grounds were rumoured to abut on to Surrey, but it was ill-mannered to say so: Surrey was lower class than Sussex. Luckily, my father supported Middlesex, which was the best sex there was.

During the later days of May, the sunshine required us constantly to water our carrots and worry about our spring onions. Each row was flagged by thrusting a stick through the Carter's packet in which we had bought the seeds from Mr McGaw. He opened a portable after-lunch shop from a big Revelation suitcase. Our purchases were entered in an account book and their price deducted from the pocket money Kept Safe until the end of term. Money was not nice to talk about; nor were we allowed to have any in our pockets.

The early summer heat was sufficient for a small fire to start in the heather on the common in front of the school. There was a call for volunteers before it spread. Relays of buckets were passed to the masters nearest the blaze, but it was already zigzagging among the roots of the heather. The horizon was unfocused by wavering air. There was no opportunity for heroism on the scale of Richardson in the lifeboat, but I seconded Mr McGaw with loyal buckets and joined him in beating out the scurrying flames that blackened the ground. 'Don't stay if you don't want to, Blackie,' he said. 'I'm all right, sir.' It was a little war and, by the time the fire brigade arrived, we could report a little victory. The blackened common was a petty presage of what was coming to London.

Preston knew about butterflies. He was one of those gentle boys who passed through the merciless machinery of an English middle-class education without incurring the malice of bullies or the coercive rectitude of the staff. If Preston had wanted to bat left-handed, I doubt if Mr Crowe would have sought to make him more dexterous. I am not sure that Preston batted, or fielded, at all. If he did the latter, it would have been deep in the deep, where the Boadicean blades of the school mower had not slashed the wild flowers or disturbed their fluttering freight of Purple Emperors, White Admirals and other gaudy lepidopterous dignitaries, including Death's Head Hawk moths, which were rare. Preston had a book in which the varieties of British moths and butterflies were extensively ranged, rather as fleets were in the copy of Jane's *Fighting Ships* which Taylor had in his locker ('And no, you *can't* borrow it'). It seemed strange, but somehow typically British, that someone called Jane should be the presiding expert on battleships, battle-cruisers, and all the intermediate vessels between *Rodney* and *Nelson* down to fleet auxiliaries. Jane even knew how many admirals Paraguay had. The general opinion was that any side that had 'pocket battleships' (only the Germans did) was a bit sneaky. They went with colonel-generals basically.

I sought Preston's company less because I shared his enthusiasm than because he was both gentle and indifferent: I was a moth attracted to his mild flame. He alleviated my solitude without intruding on my privacy. Unlike Denton, with his pitiless blue eyes, or Clode, whose shock of black hair seemed to make him eager to prove that he and I had nothing else in common, Preston was neither dangerous nor inquisitive. He captured his specimens with artfully cupped hands, so as not to damage their dusty colouring. He took so much trouble that he seemed to do a favour to those he pinned to his board. He spread their wings and braced them open, while they stiffened, with non-sticky transparent strips. The white board was scored with narrow slots, in which the insects' bodies were entrenched so that the wings could be stretched flat. Preston explained to me several times what the difference was between the wing structure and anatomy of moths and butterflies. I should not have cared to bet my life on restating it. The woods of Sussex were so nervous with now extinct specimens that we could despise prolix varieties such as Red Admirals or Cabbage Whites. The Camberwell Beauty, whose nickname was 'the mourning cloak', was still to be found, and admired.

As the German flags advanced into north-eastern France, Mr Howard was confident that the Allies were laying a trap for Master Hitler. Like the Kaiser before him, friend Adolf would pay the price for his rashness in not honouring Belgian neutrality. *Caesar oppugnat Belgas*, a key phrase in our first Latin lessons, reported an unprovoked attack which no one ever criticised, although Caesar's was scarcely more justified than Hitler's. Caesar was an irreproachable goody; his standing was a tribute less to his personal modesty than to that of his prose style.

Mr Howard's reliable sources expected that when the lines 'stabilised', a large section of the German army would be 'cut off'. Lord Gort VC knew what he was doing, even if the French didn't necessarily. By the end of May, gardeners could feel the Sussex ground pulse slightly beneath their sandalled feet. We did not quite *hear* the gunfire; we felt it in the dislocation of the heavy air. Nothing changed, until everything did. One day Mr Workman told us that we must pack our trunks and attaché cases and prepare to go home 'temporarily'. Since Copthorne lay on the likeliest flight path to London from northern France, which was falling under German control, we should to have to 'evacuate'.

Unlike Mr Moyles, Skete had made provision for what might happen if there was a war. Having taken soundings from People Who Knew About These Things, he was advised, off the record, that north Devon was an unlikely target for the Luftwaffe, if the worst came to the worst. The worst now pretty well had, so we should have to go home for 'a week or two' while as much as possible – not least the stock of grammars and textbooks – was removed to the Lee Bay Hotel, on which Mr Workman had taken an option in good time. Since no one was likely to go on a seaside holiday while there was a war on, the owners were happy to vacate it, 'for the duration'.

On the train from Horley to Waterloo, it seemed to me that the war was going very much my way. First I had been able to stay up way past my bedtime, thanks to 'the alert going', and now I was going to have an unscheduled holiday in Highlands Heath. At some point I had made a new Putney friend, another Martin to replace the one which, somewhat like a Bolton-Paul Defiant, had proved not to have the right specifications. Martin Warburton was a freckled boy, with specs and red hair; he was a mild version of Richmal Crompton's Ginger, Just William's naughty friend. Martin's mother had been 'on the stage', which explained her peroxide blonde curls. His father, who was a good deal older, had what was called a 'dry sense of humour': he 'twinkled' and 'came out' with mordant remarks. When Martin told me a joke from the First World War, it almost certainly derived from his father. A Tommy recalls how he was challenged by a French sentry: '*Qui va là?*' The quick response? '*Je*, says I, knowing the language.' Did I get it? If I did, it was a tribute to Mr Howard, who was later to infect me with a strong wish to go to France as soon as possible. This was primed by his telling us that, in a place called Normandie (which I knew only as a liner that rivalled the *Queen Mary* for the Blue Riband of the Atlantic, and failed), they had restaurants where the menu bore the legend '*Cidre compris*' which meant that the price included as much cider as you wanted. Why this so beguiled me, I cannot say; I have never liked cider.

Martin Warburton and I rode our bikes round and round the grounds of Highlands Heath. Our cheerfulness excited suspicious glares from the Brigadier, who was now on the *qui vive* for defeatists and possible Fifth Columnists, as well as for the United Dairies' horse, with its unpatriotic appetite. The *Punch* cartoonist 'Fougasse'* (just the kind of totally foreign name I could be glad my 'F' didn't stand for) had done a series of posters to deter people from 'Careless Talk' which 'Costs Lives'. He depicted Hitler's huge ear pressed to every wall, cadging vital information. Since the Germans were closing on Dunkirk and had driven the British and a large part of the French army into a 'pocket', sleeves needed to be rolled up and mouths kept shut.

David Low produced a cartoon for the advent of Winston Churchill in Downing Street: all the recognisable politicians of the day (of whom even an immigrant child could recognise a great number) were shown rolling up their sleeves while marching in step behind the new leader. 'We're all behind you, Winston', said the caption. In fact, the enthusiasm of not a few, especially in his own party, lagged a considerable way behind their leader's. My parents bought a jaundiced pamphlet entitled *Guilty Men*, in which the Tory recusants were denounced by 'Cassius', a pseudonymous Troika that included Michael Foot, whose Labour Party had voted against every increase in the defence budget. The guilt on Foot's side of the House went unremarked, despite Quintin Hogg's now forgotten counter-blast: *The Left was Never Right*.

---

*The movie *Donnie Brasco* begins with Johnny Depp playing a (fake) jewel fence who detects Al Pacino trying to sell him a 'diamond' ring which he declares '*fougasse*', fake or dodgy. Is that the origin of the cartoonist's pseudonym? It may come from the Provençal loaf of the same name.

When Martin and I tired of bicycling round and round, he taught me how to play Monopoly. It was to become the sole indoor currency of our friendship. Because I was at boarding school, we saw each other only intermittently in the years that followed. I never asked where he went to school and we never discussed anything we had learned. We resumed our property battles with a fervour worthy of a more demanding, less repetitive, game. Our dialogue consisted of 'I'll buy it', 'Rent, please', 'I'm building houses' and 'You'll have to pull down some houses and/or mortgage something'. The desire to win was less urgent than the dread of losing. We therefore evolved a banking system of modest sophistication, which made loans so easily available that our games were as endless as we chose to make them. When summoned for meals, or invited to get some fresh air, we were always able to say, 'We haven't quite finished.'

There was talk of people who had come back from Dunkirk and had 'slept non-stop for three days'. I had no contact with survivors nor any notion of how great the disaster had been. The poet laureate, John Masefield, wrote a quick, short book transforming the retreat into a miracle; there had been angels at Mons, and now God had calmed the Channel for us. The Royal Navy remained our 'bulwark' and 'unchallenged mistress of the seas'. My mother's standing rose when the Americans agreed to Lend-Lease. However, not everyone applauded a deal whereby Britain acquired fifty obsolete destroyers and the ruddy Yanks got their hands on some palmy islands in the Caribbean. Mr Roosevelt was heard on short-wave radio, telling us, in spasms of undulating unctuousness, that he sent us ... his prayers and that America – the 'bastion of democracy' – would not stand idly by while freedom was extinguished in Europe. In the meantime, he proposed to stand for re-election. One of the planks of his platform was that he would not send American boys to fight in foreign wars.

In the midsummer of 1940, when France had fallen and the Heinkels and Dorniers were beginning to bring loud danger to 'these shores', I boarded the train at Waterloo, together with Mr Howard, Mr McGaw and other members of the staff too old or too unfit for active service. How long was it before the billboards told us 'You Are Now Entering the Strong Country'? It sounded admirably muscular and reassuring. How soon did I learn that 'Strong' was the name of a West Country brewer? We went through Reading, Salisbury, Yeovil, Taunton and reached Exeter Central, where an extra engine, or two, had to be put on to climb the north Devon hills: 'One of the steepest gradients in England,' Mr Howard said. Like Dr Watson, he knew his Bradshaw.

From Ilfracombe we were driven by charabanc through the high-hedged lanes of an England unpurged by pesticides. Swatches of unripe blackberries and sloes were flattened against the windows of the bus as we dropped down towards the little cove where I was to spend most of the war. The Lee Bay Hotel was almost flush with the beach. Its porticoed entrance faced two tennis courts – soon converted into chicken runs – and was embellished with prolific fuchsia bushes, the stems of whose flowers we learned to suck. Their sweetness supplemented our rations of Fry's Chocolate Sandwich, Licorice All-Sorts and Rowntree's Fruit Gums. Quakers were good people, although they were pacifists, and particularly clever at sweets and chocolates.

Mr McGaw's portable shop came with him: in addition to sweets and penknives (the most expensive with a special hook for extracting stones from horses' hooves) he now also stocked 6d. National Savings stamps. It helped the war effort to buy and stick them in our savings books. Mr Crowe, who never seemed young enough, had 'joined up'. I did not miss his corvine presence. Mr McGaw might now teach me cricket (it seemed a mark of favour that he called me by a nickname). Alas, the valley in which the hotel stood was too narrow and the ground too tussocked for anything but rounders and a game called 'paddle-ball', which had a wicket like a noticeboard which the 'bowler' tried to hit full toss.

Indoors, the Lee Bay Hotel allowed an easy translation from Sussex. The large majority of Copthorne pupils had not deserted Mr Workman. Each of the forms still had its own room, or a section of a large room. All of us slept on the same iron bedsteads, with the same folded tartan blankets at the end. We were distributed through the various bedrooms, in smaller, friendlier groups than in the long Sussex dormitories. Since there was no chapel, on Sundays we walked to the village church, which was gaudily decorated in heavenly blue, badged with gold stars. The very old clergyman kept things short. During the day he walked, slowly, around the village in a blue cape with a gilt clasp, like the bereted curé in an old French film.

The masters again had their own cottage, on a concrete spur bracketed by the pinkish sea wall, at the right-hand corner of the bay. In summer, the estuary lapped the wall at high tide. Slate cliffs slanted into the green-black water on each side of the bay. When the tide receded, a broad tongue of beige sand glistened between toothy rocks. Facing the masters' cottage, on the far side of the beach, a one-in-five road went up towards Morte Ho. It took us steeply above the shingled roof of a dilapidated building which we were soon calling 'the smugglers' hideaway'. Years later, the Lee Bay Hotel was reported to be the discreet base of an IRA gang smuggling arms into, and out of, the country. There was a gate in the slate wall near the top of the hill, leading up sepulchral steps to a cliff-top golf course. We collected mushrooms as big as plates on the abandoned fairways. Preston taught me to tickle trout in the clear valley streams. There were different butterflies to catch and a variety of droppings to be identified: goat, sheep, rabbit, fox. On fine days, you could see Lundy Island, where the rare puffin nested.

It must have been a complex logistical operation to transport the school and so much of its equipment to north Devon. None of us was either grateful or surprised. Life resumed, with the same lessons, the same vocabulary and more or less the same diet. Lunch was our big meal. After the main course, tureens of 'soup' were put in front of Skete and the other masters who sat at the head of the same long tables we had had in Sussex. 'Soup' consisted of appropriate leftovers from the previous day's lunch, boiled up with fresh vegetables and, very often, with pearl barley. Anyone who wanted more passed up his plate. Oliver Twist should have gone to Copthorne.

Mr McGaw bore separation from his grapevine without complaint. Am I imagining that he continued to ride his motorbike? Mr Workman certainly obtained enough petrol for his Wolseley to be able to use it for emergencies. Mr McGaw's modest dignity continued to be sustained by his private income (despite 50 per cent income tax). When he presided over a table at lunch, he would ask the boy on his right to go to Mr Workman's table and request to borrow the pepper. After he had shaken it over his food, it was returned 'with my thanks'. I associated pepper with adult taste, and independent means.

The Battle of Britain had no direct impact on north Devon. We could listen to the news on Mr Workman's wireless. It was in the study where he kept the canes which, like the Roman lictor's *fasces* (bundle of rods) confirmed his summary authority. Unlike the lictors, he made no parade of them. The honest voice of the BBC announcer (Bruce Belfrage, Frank Gillard or Frank Phillips) assured us that dozens of German planes had been shot down, with much smaller losses on our side. Many of our pilots were said to be safe; none was ever said to have been burnt.

It would be pious to claim that I worried about my parents. They were directly under the bombers' path, but I had such delusions of exception, mixed with so keen an awareness of my own anxieties, that I seldom gave them much thought: I *knew* that nothing would happen to them. Besides, they could stay up as late as they liked, while I had the fourth declension to memorise: *exercitus, exercitus, exercitum, exercitus, exercitui, exercitu*. The rumour was that we would soon be doing algebra and 'trig'.

Lessons did not change; leisure time did. Since the playing field was so narrow, and the beach but a short walk away (Mr McGaw let us run there in bare feet sometimes), we spent sunny afternoons building sandcastles, and swimming, rather than learning how to play forward to a well-pitched ball or bowl a good length. Delamain, whose father was already a colonel, was patient and deft in creating villages and road systems on the black rocks which badged the sandy bed of the bay. We played in exclusive tandem, keeping away from louder, more aggressive boys. If necessary, we prised the big, ribbed limpets from their lodging on the rocks, but we tried to re-attach them well away from our building sites. Other boys made sport by throwing stones at them. They laughed as they pulsed and leaked in the ruins of their shells. We caught shrimps in the clear rock pools and took them back in string-handled jamjars to be boiled for tea.

That summer term lasted longer than any other. Boys with homes in London were 'kept back', by arrangement with grateful parents. The term seemed to go on and on, and on, although we did little work once the holidays would have begun. The masters must have rotated, so that they could have some leave, but we never noticed. Delamain and I built town after town, bridge after bridge, corniche after corniche. As the tide surged in from the Severn estuary, we constructed dams and defences which might protect our frail colonies. The next day we would find the pancaked towers of yesterday's Nineveh and Tyre. The days seemed endless. We went to bed in sunshine. Can it have been as early as 1940 that they brought in 'double daylight saving time' (to me the phrase had an American ring)? By advancing the clocks yet another hour, people could do a full day's work in the light and reach home, and the shelters, before the night's bombs began to fall, far away from us.

Mr Howard, whose urgent movements and brisk tongue contrasted with Skete's gravity, was something of an actor. When he read to us, as we sat in a circle on the grass lawn of the hotel next to the croquet hoops (Masters Only), he enlivened the dialogue with a range of accents and dramatic pauses. He particularly favoured Sherlock Holmes stories. The first I remember was *The Speckled Band*. The character of Colonel Sebastian Roylott was very much in Mr Howard's genre; the controlled menace of the man came across in the snap of his speech and the terseness of the prose. When he bent Holmes's poker, and Holmes was said to have bent it back again afterwards, Mr Howard's disbelief ceased to be suspended: he explained that it was, in practice, impossible to straighten a bent poker with your bare hands (as Conan Doyle was, no doubt, straightfacedly aware).

As the war went on, Mr Howard proceeded to a whole range of popular classics, from Victor Hugo and Alexander Dumas to John Buchan and Anthony Hope. Conan Doyle was his favourite: Brigadier Gerard and *The White Company* hardly less than Sherlock Holmes. One of Conan Doyle books was set in the Regency, during which Jew Mendoza was a bare-knuckle boxing champion. The school library was sensibly unpretentious and only incidentally instructive: you could learn quite a lot about French history from *Under the Red Robe* and other chastely racy stories by H. Seton Merriman and Stanley Weyman. There was also Francis Beeding and the Hentys, father and son, whose heroes fought gallantly for every reactionary cause which European history, and its inexhaustible antagonisms, could supply.

86

Mr Howard was a pale man who rarely stopped to talk to the boys whom he was happy to entertain. Shy of personal contact (he had no wife), he was at once present and fugitive. He opened my eyes, and ears, to a variety of dialogue and narrative; his readings made me realise that prose too can have a voice. Yet he left no affectionate impression. I could never forgive him for one piece of abrupt candour. It was in the Copthorne tradition to encourage the boys to put on plays on wet afternoons. In Sussex, one of the classrooms was built well above the floor level of its neighbour. A wide wooden wall could be folded back to make a stage on which we could improvise plays. Since there was neither script nor rehearsal, it was rare for there to be any coherence in plot or performance. Given a chance, I played shamelessly for laughs and applause. Mr Howard was often around, to make sure that no one got hurt and that the plot and dialogue were suitable. After one performance, I met him in the corridor and asked him if he had watched the show. He confessed that he had. 'What did you think, sir?' 'Some people,' he said, 'are actors and some aren't. You're not.'

It was not for lack of trying. If I was more valued for the plots I devised, or remembered, than for my capacity to get a laugh, I relished the freedom that came of saying cruel or outrageous things without being taken to mean them. In some ways, my whole life had become a performance, in which I sought to be convincing as a nice little English schoolboy. His fabricated Englishness was the unreliable shell under which a squirming limpet clung to where he had been stuck. My life was both privileged – I was loved, sheltered and educated – and arbitrary: nothing of what I was had proved unalterable, except my inescapable Jewishness. Is it ignoble to have taken so little pride in it? I had arrived in a country where a cabinet minister, who, when accused in a newspaper of being a Jew, had sued for libel. Sir John Simon was not admired for bringing the suit, nor did it wholly vindicate his gentility, but is it hard to see why, in such a society, a small boy from a non-practising Jewish home could scarcely rejoice in belonging to a race which Hitler had promised to exterminate and which could not get a round of golf at Royal Wimbledon? I was something it was undesirable to be.

I never knew when someone or something would remind me of potential pariahdom. One day, Mr Howard was reading us an A.E.W. Mason thriller, *The Prisoner in the Opal*, set in France (where, I now realise, Howard had probably been happier than in England), when the detective asked – 'sharply' of course – 'Is he a Jew?'. Was anyone looking at me? I made sure that my expression did not change. The text continued: 'The Commissaire had never forgotten the Dreyfus case.' How did I know what the Dreyfus case was? Did I ask Mr Howard after the others had dispersed or had I, as so often in life, absorbed something I had overheard while being 'good' at an adult gathering? The ability to guess the secret significance, and sense the drift, of casual remarks was the hybrid fruit of fear and curiosity.

Was any society ever so lacking in candour or so wary of forthrightness as middle-class England in the years when I first came to live here? The British prided themselves on their sense of humour, but their laughter was often primed by shame about bodily functions and by sexual prudery. 'She sits among the cabbages and peas' was a pun from an Edwardian music-hall song on which my father could rely to reduce his mother to giggles. When Nellie Wallace first sang it, she was accused of being vulgar. She then changed the line to 'She sits among the cabbages and leeks'. This was good for another laugh from Amy, if not an occasion for smelling salts. As for my father's rendering of 'From the *bottom* of my heart, dear, I apologise', nothing was more apt to bring cheerful tears to my grandmother's eyes.

The lavatory was the seat of almost all English low comedy

of the time. Cyril Fletcher, whose speciality was 'odd odes', delivered in a cheeky-chappie voice, but without Max Miller's insolent crudeness, wrote a doggerel epic about someone who sat down on a newly varnished lavatory seat to which he became adhesively attached. When someone whose help he sought affected to be shocked, the victim said, 'Haven't you ever seen one of these before?' The answer (which must have rhymed with a line I have forgotten) was 'Frequently, but never framed'.

American comedy was either too squeamish for jokes about toilets or less primly Anglo-Saxon about making sex its subject. I brought with me from New York the furtive memory of Seymour Wallace, the comedian in my parents' set, telling a story about a man who, when asked to go to a ball game by his best buddy, replied, 'I'd love to come, unless Levinski's playing that night.' With a name like that, Levinski had to be a violinist, of course. This routine recurred a few times. Finally the guy's friend got tickets for the surely irresistible final game in the World Series. Once again, he was told, 'I'd love to come. Unless Levinski's playing.' Exasperated, the friend says, 'This Levinski, what and where's he playing that's better than the final of the World Series?'

'*Vot* he's playing,' his buddy replies, 'who cares? *Vere* he's playing, who knows? But *ven* he's playing ... ! I sleep with his wife.'

Seymour told the story with the obligatory Jewish accents. Everyone laughed except me; I understood that I was too innocent to understand, just as I was, supposedly, too young to know who was fat and forty and slept with 'cats'. The answer was, 'Mrs Katz and sometimes Mrs Nussbaum.' Only recently, I tried this joke on a number of people in a dream. Even when I am 'safely' asleep, I feel the need to entertain the company. How is it that, insulated inside my own head, I can still be impelled to generate an unfriendly ambience and then try to placate it?

Once we were settled in England, my father's risqué jokes lost their ethnicity. The first I heard was about the parrot who lost his mate. His owner went to the pet shop and tried to find him a second wife. Being out of parrots, the shop-keeper suggested that an owl would be just as good. The owl was put in the parrot's cage and sat nervously blinking on its perch. The parrot regarded it without appetite, but finally sidled up and said, 'I'm going to do you.' The owl said, 'Oo,oo.' The parrot said, 'You, you flat-faced fool.' In the same spirit, when Mrs Mopp came bursting into Tommy Handley's office in the weekly radio comedy series *ITMA*, her catchphrase was 'Can I do you now, sir?' It never failed to get a laugh. Puns were trapdoors into the basement where the Englishman's *id* was darkly lodged.

The long summer of 1940 seems, in retrospect, to fuse with the one that followed. My mother made the six-hour journey to see me, and stayed in lodgings in Ilfracombe. I soon acquired the habit of boarding-school boys who at once long for a parent's visit and derive small joy from it when it takes place. While seeking to honour Mummy's eagerness to hear how happy I was, I was nervous of what people at school might be saying about me, or her, behind my back. I could scarcely finish my strawberries and clotted cream. It did little for my appetite to think of the starving millions in Europe. Returning to school after being 'out' was always alarming. Had Delamain made a friend with more engineering resource than I? 'Was that your *mother*, Raphael, or what?' Taylor might ask, pronouncing me 'Ray-fle', quite as if Irene, who was young and beautiful, were some kind of apparition.

No one could be as emblematically ugly as 'the hag', Miss Lever, the school nurse. For a time, she had the nickname 'the Toop', which derived from one of the first books I read in the school library: *Excess Baggage*. The text is lost to posterity except for one unforgettable line: 'He saw the Toop arrayed for bed, and never smiled again.' Miss Lever wore a pale mauve uniform with a starched white collar. She administered daily doses of Radio Malt with a tablespoon. If you had a boil, she would lance, and disinfect, it. I was more likely to have a poisoned toe. I picked (and sometimes even managed to bite) my toenails – as well as my fingernails – with assiduous, often bloody, persistence. My big toes often turned septic and bulged with shiny sacs of pus. I limped with pleasure as they gained in volume, until the sweetly painful moment when I could squeeze them until they ejaculated their yellowy poison. When they failed to heal, I would tell the hag that I must have stubbed my toe, because 'Look, Miss Lever'. She boiled water and made me stick my toe in while it was still very hot indeed.

My father always attached great significance to the look of people's hands. My mother's nails were always brilliantly red and watchfully unchipped. Cedric hated dirty nails, but he despised bitten ones. He liked to think that I had 'surgeon's hands', but the condition of my nails, not only bitten to the quick but also with the cuticles torn red and ragged, affronted and disgusted him. He offered to give me a good manicure, at the tiled barber's in Little Windmill Street – where George, whose speciality was 'singeing', gave him losing tips on the horses – if I could show him a pair of unbitten hands, with fully grown nails. It never happened. I was Terence's *Heauton Timoroumenos* ('the Self-Torturer') come again; pain was the greater pleasure.

'Sick room' was one of the nicest bedrooms in the Lee Bay Hotel. Unless 'bilious' (when you received nothing but Bovril and two dry biscuits), you were sure of good food and of immunity from boys such as Denton and Clode, Taylor and Macpherson. They were the thuggy kind who never got ill. Seeking pampered sanctuary, I once claimed to have whooping cough when it was 'going round'. I cannot swear whether my realistic coughing fits were fabricated or not; who can tell the actor from the act? If fake, my whoops were so realistic that I duped even myself: presuming myself immune, I never caught whooping cough when it came round again.

Imposture became a part of my life as soon as I reached England. I never thought to be anything other than myself in America. As an 'Englishman', I was always in dread of being unmasked. Acting what I really was gave me a sort of duplicitous integrity: I was not a liar, but I had to be – and remained – a bit of a performer. My accent had a false nose; it was straight.

Many years later, I saw *Il Generale della Rovere*, a minor film directed by Vittorio de Sica, and recognised aspects of myself. De Sica played a confidence trickster who poses as a resistance hero in the gaol where he has been confined for some ignominious fraud. At the crisis of the plot, an Allied bombing creates panic and an opportunity for a mass break-out. De Sica's character rallies his fellow prisoners by taking the lead. '*Sono io il generale della Rovere,*' he cries. The others recognise a man born to command and escape. The 'general', however, is shot and killed in the brave process. The fake receives a funeral worthy of the genuine article, which he has become. All style carries a zest of imposture.

The Emperor Augustus admitted as much on his death bed when, like Byron in Missolonghi, he announced that the comedy was over. Augustus said that he hoped that he would get good notices for his long and empurpled performance. How appropriate that the emperor should have succeeded a 'father', the divine Julius, who was in fact his uncle, and whose supremacy, like his nephew's, was the result of self-righteous usurpation! Even Churchill, in order to rally his compatriots, wrote himself a series of speeches in order to be sure that he had an eloquent part to play. The old injunction to those who have a certain standing – 'Remember who you are' – implies that worthy behaviour can require conscious recollection.*

We continued to do plays at the Lee Bay Hotel. The sun lounge was our stage; the residents' lounge, which had been converted into a shrunken version of Big School, was the auditorium. Sliding glass doors separated them. Either I was too innocent to observe what went on or Copthorne was a school remarkably clean – the late Simon Raven might even dare to say 'deprived' – of sexual activity. In one of my dorms, there was a brief period of playing doctors and patients, but the scrutiny to which we were subjected, by each other, was without any but curious motive, or result. I do, however, recall doing a play in which a boy called Strangways resurrected me, after I had been murdered, by hauling me to my feet by my penis. The moment jumps back into reality with much the same speed as I did. Strangways, with his rumpled, elderly face, had one more significant part to play in my schooldays.

Life is a film in which characters often appear without preamble, become briefly important and then disappear without clear motive or explanation. How did I become friendly with Goschen, and how long did it last? He must have been in my form, but was he clever or stupid? A tall, fairish boy, with curly hair, there was something attractively gauche about him. He broke the rules, more with guffawing inadvertence than from wilful rebelliousness. His attitude and person did not seem wholly English, but he had no

*The French collaborator Benoist-Méchin records in his memoir, *De la Défaite au Désastre*, how Marshal Pétain was overheard one day, as he came down in the lift in the Hotel du Parc at Vichy, wearing the full uniform of his rank, asking his aide-de-camp, in a nervous voice, '*Qui suis-je?*'. It was as if he were an old actor who needed to be reminded which role in the repertoire he was supposed to be playing at that particular matinée.

obvious strangeness, apart from his name. Was he of the same family as the minister whom Lord Randolph Churchill so famously 'forgot'? He never mentioned it. The Germanic form of his name did not, oddly enough, excite the alert malice of Denton or Clode. There was nothing dangerous about Goschen's physical attributes (he was gangling and ill-coordinated), but unpredictability exempted him from persecution.

On wet afternoons, Big School became a miniature munitions factory. Planes and ships were put together from kits of greater or less complexity according to the competence, and purses, of the workers. My preference for model ships was sharpened by the ambition to wear a cap like Gerald Lewin's. Gerald was my parents' friend and dentist. A handsome man, whose profile resembled Cary Grant and whose voice recalled James Mason's, he drove a Jaguar and, before the war, had married a beautiful German blonde. He divorced her when she proved to share the views of the Führer. In 1939, Gerald joined the Navy. He was wearing his uniform when he came to visit my parents sometime when I was allowed back to London. His cap was identical with that of other officers, but the gold braid on his arm was intercalated with orange ribbon, signifying his dental speciality. While he was talking to my parents, I coveted his hat and finally, left alone with it, I put it, with a pumping heart, very briefly on my own head. It fell to my ears.

Mr McGaw must have sold kits for making HMS Nelson (nine sixteen-inch guns) or HMS Hood ('The Pride of the Fleet') or destroyers such as HMS Achilles ('Victor of the River Plate'), since most of us seemed to be engaged on their construction. The balsa wood was easy to work, and to split. The best fun was painting the finished article, but if you had not sanded it properly, the paint bobbled. Delamain preferred making aeroplanes. He was capable of patient accuracy and when he glued, there were never any unsightly blisters. Not long ago, when a product called New Skin came on to the market (it paints an antiseptic, stingingly effective gloss on small cuts), I had only to sniff it to have a Proustian recollection of models past: the smell recalled the tubes of colourless glue which Delamain sealed, after use, with an accurate pin. My tubes had a way of unravelling at the bottom and covering my awkward hands with prototypical new skin, which later peeled off, deliciously.

Goschen had no time for modelling. His indifference was never aggressive; he managed to condescend from below. No one feared him, or paid him much attention, but his reluctance to share our pursuits was – what? – embarrassing. When he looked at what you were doing, he was neither envious nor admiring; he grinned and opened his mouth without making a sound.

Mr Drake's disdain was less nuanced. He was one of the masters who stood in for those who had been called up. Like our cabbage-growing neighbour Brigadier Morgan, he had a gammy leg; with Drake, however, sarcasm served for rage. He had been a headmaster himself but, like Mr Moyles, lost his livelihood, and autonomy, because of the war. If Mr Workman had done him a good turn by giving him employment, gratitude was not his first reaction. His face was pulled down and sideways by the tug of resentment. He scorned small boys who made baby battleships and who played on the beach 'like girls'. He also deplored the way Copthorne School was organised. The name Drake gave him a bucaneering air: 'Effingham, Grenville, Ralegh, Drake/Admirals all for England's sake' was part of our earliest 'repetition', as Mr Workman termed the poetry he set us to learn by heart. To add to Mr Drake's false lustre, the local manor house – visible through the winter trees on the far side of the valley – belonged to a family called Tyrwhitt-Drake. It seemed to reflect hyphenated glory on the sour master.

Mr Drake believed in competition. He pressed for the school to be organised into two 'Houses', the Red and the

Blue, which should compete both in the classroom and on the sports field. Since cricket was out, and football rather a shambles, Mr Drake instituted an elaborate system of athletic 'standards' and 'merits', which earned points for your Colour. He must have been a forceful presence at staff meetings: not long after his arrival, he imposed his version of the corporate state on Mr Workman as well as his pupils. He hung large charts on the wall of Big School, on which each individual's contribution to his House was denoted by a line which grew longer as more 'merits' were won. Life was a race, and it belonged to the swift.

There was something which we might now call Buñuelesque about a cripple contriving a society in which fleetness of foot and physical fitness were the mark of excellence. When I had to run the hundred yards, it seemed that the finishing line was on the horizon. The long meadow grasses swished against my legs as I stumbled over the molehills towards where Mr Drake and his implacable stopwatch demarcated sheep from goats.

When it was his turn, Goschen ran like a lurching clown. Mr Drake said that he was 'the kind of boy who will never learn to march in step'. Goschen wished a plague on all available Houses. If he had little, except his curls, in common with the small boy who pissed on the carpet in St Louis, Goschen's mockery of what others took seriously excited similar feelings in me, of envy and of embarrassment. Boys spoke little of their homes, or what their fathers did, unless they had military rank. Goschen was no exception, but I gathered that his family would share his lack of interest in the high jump. His clumsiness on the athletic field, like his unkempt hair, infuriated Mr Drake. Goschen became his easy butt, all the more annoying for his refusal to be chastened and for his capacity for making the rest of us laugh, partly at, but also with, him. Whenever Mr Drake made a fool of Goschen he also, somehow, made a fool of himself.

His refusal to be mortified by sarcasm, conscripted by imposed loyalties or impressed by 'efficiency' of any kind (for instance, my mounting unsplit gun turrets that could also swivel, on my HMS *Hood*) turned Goschen into the exception which, had I had more courage, or less ambition, I could imagine myself being. I did him a favour by being his friend, while feeling secretly privileged (and furtively bold) in enjoying his company. He told me one day that he was not interested in model planes and boats, with silly wooden guns on them, because at home he had a 'two-two' and a pair of duelling pistols. Did I say 'I'll bet'? (I was familiar with duelling pistols from Mr Howard's choice of reading, but how did I know what a 'two-two' was?) 'If people go on picking on me,' Goschen said, 'I may have to take measures.'

One of the other wartime masters who had come out of retirement was called Mr Lefroy. He was suspected of being a bit French. He was amiable to everyone, not least Goschen. We did not bait him, as we later did Mr Griffiths (the booted Welsh maniac), but we played on his guilelessness. He was once taken short and locked himself in one of the downstairs bogs which masters never used. His presence was instantly relayed to Clode, Strangways, Gilmour and company, who went, one after the other, to knock on the stall door and ask, 'Who's in there?'. He replied patiently, and politely, each time, 'Mr Lefroy.' His persecutors were doubled up in silent straight-faced laughter. The door of the stall was opened by a toothed bolt which turned a cog that rotated the brass-framed signal outside from 'OCCUPIED' to 'VACANT'. Mr Lefroy emerged, red-faced, but unsuspecting. He washed his hands and went to take his class.

Goschen came back at the end of one holiday with a large wooden box, with chasing on the top. He kept it in his locker. Occasionally he would be seen to open it, and look at what was inside, without taking it out. Having created an atmosphere of mystery, he waited for me to ask him what he had in there. When I did not, he volunteered to show me something if I didn't tell anyone else. He unlocked the lid of the French-polished box and disclosed two long-barrelled antique revolvers, packed nose to tail in crimson-felted crevices. 'What did I tell you?' he said. There was also a hinged ramrod, which unfolded and clipped into rigidity, and six what-looked-to-be silver bullets. The cylinder of each revolver rotated with smooth clicks, like the lavatory door when Mr Lefroy came out. I said, 'You're not supposed to have anything like this, are you?' 'Supposed to!' Goschen said.

Once the guns had been removed from their cache, Goschen began to play with them more openly; that is to say, more openly to me. He threatened whoever threatened him – Denton or Drake or anyone else – by revealing to me that he had the means to make them sorry. They remained unaware of his armoury. He reminded me of the 'Q-ships' to be found in G.A. Henty's books; they were the disguised merchantmen who, in the Great War, lured submarines to the surface, by appearing to be defenceless. Unwilling to waste torpedoes on petty targets, the U-boat captains preferred to surface and sink them with gunfire. Once the subs 'blew their tanks' and became sitting targets, the crew of the Q-ship threw off the plywood and canvas cladding over their 4.5-inch guns and opened up on the 'ferret turned rabbit'.

Some local farmers in north Devon still hunted by putting the sleek and sly-eyed yellow beasts into the warrens and waiting for the terrified rabbits to break cover. The ferrets were transported in twitching sacks. Others caught their rabbits in steel-jawed traps. On our walks to Happy Valley (beyond the village church and turn right), we sometimes found a half-dead captive, trying to chew off its own leg in the effort to get free of the clenched metal jaws. Preston was callously compassionate. He extracted the wounded creatures, held them up by their ears, and put them out of their misery with an abrupt rabbit punch. I couldn't look. I took refuge in a ruined shepherd's cottage, furnished with an old chair and table and fountains of bramble.

Goschen sat near me in class. One day, at the start of Mr Lefroy's geography lesson, he hid one of his revolvers on his lap. With a mixture of insolence and indolence, he ignored the blackboard and unfolded the ramrod. I managed to be two-faced enough both to observe where New South Wales was and to keep an eye on Goschen as, with his vacuous smile, he started to clean the revolver. As he thrust with the ramrod, he tightened his grip on the butt. Suddenly there was a very loud bang. Mr Lefroy turned from the blackboard, flipped the chalk back on to it, and collapsed. It seemed that Goschen had shot him.

Goschen was hunched over his desk, holding a newly red hand against his breast, deadly pale (even his curls looked white). He had shot himself through the fleshy part of his thumb, a wound as dramatic as it proved trivial. Mr Lefroy had not been wounded in any way. He had collapsed with a heart attack.

Goschen was led to the sick room for Miss Lever to bandage his hand. I doubt if he was ever punished; the shock had been too great and his wound too alarming. Mr Lefroy was removed by ambulance to Ilfracombe hospital. We never saw him again. The one person, staff or pupil, whom Goschen had no wish to harm was the only one, apart from himself, to suffer. The revolvers were put in Skete's safe. The bullet stayed in a hole in the hotel ceiling. Mr Drake no longer treated Goschen with open derision.

Sometime during the war, Goschen invited me to go and stay with him during the holidays. He lived in a house in the country. There was a wooden fence between the back garden and the surrounding fields, on which we lined up a row of tins and bottles before loading the .22 (he really did have one) and shooting them to pieces or potting holes in them. I

99

have no memory of his parents, or of his siblings, if any; I see only a solid, unspectacular, modernish house; the raw wooden fence sloping slightly up an incline; the bottles and the tin cans on it and the green thrill of splintering glass.

In the early spring of 1941, I was called to Mr Workman's study. I was so conditioned that my posture, as I went through the coloured glass door of what had been 'RECEPTION' when the hotel was in business, was that of a boy who had done something wrong, even though I had not. The Headmaster's study was on the right. Later I should become used to its orderly clutter, since Mr Workman took the higher forms for Latin and Greek, but at the time it was intimidatingly unfamiliar. Skete was alone, but the gentleness in his voice promised that I was not about to be accused of anything. A bomb had fallen on Highlands Heath and my parents' flat had received a direct hit. I had no reaction of alarm, nor of any emotion that remains with me; I listened and I was interested. The Headmaster's tone made it clear that nothing terrible had happened. Although our flat was indeed in the block that was hit, it was on the first floor; our ceiling had not been penetrated; my parents were unhurt; even our dachshund, Toots,* was unscratched. The building, however, was declared unsafe and, since the water tanks had been in the attic, our entire flat had been flooded. The people on the floor above my parents had been killed. Cedric and Irene had been in the flat, with a coal fire burning in the grate. When the bomb exploded, the fireplace was blown

---

*Toots survived the war, and many years after it. My parents once left her in the company of a live chicken with a broken leg, the pet property of a friend, before 'going on duty'. The injunction to Toots to take care of the lame bird failed to mitigate the instincts of centuries. When Cedric and Irene returned, after the All Clear, Toots was still there, wagging her tail; only a few feathers, and its splint, were left of the chicken. Bad dog!

several feet into the centre of the room and was then sucked back into its proper place.

When I returned to class, my appearance advertised an air of secret grief. I confess to a small sense of anti-climax. There was a measure of imposture in my show of bravely controlled distress. There was, in truth, little to control; I played, modestly, on the sympathy of my fellow pupils. There was more pleasure from the manipulation of their feelings than anguish at the thought of what might have happened to my parents. The belief that they could never really be taken away from me licensed fantasies of bereavement. The imagination is a seditious scoundrel; what tragedy ever failed to precipitate comic possibilities? The Greek satyr play, which followed every tragic trilogy and lampooned its solemnities, admitted − not to say celebrated − the fact that there is no horror from which a writer cannot derive some facetious dividend. Even as I rejoiced at my parents' survival, I could imagine playing the noble orphan. How often the fortunate entertain the despicable grievance that they might be missing something! The Jews, such people say, are lucky.

Mr Howard told us at lunch, in June 1941, that the Germans had invaded Russia. The solemnity, and satisfaction, in his voice implied what I can almost believe that I knew instantly: that this was a vital moment in the war. The *Daily Express* maps had not come with us from Sussex; after the débâcle in France, they lost their charm. The war was and was not constantly in our thoughts; there was something dutiful in how seriously we took it. Mr Howard was confident that the Russian campaign would divert Hitler only temporarily from attacking England. 'How long do you think Russia will hold out, sir?' He wrote something on a piece of scrap paper, folded it, and left it on the table while he hurried on to do something which would exempt him from puerile company. When unfolded, like a betting slip, the pencilled prediction was 'SIX WEEKS'.

The departure of Mr Lefroy had been the direct consequence of Goschen's revolver shot. That of Mr Drake, almost as abrupt, owed nothing to what any of the boys had done. Mr Drake was there, scornful and dominant, one week and a week later he was gone. His colourful wall charts were unpinned; the whole system of merits, and of imposed House allegiances, was dismantled. It was a petty presage of what would happen in Germany when Hitler was finally crushed: once loyalty to the system was no longer at a premium, few could explain what had impelled them to it. Meanwhile, there was something darkly attractive about the Nazis; the equipment and insignia of the Afrika Korps made them, rather than the Eighth Army, into the regular subject of my caterpillar-tracked drawings and haughtily capped doodles.

I was an earnest and able pupil, seldom accused of inattention and usually at the top of my small class. Yet I see myself as the nervous outsider, forever apprehensive of those who should have been my friends, menaced by the cant vocabulary that made a pariah of what I was supposed to be proud of. Unfortified by spiritual conviction or sense of community, I lived as if imposture were my nature. It is, however, unlikely that I was seen as this frail character by those who had problems of their own, one of which may have been me and my too-quick tongue.

Life, like all ill-made dramas, has its share of characters who seem defined by a single characteristic. Grubb, for instance, read the Bible. He underlined key passages, using a pencil which had a fat barrel containing leads (supplied in little tubes by Mr McGaw) in a selection of colours. Grubb's copy of the Bible had a number of different-coloured ribbons, by which he could flag crucial texts. Grubb read the Bible with true single-mindedness. The only other thing I remember about him was his excesses of rage should anyone mock him for his piety. He scratched; when he did it to me, his long nail extracted a sliver of flesh. Interestingly, the white wound began to fill with blood only several seconds after it was inflicted.

Mr Workman had not infrequently to replace masters who were either too old or too decrepit to continue or who found remote north Devon unendurable. In the winter, clouds bundled low along the hills or spilled, in grey and dank billows, into it. The foghorn on the Morte Ho lighthouse moaned sleeplessly in the night. We could imagine the hound of the Baskervilles loping in the brown, obsolete bracken. Nothing seemed to happen in the cold months. We made models; we did stamps; we put on plays.

As the Russian resistance outlasted Mr Howard's prediction, he told us that the Germans, like Napoleon, had not reckoned with 'General Winter'. The prolonged Russian campaign helped to abate the bombing of London. I was again able to go home for the holidays. Sometimes I could buy my mother a freshly killed chicken from Mrs Workman's poultry run: two and sixpence. After being bombed out, my parents had had no trouble in finding a new flat, half a mile from Highlands Heath. We even kept the same PUTney telephone number (not that I ever called it). Our furniture had been cleaned and dried. The new flat, in Manor Fields, was a step higher on the social ladder, especially since Highlands Heath had been partly requisitioned to house 'Gibbies', refugees who had been more or less forcibly deported from Gibraltar.

Our new flat was in Balliol House. I knew Balliol to be the name of an Oxford college, adjacent to my father's. He and his friends had called it 'Bloody Belial', but it had a classy ring. Even my father conceded that a Classical scholarship at Balliol was worth more than any other. I was reminded, frequently, that my scholastic future depended on scholarships: first Winchester, then Oxford.

We were still living close enough to Highlands Heath for Martin Warburton and me to resume our Monopoly sessions. How young was I when I first began to use my bicycle 'outside the gates'? There was so little traffic that Martin and I were quite soon allowed to go exploring together. As we got older, our sorties became increasingly explorative. The whole of south-west London, as far as Epsom and Twickenham, was later within our pedalling province, though not a single one of the places – from Tooting to Mogador, Balham to Battersea – figured on the Monopoly board whose makers, like the legendary north London Jews, must have imagined that if you crossed the Thames you fell off the edge of the world.

On one occasion, we went into Richmond station, for some reason, and I bought a short-story magazine at the newsagent's kiosk. I had become an admirer of the short-story writer whose pseudonym was 'Gun Buster'. Unlike Flying Officer X, who was later unmasked as H.E. Bates, Gun Buster maintained his anonymity until his recent death. He was then revealed as a Colonel Richard Austin; his trimly realistic stories pandered little to British conceits. I shall never forget the one in which a British tank crew, in the western desert, was confronted by a number of Italians, who climbed out of their trench with their hands up. The tank commander had no way of accepting their surrender, so he ordered his driver to run them over, which he did. Gun Buster's narrative had something of the terseness of Hemingway's In Our Time, and a similar unblinking callousness.

When, in my innocence, I mentioned to my parents that I had bought a magazine at Richmond Station, I was amazed by the violence of my father's reaction. He was rarely interested, still less distressed, by what I was reading. This time, he demanded to see the magazine and, on glancing at the lurid cover, declared it confiscated. Without looking inside, he told me that I should never again spend my pocket money on such trash. What can he have thought that it contained? I cannot believe that anything remotely pornographic was available on Richmond station. He soon discovered, and conceded, that the stories were harmless. Almost shamefaced, he returned the magazine to me. I looked at it again with new, slightly disappointed eyes. My father's muted outrage made me aware that there must be magazines with more dangerous contents than True Story. I looked forward to the chance to buy one of them.

I was soon allowed to go on my own to see my grandmother in Dorset House. It would be comely to attribute my solicitude to affection for the old lady, but what I enjoyed were the long journeys, sometimes by bus (the 74 went all the way from The Green Man, at the top of Putney Hill, to Baker Street), sometimes on the underground, via Edgware Road. I read the ads ('Is Your Journey Really Necessary?', 'A Pickford's Van, a gentle giant/The job is done: a satisfied client') and I scanned the grey ruins of London through lozenge-shaped spyholes in the green-meshed windows of trains and buses. My favourite hoarding showed an ostrich with a glass-shaped deformity in its long throat. The caption? 'My Goodness My Guinness', of course. 'We Want Watneys', on the other hand, appeared to have been whitewashed, like a political slogan on brickwork. 'Don't be Vague, Ask for Haig' completed the incitements to revelry. Many of the bombsites had big metal tanks installed on them with 'EWS' (Emergency Water Supply) stencilled on the sides. Who knew when the Luftwaffe would be back? Meanwhile, it was 'Business As Usual', especially on boarded, windowless shopfronts ('Second Front Now' came later).

There was a sweet sense of safe danger in these trips, alone, through wartime London. I savoured the different feel of various districts: South Kensington was guttural with square-hatted Polish officers, for whom I felt more fear than admiration. How did I know that Jews and Poles had small affinity? Later, someone chalked 'PROSTIES AT THE THREE BELLS' on the wall of what is now a Chinese restaurant. I knew and did not know what it meant. The multiplicity of Allied uniforms promised that, if the war had not yet tilted in our favour, too many people were intent on Hitler's defeat for him to have any hope of prevailing.

North London was *terra incognita*, so full of foreign refugees that bus conductors were rumoured to call out 'British North Hampstead'. It cost eight pence to ride all the way to Baker Street from Putney. There was something quite grand about requiring the 'clippie' to extract so exotic a ticket from her rack. Each ticket was differently coloured; the more sumptuously tinted, the more expensive the denomination (a word I learned from Stanley Gibbons' stamp catalogue). The value of the ticket was announced in a large, hollow figure on top of the grid which boxed off each 'stage' on the journey. The clippie braced herself against a seat while puncturing the appropriate fare stage. I learned cockney from the voices I heard saying 'ay nank kew', 'pass rye dow inside nah pleece' and 'hupstairs only nah, peace'. One rarely heard the mildest swear word; never an obscenity.

One winter term when we went back to Devon, there was yet another new master. Mr Pears was pale skinned but dark haired, with a curved, shiny nose and eloquent black eyebrows. He was soon known as 'Herr Kurt Vogel' (a name taken, I think, from one of Sapper's righteously xenophobic Bulldog Drummond books). Although it was almost certain that he was a German spy, we rather liked Mr Pears, perhaps because he took our accusations with enough good humour to offer small clues that it *might be true*. Of course, he was no such thing.

Another of the temporary masters, who came late in the war, was the square-headed Welshman, Mr Griffiths, whose heavy boots, cropped grey hair and explosions of rage proved him to be of another stamp; on some floors, his hob-nailed boots literally struck sparks. With cruel justice, he was given the nickname of 'The [Ze] kommandant'. The poor man could neither keep order nor acquiesce in disorder; without the wit to teach, he lacked the charm to amuse. When goaded, he would kick our benches. His boots were so rigidly capped that he never hurt himself. He rarely hurt us, except when we were using the wicker-seated chairs left behind by the hoteliers. In that case, his boot could leave quite a bruise, unless you were agile and rose – with a realistic yelp and timely simultaneity – as he put the boot in.

The only lessons which left an instructive impression were Mr McGaw's maths and Mr Workman's Latin and Greek. Skete leavened severity with sport. During the last quarter of an hour of each morning's lesson, he would have us arrange our chairs (he taught in his study) in a row. There were never more than eight or nine pupils in a class, so we could quickly resume the places we had occupied at the end of the previous session. There followed an implacable, but playful quiz. The boy at the top of the line was asked a question (the Greek for messenger, for instance) and if he could not answer, the next boy had the chance, and so on down the line. If you were languishing at the dim end of the ladder, you could – provided no intervening boy knew the answer – be translated to eminence at a stroke. You waited in controlled excitement as the question travelled towards you. If you got the chance to give a correct answer, Mr Workman would say 'Go up' and you took the place of the person first questioned. If he was at the top of the class, you supplanted him and everyone else budged down a place. Should the bell go while you still had tenure, you got as many marks as there were pupils in the class. As you went down the line, so did your tally dwindle.

Early in our Greek studies, my joy at knowing the word 'messenger' (*angelos*) was tarnished when I was asked to spell it. In the innocence of which Mr Workman was seeking to disembarrass me, I began confidently, 'Alpha, nu, gamma'. 'Next.' 'Um.' 'Next.' 'Alpha, gamma, gamma, epsilon, lambda, omicron, sigma', said the next boy. Which was, of course, the right answer. Since it was pronounced *angelos*, the word sounded as if there had to be a nu (n) in it, but the subtle Greeks had set a trap for generations of naive little boys. That was part of their educational usefulness. If I never made that mistake again, and I never did, many others were available (what other language attaches a singular verb to a plural subject, but only if the latter is neuter?).

At the end of 1941, my mother was purged of the stigma of being American by the attack on Pearl Harbor and the immediate and, it seemed, whole-hearted entry of the United States on 'our' side. Irene not only had ARP on her nightly tin hat (the plastic model had been replaced by something that dented less easily); by day she also wore WVS uniform. The local WVS was quartered in an empty shop in Putney High Street. They ran a car pool, and emergency aid, especially clothing, passed through the office on its way to Wandsworth, a regular target of the now less frequent German bombs. These were probably aimed at Battersea power station, the location of which no blackout could conceal: the silver thread of the moonlit Thames led the Germans right to it.

The WVS office was furnished with trestle tables. There were several borrowed typewriters. When one was out of use, I was allowed to feed scrap paper into the roller and tap out letters to my grandparents in Kansas City. Sometimes I wrote stories, such as 'The Tale of a Handkerchief', a laundered version of *Black Beauty*. Luckily, no trace of it has come down to us.

My one vivid memory of the Putney WVS is of helping my mother to count the proceeds of a Flag Day. The contents of several slotted tins were tipped on to a tray and, being good (thanks to Mr McGaw) at adding pounds, shillings and pence, I was allowed to take part in the tally. As the coins were poured out in front me, the big brown pennies (some of them still had a bun* on them) and ha'pennies and silver coins made a heavy rain. They must have reminded me of something that my father had said, or done, in the secrecy of our flat. Telling Jewish stories was one of his ways of 'confessing' his Jewishness while also distancing himself, and us, from its folkloric manifestations. The 'narcissism of small differences' works with steadily fractious force within the Jewish world no less than elsewhere.

Faced, like some small Fagin or Shylock, with a sight traditionally held to be especially dear to a Jew's eyes, I did something which I took to be an imitation of my father in his story-telling mood: I spread my hands in a Semitic gesture (no nice person 'used his hands' when speaking) and, in a mimicked drawl, uttered one appalling, too loud syllable, '*Vell!*' I shall never forget the expression of horror and loathing on my young mother's face. She looked round to check whether any of her greenly tweeded colleagues – busy bundling relief for bombed-out families or loud, ungrateful refugees from 'Gib.' – could possibly have been the witness of my obscenity. 'Don't ever do that again,' she said. 'Ever.' I had betrayed her more seriously than if I had 'done a blow', even a really loud and smelly one, or pissed on the floor. I blushed and was angry with myself, and with her. I started, joylessly, to stack the coins in turrets of a shilling's worth each.

---

*A 'bun' penny carried the profile of Queen Victoria with her hair in a bun at the back. Although still legal tender, like the sovereigns which Sherlock Holmes promised cabbies when in a hurry to catch a train picked out from Bradshaw by Dr Watson, bun pennies were said to be worth more than their face value.

In the summer holidays of 1942, when I was eleven, I made a new friend. His name too was Martin. He had come to Manor Fields for his holidays from Dartmouth. No more than fourteen or fifteen, he might as well have been a generation older than I: he wore a uniform, with anchored brass buttons, almost indistinguishable from that of a naval officer. He already sported a cap like that of my parents' friend Dental Lieutenant-Commander Gerald Lewin. Martin was quite tall, but I was not that much shorter. For want of older company, he was glad to spend time with me. One day we went for a walk on Wimbledon Common. There was a lake in a remote corner with an abandoned anti-aircraft post near it. Thinning sandbags and rusty barbed wire surrounded the empty pit where the guns had been. We had visited the spot before, drawn to its unalarming spookiness.

This time, as we approached, squares of paper were fluttering on the wire. When we were near enough, we could see a number of black-and-white photographs pronged on the barbs. Closer still, we gazed in silence at what the photographs revealed: men and women, some naked, some half-dressed, in a variety of poses, sometimes of two, sometimes of more people. Few were beautiful; some seemed quite old; most were fleshy. Their sexual conjugations stayed with me less than the smiles – at once fatuous and inviting – which almost blurred their shameless faces.

We walked from one picture to the next as they twitched on the wire in the mild breeze. The artless candour of the exhibition was a rude (and grateful) education. The want of subtlety announced that this was the hairy truth. I assumed that Martin, being older, would be neither shocked nor surprised by what we were looking at. In fact, perhaps because he was older, and physically excited, or appalled, he was keener than I to get away. It may be that it was a serious offence at Dartmouth to look at even the mildly erotic photographs in magazines such as *Lilliput*, which featured one bare-breasted girl a month, with her pubic hair air-brushed out. Lilliput also pioneered double-page spreads of photographs showing unlikely, but unmistakable, similarities: for instance, between Neville Chamberlain and 'the beautiful llama'. The Incas' sacred animal and Britain's sorry ex-Prime Minister clearly had the same dentist. Lilliput also regularly featured the adventures of 'that naughty girl Monica', whose misdeeds were either too subtly coded by *double entendres* for me to decipher them or were unexceptionally skittish. It was impossible to imagine Monica doing anything of the sort that I saw pictured on the wire on Wimbledon Common. Years later, when Bernard Braden, a Canadian radio comedian, did a spoof shampoo commercial with the refrain, 'She's lovely, she's popular, she uses...Wimbledon Common', I was in a position to know that she was not the first.

The photographs reminded me of the one copy of our maths textbook with Answers At The Back; Mr McGaw kept it in his briefcase. They gave blunt and undeniable answers. I had never seen a naked woman. Because of my Caesarean birth, and the 'complications' which followed it, I never even fed at my mother's breast. My cosseted isolation began at birth. It is not remarkably sad, but it is true. I could tell that the people in the photographed poses were 'lower class'. You could almost see that they would have accents like the Martin with whom I had been forbidden to play or the clippies whose voices I mimicked. I felt less disgust than wonder at their shameless ostentation. I gorged on what I saw with urgent eyes, fearing only that a policeman would snatch them away before I had slaked my ignorance.

Martin was afraid that we should be blamed if anyone came along, or taken for disgusting boys. I think that I was the first to say anything. Whatever it was, my informed nonchalance was explicit enough for a naval cadet to be surprised that I knew about 'that kind of thing'. As we walked home from the Common, he asked me where I had learned 'those words' and what they meant. For all I know, my understanding of what those people were doing in their black-and-pork-white nakedness and their terrible under-wear came to me by inspection. What was being enacted added more to my knowledge than to my appetite. Obscenity breaches the veil between what others have decided is good for them and what boys suspect the truth to be. It pokes holes in the formal logic of society and makes 'dirt' a function of liberty. A French philosopher has called obscenity 'a sun'. It came out for me that day.

Having had small access to the gutter, in the normal way of things, I was not going to miss an opportunity of learning what it had to teach. Copthornians spoke with apprehensive prurience about the 'leaving jaw' which Mr Workman deliv-ered to those who were about to depart to their public schools. Apparently what he disclosed was particularly 'juicy'. I did not like that word; all words beginning with 'j' made me anxious: so did the way some people said 'due' or 'dew'.

A few days later, Martin and I went for another walk. I suggested that we return to the pond, 'for fun'. He was reluctant, but I prevailed (as the younger often does, if only because indulging him gives an excuse to his senior). What kind of excitement was it that moved me as we saw the gleam of the brackish water through the trees and the settled shudder of a swan as it adjusted its wings? The forbidden and the unspeakable were more of a lure than the sexual. The wire was punctuated only with brief commas of torn paper but the photographs had been removed, either officiously or as collector's items. Martin said, 'Just as well really.' He looked at me with the reproach proper to someone who was relieved not to be led further astray. I scarcely ever saw him again.

How soon after this was it, I wonder, that I saw another

picture of a naked woman? She was sitting on a bed and the photograph had been deliberately torn into several pieces. It comprised one of the cleverly 'authentic' clues in a detective story, by Dennis Wheatley, which took the form of a dossier of evidence. One of the racier Copthorne boys must have brought it back after the holidays. Also included were clipped train tickets and sheets of apparently typed reports, all slotted into cellophane sleeves which were bound into the album-sized book.

It added to the titillating pleasure of the woman's nakedness that it had to be pieced together. The photograph was advisedly blurred; its reality was enhanced by its seeming amateurishness. The woman was the more real, and hence the more naked, and the more thrillingly revealed, because it appeared that she had been photographed without her knowledge. Unpreparedness took another veil from her. There was a tincture of rape in the ripped image: something had been done both to her and to the picture. What her place was in the story, and what the story itself was, escapes recall. She sits, forever archetypal, in a basement room of my imagination, slightly hunched on the sagging, unmade bed, without doubt having recently made love, whatever that was, with some forgotten character. Dennis Wheatley was a shrewdly calculating writer whose many best-sellers were, for the more part, Gothic absurdities. Yet they hinged on to reality, by the gimcrack elegance of their details. Their air of almost convincing worldliness meant that reading Wheatley was a little like smoking: it was not entirely pleasurable, but it had a sulphurous whiff of wickedness.

In the autumn of 1942, the first American soldiers began to arrive. Even in Devon their presence changed everything. The ruggedness of the landscape, and its remoteness both from German bombers and from metropolitan temptations, made it suitable for training raw soldiers. Only four years before, I had been a little New Yorker, but I did not hear those first American voices with any sentiment of nostalgia or affinity. I was struck more by their clarity and their un-English volume. Americans talked faster and louder and with sharper consonants than we English, who had been taught not to raise our voices. The appearance of American soldiers – not to be called 'doughboys' this time, but not yet known as GIs – had a rumpled and unrationed bigness: they wore paler khaki uniforms, with dusty-white gaiters. Their lustre-less brasses did not gleam like those of English soldiers. Pudding-basin tin hats dangled from unrigid knapsacks. Netted water bottles widened their hips. Their rifles were smaller and less antique than the British .303s. They chewed Wrigley's spearmint (from packets) or Chiclets (from flat boxes).

Mr McGaw's classroom was in the semi-basement of the hotel. The Ilfracombe road sloped down past windows which could be opened by the (Masters Only) manipulation of a system of pulleys. By turning a long arm with a hinged metal handle, the windows were tilted inwards from the top. They were braked, at the limit, by a curved brass bracket. One day, during a maths lesson, we heard the slurring tramp of military feet – Yanks did not march with the heavy-booted crunches of the English and the Canadians – and an unaggressive cry of 'Halt', followed by, 'OK. Take five.' There was a corporate expulsion of breath from the street and the double clunks of rifle butts and unslung packs hitting the macadam (named, we had learned in geography, 'jog', after the – British, of course – inventor of properly drained and surfaced roads). Then a voice said, 'Oh my fucking back.' The words flew through the open window into our ears. Our smirking schoolboy response was unlike that of the soldiers, who laughed, but in a very young way. How many were more than ten years older than we were? I filed 'fucking' in my secret vocabulary, certain (if only from the kind of laughter it provoked) that it bore on the activity of the figures in those fluttering photographs.

It was not long before the Americans were often to be seen, feet up except for the driver, in the jeeps which were soon ubiquitous. *Ubique* was the motto of the Royal Artillery, but we saw few English gunners in Devon. There were more Italians; they worked on the urine-puddled dairy farms which we walked past on fine days, on the way to picnics. Mr Workman would take hampers and canteens of drink in the Wolseley to a pre-arranged rendezvous. The Eyeties wore overalls with large white targets on the back. Dark and unsmiling faces regarded us without shame or hostility. The wops lived for the day when they would return to vines and olives, instead of toiling in the bracken and oak and the coarse pastures on steep, cold, alien hillsides.

We walked towards Woolacombe Sands along the unfenced cliffs adjacent to the abandoned golf course where wide mushrooms grew. The masters must have been unobtrusively vigilant, and the boys very orderly; there were no accidents or alarms. Because we had to keep to narrow tracks, we often went in single file. If you were talking to the boy behind you, it was natural to turn your head and rely on the shadow of the person in front to keep you in line. On one occasion, I was ahead of someone who was chatting to the boy behind him when I came to an almost right-angled bend in the path. If you went straight ahead, you would walk over the edge of the cliff. As I made the turn, I looked back and saw that the next boy was about to walk blindly on. I called his name urgently; he glanced round and easily corrected his path. 'Thanks, Raffers.' In the least meritorious way possible, I had saved his life. 'It's OK.' It was rather embarrassing.

Clothes rationing imposed tight limits on our wardrobes. Ingenious lengthening and repair jobs were done by Miss Banks, Miss Lever's slightly more comely, and more amiable, assistant. However, we still strictly observed the distinction between indoor and outdoor shoes. Mr and Mrs Workman insisted that we respect hotel property, no doubt in the hope that their school buildings would be cared for with the same scrupulous attention by the Royal Air Force, which had requisitioned them.

One day, in the middle of a morning French lesson with Mr Haughton (whose shaving regularly left bloody divots on his face), we were told by a calmly panting Mr Howard to leave the premises at once, *without changing our shoes*, and line up in the drive ready to move off as soon as possible. Within a few minutes, all sixty-eight of us were in marching order near the fuchsia bushes. Mr McGaw and Mr Howard led us off, escorted by members of staff with the stamina for a long hike. As we walked up the incline on the Ilfracombe road, the word passed that there was a mine in the bay. Was there a point where we looked back and saw the spiked black globe floating in on the tide? One of its prongs had only to butt the rocks to provoke a huge explosion.

We walked without undue haste, but briskly, until we had gone a mile or so inland. A truck with 'RN BOMB DISPOSAL' on a board at the front came down the hedged lane with a serious, blue-sweatered quartet of experts in it. We walked on, and on. Eventually, we came to an area where we had never been before, with rocks and open fields shiny with marsh grass. Mr Workman was there, in the Wolseley, with the usual hampers and canteens. We had an unforeseen picnic while waiting for the distant bang which would prove that the mine had been 'detonated with rifle fire' as was sometimes done. No bang was heard. We sat around for a while, and then we were on the move again.

All afternoon we waited for what Holmes might have called the mine that went bang in the day. Like the dog in *Silver Blaze* who did not bark, it was loud in its silence. The word came to Mr Workman that we could not yet return to

Lee Bay. By some typically British means, it was arranged that we should go to the Hall for the night. We straggled, blistered and wearily gallant – it *was* an adventure – under sombre pines along the driveway and into a roomy, gloomy building. Suits of armour stood in the checkered hallway. Halberds, so Delamain told me, were grasped in their jointed gauntlets. Frayed and faded banners hung from the rafters in the main, cathedral-ceilinged hall. It was a petty museum of English chivalry, as old as its dust.

Most of us slept on the floor in the Great Hall. A few may have been put in upstairs rooms, but I was so tired that I cannot remember if we had tea or not. The breakfast I shall never forget. There was a large refectory, with long-benched tables very like those at which we usually sat. What was memorable was not the racks of toast nor the extra butter and marmalade. After creamy porridge, we each had a freshly boiled egg put in front of us (can there have been enough egg cups or was one simply put on my plate?). Mr Workman sliced the top of his egg with a deft flick of the wrist. I tapped mine, as Mr Howard did his, with the flat of my spoon. No sooner had I broken the shell than I smelt the pong of sulphuretted hydrogen. Everyone else was spooning yolk or dipping soldiers into their eggs. I put up my hand. 'Please, sir, I don't think my egg is very good.'

'You and the curate,' Mr Howard said.

He sniffed my egg and had to agree that it was not edible. I waited with the naive conviction that it would be replaced. As it happened, there were no more eggs in the kitchen. Something in my stars made me the sad exception. Does being a bad loser have something to do with the confirmation which defeat seems to supply that the world is rigged against one? Triumphs, should they occur, can be a reprieve; catastrophes are proof of one's true standing.

There was no climactic explosion of the mine in the bay. When word came that it had been successfully defused, we trooped back to the hotel, wiped our house shoes on the mat before going in, and resumed lessons. 'Where was I?' Mr McGaw said.

The four years in north Devon are now impacted into a clamp of memories without reliable order or distinction. When was it that I was in the big field, with Delamain, on a cloud-heavy afternoon when all of a sudden we heard the pulsing drone of an engine whose note he immediately identified as 'enemy'? We looked up and saw a dark aeroplane with a glassed 'blister' at the front; it displayed a gunner crouched behind his machine gun. Coming in from the sea, the plane flew directly at us. 'Heinkel,' Delamain said. We could see the gunner, in black leather kit and ear muffs, only a hundred and sixty yards or so above us. The plane droned overhead and was blanked by cloud. It was the only time I saw a German serviceman during the whole war.

Delamain's father was now a brigadier. He worked at the War Office and led quite a social life in London. His rank (and income) secured him entrée to the Ritz, but was insufficient to give him priority. On one occasion, he waited for a very long time to be fed. Diners with higher ranks or grander titles, who had come in after him, were served before him. The Brigadier took the tall jug of water from his table and poured it, with its ice cubes, on to the floor. He did it, so his son said, calmly and without haste. He was served at once. It was another enviable example of conduct I feared that I should never have the nerve, or the status, to emulate.

There were rumours at one point that my father might have to go to Russia to assist them in managing their oil supplies. He was to be given the rank of colonel (decked with red tabs) to lend military authority to civilian expertise. To my disappointment, nothing came of the project. The mission would probably have been both dangerous and futile: my father had no foreign languages and would, presumably, have had to fly over the battlefield. I less feared for his safety than regretted the cachet which his crimsoned rank might have lent me.

Of all the battles of the Second World War, none captured the imagination more than Stalingrad. 'House-to-house fighting' had a domesticated vividness which evoked endless illustration. My desire for an Allied victory was as whole-hearted as it was confident, yet I rarely drew pictures of the Russian soldiers whose tenacity earned 'Uncle Joe' Stalin our government-sponsored admiration. The equipment and uniforms of the German army figured almost exclusively in my doodles. The shape of their coal-scuttle helmets and the ingenuity of their half-tracks, the booted officers with wide-lapelled great coats and chested binoculars, gave them a devilish allure which trumped patriotism.

Many years later, I heard a story about General de Gaulle when he was taken on a post-war official visit to the Stalingrad battlefield. His Russian guide showed him how far the Germans had penetrated and told him with what obstinate courage they had defended themselves when finally entrapped, before going on to vaunt the achievement of the Red Army in winning so remarkable a victory. De Gaulle gazed at the scene and murmured, 'Quel grand peuple!' The Russian thanked the general for his admiration, whereupon de Gaulle said, 'Les Allemands.'

His compatriot, the collaborator Benoit-Méchin, in his self-justifying *De la Défaite au Désastre*, tells of how the German commander von Paulus flew three times from his beleaguered position to Hitler's headquarters, in order to plead to be allowed to break out while there was still time. On each occasion, full of soldierly determination to save as many of his men as was still possible, he steeled himself to confront the Führer. On each occasion, he dared not oppose Hitler's disastrous insistence that he fight to the last man. When all hope was gone, Hitler promoted von Paulus to Field

Marshal, in the expectation that he would die a happy hero. Surrounded and without hope of supply or escape, the new Field Marshal saved his men, and himself, and surrendered.

The fate of the Jews under Hitler was little mentioned in the newspapers left on the table for us by Mr Howard, a day after he had bought them. Wartime economy impelled him to do The Times crossword in pencil, very lightly. Once he had completed it, he rubbed out his solution and passed the puzzle to Mr McGaw, who could then solve it yet again. Sometimes a few of the clues were left unanswered when the paper reached us. Delamain and I debated possibilities and, occasionally, composed amateur (asymmetrical) puzzles of our own.

The world itself was revealed more with clues than with explicit answers. I cannot recall any greater interest in sex than in whatever other topic either policy or prudence veiled from proper attention. It was an incurious epoch; conformity was an intellectual no less than a social habit. Patriotism and credulity went together: Churchill and Roosevelt were held to be close friends and – after 1941 – Americans were our no less close, and admired, cousins. What our betters declared to be good was good; their accolades guaranteed merit: once Jacob Epstein was knighted, he became a great sculptor. To be On The Radio was fame.

My mother's kudos was enhanced by the evident power, and wealth, of the United States. When American soldiers began to arrive in large numbers, several turned out to be old friends from Chicago and Kansas City. Our flat, to which I returned for longer periods during the quieter weeks of 1942 and 1943, was often visited by Chuck or Buddy or their friends, always with a sack of PX goods: Hershey bars and cans of Hormel ham and del Monte Yellow Cling Peaches. (Why 'Cling'?)

My mother's kid cousin, Irvin, was a pilot in the Army Air Force. He was about ten years younger than Irene. Since they were both only children, they treated each other as brother and sister. I was almost jealous. In general, however, there was something exhilarating about the Americans who came and went, so generous, so smiling, so fearless. How many had ever been to Europe before? The war was an adventure as well as a test. Irvin was a lieutenant, silver bars on his shoulders. His dark tailored jacket and slick, lighter trousers contrasted with the hairy khaki of the British Army. His golden wings and healthy enthusiasm promised that the war would soon end. I did not renounce my desire to become a British naval officer, but I did admire his permanently knife-edged trousers. He gave me gum and candy bars (I didn't like the coconut) and a spare set of wings and US lapel badges, as well as some 8th Air Force shoulder flashes. For the first time in five years, I felt the pull of America; I was proud to have connections with the Yanks that almost everyone admired. If it was said of them (and it was) that they were 'overpaid, over-sexed and over here', I knew nothing of it. GIs and officers were democratically unembarrassed to talk to me and they told my mother all the things she wanted to hear about Home.

My father was always glad to see Irene happy. For the rest, he went about his English life like the assiduous hedonist that he was, *meeden agan* his golden rule. He played bridge and golf; he worked dutifully and intelligently; he visited his parents. From time to time, he would return to the flat with a package of cold fried fish, a speciality of the kosher food shops in the East End. He never disclosed why he had been in the East End. His purchases were certainly without any pious motive. One evening, as he sat in an armchair reading *The Evening News*, he began to cluck quietly. Soon his clucking became more vigorous and agitated and finally, with a squawk of triumph, and relief, he 'laid' three eggs. He must have scrounged these rarities somewhere in the City. He would not accept that they were 'black market'; he would never have anything to do with that sort of thing.

One day, in 1943, he told me to put on my best suit; he was taking me with him to a service. Although they rarely went there, my parents were members of the Liberal Jewish Synagogue in St John's Wood, opposite Lord's cricket ground, a destination which my father greatly preferred. He was a Middlesex man whose favourite batsman had been 'Patsy' Hendren. Our destination on this particular day, however, was the bombed ruins of the Great Temple in the East End (reached by tube to Aldgate East).

The Great Temple had been a centre of Orthodoxy, which was not my parents' style. Had they not been 'Liberal', they would never have sent me away to Copthorne, where I ate cold ham, once a week, with salad and without complaint. Unlike pork, ham was unrationed, and hence rarely obtainable in big cities. A local farmer must have made it available to the school. I dreaded its thick margin of white fat. Every blanched inch had to be eaten, in honour of the starving millions in Europe. 'You lucky people!' was Tommy Trinder's catchphrase, and Miss Lever's.

My father wore a black homburg and I my school cap (black with red braid). As we came out of the sandbagged tube station, we met other men and boys, all formally dressed and hatted, walking towards what was left of the Great Temple. Its jagged walls surrounded a big bombsite already feathered with weeds and wild flowers. Remains of burnt roof timbers were stacked against the walls. Compressing his lips against the twitch of emotion, my father left me to be informed by the occasion itself.

Dr Israel Mattuck, the Liberal rabbi from St John's Wood, was part of the platoon of ministers of all persuasions, from Liberal to Orthodox, via Reform, who came together, in rare concord, to pray for the Jews of Europe. News of their systematic extermination was current, though not widely believed. The dignitaries (including Colonel Louis H. Gluckstein, a Liberal luminary) stood against the skyline, in their various gowns, uniforms, hats and caps. I was part of something I did not understand, but felt. My father's clenched solemnity forbade, and somehow answered, questions. Something very terrible was happening somewhere, and I had some connection with it.

Dr Mattuck spoke in tones of intimidating imprecation which combined the wolf and the lamb. Other rabbis, in their lettered silken shawls, were ritually incomprehensible in Hebrew. What could they have said? Jews did not expect to be saved; pride and resignation went together: they lamented, but they did not complain. The Christian God moved in a mysterious way; the Jewish God was more immutable. He could be flattered with generous qualities, but nothing was expected of Him, except that He give us 'peace', a word which, on Mattuck's lips, was protracted into a polysyllable.

A few days later my father took me to the Wimbledon Park Golf Club (district line to Southfields) where I enjoyed supervised access to the putting course. On our way home, we had to catch a bus (85 or 93) up Putney Hill. The first one was full; so was the second. My infatuation with the paraphernalia of Nazism may have influenced me to say, 'If we were in Germany, we could pull a few people off and get on ourselves.' 'If we were in Germany,' my father said, 'we would be dead.'

I was put in my place by a mixture of curt anguish and accusing scorn. Cedric's tone repressed a fury which he knew that England would not tolerate in public. His anger was vented, tersely, on my innocent affectation of exemption from our inescapable Jewishness. I was startled by his vehemence in the face of my unvoiced wish not to be included among those for whom Dr Israel Mattuck and the other strangely foreign people, in their tasselled scarves and homburg hats, had prayed with such coercive, and often unintelligible, earnestness. If I was attempting some kind of flight from the threat of innate difference, my father pulled me back, irrevocably, into the ranks of the doomed. My silly remark proved how tempting it must have been to be a bully if there was nothing to stop you.

My schooling was calculated to make me the English gentleman whom my father believed I should become. Although I never bowed my head in the Creed, when it was uttered by the funny little parson in the florid village church, I did my unmusical best to join in the hymns, muting the Jesus Christ bits if they came along. By the force of osmosis, I became chapter-and-versed in the New as well as the Old Testament.

On Sunday evenings, we had Prayers in the dining room of the Lee Bay Hotel. Older boys were encouraged to read bits of the Bible before Mr Workman did his solemn stuff. One summer's evening, when I was old enough, Skete told me that it was my turn to read the lesson. Delamain, Sneyd and I were building a huge sandy village on the rocks. We stayed as late as we could, constructing yet another futile, slate-backed dam to protect it against the tide. I had to run back to school to be in time for the service.

When the cue came to read my verses from 2 Kings, my chest was rigid. I couldn't draw breath. Was the congestion of my lungs due to stage-fright no less than to haste? I could hardly make a sound. I panted and gasped my way through the words (to which no one listened with any great attention) and finished in a state of raucous aphasia. My undulant inaudibility must have sounded like Franklin Roosevelt when he broadcast to England on short-wave radio. No one jeered, but I was so humiliated that I continued, for years, to panic when asked to do any public reading.

Acting was different. Assuming a character made the impersonation of others more attractive, and plausible, than the pretence of being myself. Towards the end of our north Devon exile, I read Anthony Hope's *Rupert of Hentzau*, the sequel to *The Prisoner of Zenda*, and conceived the ambition of making it into a play. Unless – in the tradition of screenwriters, and of directors – I have repressed the memory of some nameless collaborator, I wrote the whole script myself. It is a tribute to Copthorne School that Mr Workman endorsed the project of putting the show on and allowed me to send to Monty Berman's for appropriate costumes (I cannot say who bore the expense).

When the hamper of swashbuckling apparel arrived, I felt all the pride, and alarm, of the producer/director/writer obliged to match achievement to vanity. Who had agreed to be in my cast, and how far our rehearsals went, is covered by a veil of oblivion. Among the props which I had ordered was a range of weaponry including the necessary swords with which Rudolf Rassendyl (was that going to be me?) and Rupert of Hentzau (or was that going to be me?) were to be armed in their climactic duel. The swords were not, as prudence might have dictated, made of painted wood; they were steel, and had lethal tips. 'Buttons' had been supplied to render them harmless, but Skete was not to be argued or pleaded with: they would all have to be returned forthwith. The production was cancelled.

Since then, it has happened on several occasions that some ambitious plan of mine has been aborted, or abandoned, for one reason or another. Only rarely have I felt that almost uncontrollable indignation which too often follows getting inconvenient letters at Scrabble or hitting an easy backhand into the net. When I was about to direct a movie, with a big star in it, and it was cancelled because the studio did not have the money to honour its promises, I was secretly almost as relieved as I was publicly mortified. Frustration is what I expect, and (it seems) imagine that I deserve: self-doubt, no less than ambition, is part of the character I have been allotted to play. My father used to say, 'Remember, you always come third in this family.' I could come first only in class. I was a timid Oedipus, licensed to solve the riddle of the Sphinx, if there were marks to be won, but reluctant to harm the father who kept me in my place.

By 1944, it was manifest that Germany was going to lose the war. Rumours said both that the invasion of Europe was imminent and that Copthorne would soon be returning to Sussex. North Devon was a huge camp; bulging trucks often throbbed in the high-hedged lanes. The hooped white star of the US forces was stencilled on their canvas sides and pulsing bonnets. Yet schoolwork went on, quite as if nothing had changed or could ever change its rhythmic cycle and repetitive content: *Tollo, tollere, tuli, latum* would, for some reason, always be worth remembering.

On the penultimate day of term, Mr Workman always set us pieces of 'repetition' to learn. The younger boys were required to master some Keats or Milton; fragments of *Lycidas* remain lodged, like benign shrapnel, in my mind. As we got older, he set us chunks of Virgil ('*Panditur interea domus omnipotentis Olympi ... aut hos aut hos arma sequi bellumque incesse Latinos*' etc.) and of Ciceronian prose, which was much easier to memorise than dread suggested. The gender rhymes at the end of Kennedy's *Latin Primer* were a doggerel delight: not only did we learn, for ever, that 'abstract nouns in -io call/*Feminina* one and all' but also that 'masculine will always be/Things that you can touch and see/...Also *Hadria*, the Adriatic Sea'. In addition to genders, we learnt lists of pronouns which took the accusative or the ablative case ('*A, ab, absque, coram, de, palam, cum* and *ex* and *e*', etc.). There was nothing punitive in this terminal test. We were being prepared, little by little (*paulatim*), for our scholarship examinations. Copthorne was, after all, a preparatory school: its reputation, and honour, depended on the awards we would win for ourselves, and for it.

The last year, in the top form, was devoted to regular rehearsals of the real thing. Mr Workman had accumulated stacks of scholarship papers from previous years. We answered foxy, foxed questions from Eton, Winchester, Clifton, Stowe, Repton, Rugby and, presumably, Charterhouse (I remember none). My sights were set on Winchester, the intellectual apex. I feared many things, not least what, in a vestigial diary I discovered not long ago, I abbreviated to JB: it stood for 'Jew Business'. Examinations more excited than alarmed me. I was alone with my task, in a policed cocoon of silence. The effort to get things right in an abstract way, to please my masters, was much less nerve-racking than contact with my fellow pupils. It was easier to recommend myself to my elders than to secure the friendship of my peers. Precocious questions to Mr McGaw or to Mr Howard provoked little smiles or teased revealing answers. If I said something amusing, they might consent to look at me with wary appreciation.

I did have a few friends among my fellows (Sneyd and Delamain). I acted as if others (Clode, Denton, Gilmour, Strangways, Taylor) accepted me rather than with confidence that they did. I heard menace in their murmurs and saw hostility in their cold blue gaze. I was at ease only among the more gentle boys, whose company never quite satisfied me. Quick-witted as well as uncertain, I developed the unwise habit of recruiting the temporary favour of dangerous boys by sharing my jejune sarcasms with them. Apprehension made me alert to the nuances of childish and adult speech; the wish to be armed against other people incited me to note (and embroider) their weaknesses and foibles. I should have been more guarded in mocking their absurdities, but the desire to entertain led to recklessness. When I was prudent, it showed itself in demeaning attempts to ingratiate myself with those who, like Steve Taylor, I feared for some earlier casual remark, too often about Jews, which probably meant little to him. I rarely forget what others find negligible. Vladimir Nabokov advised that a writer 'caress the details'; mine are often thorns.

As the war entered its last phase, food shortages abated. Mrs Workman moved her chicken run from the tennis courts to another part of the hotel grounds. In the summer of 1944, the courts had been regrassed (preparatory to the premises being handed back to its owners) and, since we still could not play cricket, we were given rudimentary tennis lessons.

On the morning of 6 June 1944, Mr Howard informed us – almost three years after he had told us that Hitler had invaded Russia – that the Allies had landed in Normandy (where the menus, he had by now told us, advertised '*cidre compris*'). Despite the disasters of the last four years, I retained an innocent faith in the irresistibility of the Allies, and in their cohesion. What schoolboy, however shrewd, could have guessed that there was any tension between 'us' and the Russians, still less that there was any between Eisenhower and Monty?*

Because the Americans were on our side, it did not occur to me that the Normandy invasion was hazardous or that there was any risk of repulse (some two years earlier the battleship of that name, HMS *Repulse*, had been sunk by the Japanese, who were horrid, but lacked the proximate menace of the Nazis).

It was a fine, hot June. I partnered Steve Taylor** in the

---

*I was now British enough to assume 'our' military superiority. Field Marshal Montgomery was so manifest a hero that his personal foibles, not least his asceticism and plethora of beret badges, passed for virtuous eccentricities. A row had broken out in a secret session of Parliament when it was learned that, at the end of the African campaign, Monty had invited the surrendered German commander, General von Thoma, to a meal in his caravan. Churchill is said to have commented, 'Poor von Thoma! I too have dined with Montgomery.' Such remarks never reached tender ears.

**Thirty years later, when writing a television series entitled *The Glittering Prizes*, I gave the name Stephen Taylor to an English Fascist, whom my hero goes to quiz in his truculent retirement. Adam Morris's provocative deference reflects that mixture of aggression and tennis tournament. He could run very fast, although with his behind strangely stuck out. We never played singles, both because there were only two courts and because it was more morally uplifting to play in a team, however small, than to win on one's own account. One box of Dunlop balls lasted all summer. As the court dried out, the balls were left greener than it was.

The only sporting activity in which one was quite alone was boxing. If I continued to see myself as small and defenceless and deserving of favour, as I sometimes still do (the common fate of only children?), I had become one of the tallest boys in the school. The tallest, by far, was Mackinnon. The boxing ring was in the hotel garage, which had a corrugated iron roof. There was space for the ring to be roped only on three sides. The fourth was against the wall at the back. It was cushioned with sacking stuffed with straw, in order to prevent heads being banged against the bricks. At the beginning of the term, the cushion was evenly plump, but as the weeks went by, the straw settled, and the canvas sagged and bellied. If you were tall enough to have regularly to fight Mackinnon, you were likely to find that his long left jab cracked your head against canvas-covered brickwork.

Mackinnon was neither very powerful nor vindictive; he boxed against me because I was boxing against him. If his arms were longer than mine, what could I do about it? If my head was knocked against the wall, then it was. I did not learn the art of self-defence, despite honest efforts on the part of some master or other; I learned that it was unfruitful to trade punches with people who were bigger than you were. I did not cry a lot, out of pride rather than courage, but I inferred that the world was always likely to be rigged against me; only subtlety could escape bruising consequences. I had

ingratiation with which I have too often confronted, and also sought to pacify, those whose admiration I craved, even as I denounced their vanities.

yet to read the *Odyssey*, but I later recognised that it was no accident that its hero was the cleverest, and hence the most durable, of the Greeks who went to Troy. He did not trade punches with the gigantic cyclops, Polyphemus; he sharpened and stuck a red-hot pole in his eye. I became a writer.

There is a categorical distinction between Confessions – in which disclosures, and boasts, not least sexual, are to be expected – and autobiography, which can be more discreet. I have no aptitude for confessions, and small history to warrant them. If I fail to expose every displeasing detail of my remembered life, it is more from fear of boring the reader than in order to add false lustre to my reputation. I am trying, in part, to get to the root of the persistent dread which has haunted my life, despite its joys, blessings and petty achievements, ever since I was brought to live in England. Unlike many of the refugees who came here at more or less the same time, I do not feel compelled to eternal gratitude; I may be fortunate, but I was done no favours; if I remain a metic, I am not a refugee.

In regarding England through one jaundiced and one rose-tinted glass, I follow many of the native writers whom I admire. Irony is implicit in English usage; the Classics are its common source. I am and am not at home in my father's native land, but I am sufficiently secure, in my uncertainty, not to affect unalloyed allegiance either to Britain or to the US. At my age, I am timidly brazen enough to say that, much as England means to me, I have signed no contract requiring me to obsequiousness. Nor am I paying off a debt. I arrived here/there in consequence of a necessity which I could not resist; I remained because a murderous war broke out, during which I was unscathed but exposed to a way of life alien to anything I expected during my earliest years. Would I have been much the same person whether I had grown up in the US or in the last years of British supremacy (or at least during the last years when the British imagined themselves supreme)? Who knows? Old England certainly intimidated me into deferential resentment. Solitude – masked by a pose of wary self-sufficiency – impelled me to mimic a style that has never been wholly natural to me. In art, this may matter very little (sincerity is not a method in literature); in life it means that I am rarely at ease, except with the very few people whom I dare to trust. Even then, I am half-inclined to believe that they may, at any moment, turn their backs. I lack the vanity to be certain that they would be mistaken to do so.

By becoming a writer, I sought to immunise myself, if not against rejection, at least against ostracism. In a club of one, my membership is unchallenged. The Wykhamist motto 'Manners makyth man' is very much to my taste. Manners have nothing to do with sincerity or belief in eternal values. They are the evidence of knowing how to behave, not of what one believes. There is shallow, but rich, pleasure in honouring a code for no reason; manners are the grammar of behaviour, arbitrary but nicely articulated. The rules are the rules; cricket is cricket, or was.

All courtesy contains a tincture of irony: we respond not to what a person merits, in the way of attention or civility, but to what he and/or she *would* merit, if they merited it. To stand up with the same promptness when a plain as when a beautiful woman comes into the room, or when a bore no less than a wit comes to your table in a restaurant, is to visit on those whom we secretly despise the same apparent attention as on those whom we deem worthy of it. In polite societies, sincerity and insincerity wear indistinguishable smiles, and tip the same hat.

English life, in the days of social stratification, was seasoned and spiced by undetected condescension or deference. All but the grandest and the most abject were involved in a ceaseless interplay of the affected and the genuine, the conventional and the genuine. English prose was trapped with double meanings and nuances of greater or less significance. When an official signed a letter, as he often did, 'Your obedient servant', he promised neither obedience nor service; when an editor sent you his compliments, on rejecting your manuscript, it was always uncomplimentary: only a clown would ask him (as I once did the editor of *The Evening Standard*) to be more specific with his compliments.

Evasiveness within the limits of what one's peers or masters would abide (or never discover) was part of school life. There were certain acts to which one owned up; others which it was legitimate to deny. A.H. Clough's 'Thou shalt not kill; but need'st not strive/Officiously to keep alive' is a very English scholarly sentiment; it may be heartless, but it scans.

A shrewd, or impatient, reader will have guessed that all these lucubrations must be the prelude to something. It is more shameful than sensational, though I am not sure precisely what it is. Here is what I remember: Strangways – the oddly old-faced boy who once hauled me to my feet by my penis – and I together broke some rule which no amount of introspection can retrieve. I doubt if we were exceptionally wicked, but somehow the offence was traced to Strangways, who neither denied it nor hinted that anyone else had been involved. It was clear that Skete took a serious view of whatever it was and that he intended to spong (cane) my confederate. The question was, should I confess what I had not been called upon to deny (since I was not suspected) or should I remain ingloriously silent?

I discussed the question with Strangways and said (albeit in what Homer might have called 'unwinged words', that is, in this case, without pressing sincerity) that I would tell Skete that I had shared his guilt, if he thought it would do any good. Can I have failed to realise that I was going through the motions of true fellowship? Why else put the issue in such a way that my friend was forced to make the decision whether I should share a fate which my confession could do nothing to mitigate? I contrived to make Strangways, not myself, responsible for my decision. Like Odysseus of the many ruses, I combined standing by him with deserting him.

There was something in the characters we had both played through our time at Copthorne which – though no excuse for my conduct – does something to explain why I did not confess. It was not that I feared being caned (there was a certain fascination in being the victim of such a fate); it was rather that I dreaded being revealed to Mr Workman as a 'bad' boy, when – since I was diligent and always had a good report and was slated to take a Winchester scholarship in 1945 – he had always taken me for virtuous. Strangways was not wicked, but he had a cheeky face. Mr Workman would punish him without being disappointed in him, and without the vigour which disappointment might provoke. In the event, Strangways was caned; I was not. When he showed his dormitory the marks, he was the brief object of admiration. I was burdened with secret shame, and envy. Strangways appeared not to resent my – let us say – reticence, but it would have consequences in another part of life, and in another school.

Apart from his ability to bang my head against the softened bricks of the garage wall, Mackinnon plays no part in my schoolboy memories. He had freckles and a very white skin. Was he clever or friendly? Was he in the cast of my aborted production of *Rupert of Hentzau*? I cannot say. I went three rounds with him and that was that. Similar inconsequential scraps litter the cutting-room floor of memory. What became of my friendship, both nervous and intense, with an aloof boy called Carn, whose name remains fresh, perhaps because of *caro, carnis* (f.) meaning 'flesh' (and 'of flesh') in Latin? Carn was not fleshy at all; his leanness chimed with his monosyllabic surname. He belonged to no group, affected no enthusiasm. He seemed set on a different course from the rest of us. I used his name, years later, in a novel called *A Wild Surmise*, though the character to which I attached it belonged to someone of similar style whom I knew later.

At some point an American boy called Outwater came to the school. Was he the son of a diplomat or a soldier? He did not disclose his origins; he had a smiling face, dark curls and an accent which he made no effort to anglicise. As with those whom I knew or suspected of being Jews, so with this American kid: I had no aptitude for solidarity; I made no effort to befriend him. There was another boy who, like me, had an American mother and may well have been Jewish. One day, when we were having showers, he put his hand over his penis and balls and pushed them upwards. 'Women look like this,' he said, 'down there. But they have round-heads and cavaliers too, underneath.' 'I know,' I said, as if I did.

I look back on the landscape and the details of my wartime schooldays with accurate indifference: the bracken on the golf course and the improbably steep layout of the links themselves; the cataracted valley streams that flashed with trout and minnows; the broad-brimmed mushrooms with their darkly fluted undersides; the wrecked steamer against the rocks below the cliffs, its cargo of salted oranges bobbing in the shuffling water; the little tea shoppe in Lee village where I ate strawberries and clotted cream and tried to be happy with my visiting mother; the long summer evenings in the dorm, reading Arthur Ransome, with a mixture of impatience and fascination (I knew the books were no good, but I wanted to know what happened); blue-mackintoshed walks up one-in-five lanes; the crash and vaulting spray of the spring tide against the pinkish sea wall (sometimes the force of the water was strong enough to kick lumps of con-crete into the roadway); the wide sickle of insurgent water as you looked down on Woolacombe Bay notorious for quick-sands; the flash and distant grumble of air raids on Cardiff; two strangely accented foreigners who sold us French flags (on the usual pins) badged with the cross of Lorraine, after singing a medley of embarrassing songs ('*Gentille Alouette*' among them), culminating with the Marseillaise, which made the lady cry; P.P. 'running away' and being caught and brought back in privileged disgrace. I envied his mad nerve and knew that I lacked it; besides, where was there to run to? A nagging question remains: did my quips contribute to the misery which impelled him to do what he did?

All these scraps amount to a montage without any cumu-lative sense or narrative thrust. Yet I have little doubt that I appeared a well-behaved, normal little boy, of eager intelli-gence and ambition. How many of my contemporaries would recognise me as the anxious, docile solitary that I have described?

My home life was hardly more gregarious. Since I was an only child, I played a great deal by myself. In the small room at the end of the corridor, I spent hours reading William and Biggles books (years later, I could still think of the reserve petrol tank in our 1960 Standard Ensign as the 'gravity' tank). I wept when Ernst, in *The Swiss Family Robinson*, had to watch helplessly as the anaconda swallowed his honest donkey. Most of my time was spent in building model vil-lages, out of wooden bricks which we had brought with us from New York, and driving my Dinky toys through car-peted streets. I invented scenarios for the Dinky people to enact; I bombed their houses and I raced ambulances to save some of their lives; I was the enemy and I was the hero, the creator and the observer of their dreamed-up dramas, a god till it was time for me to walk the dog, again.

Sometimes I did go out to play with the other children who cycled or ran around the secluded grounds of Manor Fields. The flats were said to be built on an estate which once belonged to Lord North, forever stigmatised for having lost the American colonies. The various blocks almost all bore the names of Oxford (and a few Cambridge) colleges, though only of those with non-religious connotations. I felt no easier with the children whom I met during the holidays than with my schoolfellows. If less threatened, I was no more sure of their goodwill. We played at war in picked-up gangs. Our spears were the long bamboo canes left over after the gardeners had tied up plants. Our battles grew fiercer as the day dragged on. One afternoon, I led a charge on the enemy's hideout and had a spear flung at me with whirring accuracy. It struck me on the upper lip, below the nose, penetrated the flesh and lodged there, in all its horizontal length, quivering. I walked back to Balliol House with the cane drooping only slightly. Did I pull it out finally, or did my mother?

The bamboo left a few splinters behind, which Dr Millis extracted with tweezers. Like Skete, he had won an MC in the Great War. My injuries did not alarm him. He gave me a tetanus shot and that was soon that. If the spear had hit me with the same velocity three inches higher, it might have pierced my eye and killed me, like Harold at the Battle of Hastings (whose displacement by William I triggered the list of England's kings 1066–1087, 1087–1101, all the way to George VI, 1936–, a small proportion of whom were indeed English).

My sole reliable friend was still Martin Warburton, who continued to live in the block of flats from which we had been forced to move. Our friendship had a pastoral timelessness: we played Monopoly and we went on longer cycle rides, but we developed no maturing intimacy. If he came to our flat, I was reluctant to confess how much I still enjoyed playing with my toys. He brought the Monopoly. I chose the battleship; he was the boot.

In the summer holidays of 1944, the 'buzz-bombs' made

it too dangerous for me to return to London. My mother and I went to stay in Felpham, a seaside village outside Bognor Regis, where we shared a rented house. It was a naive choice of retreat, since it lay on the direct line taken by the buzz-bombs (the primitive, unguided missiles officially known as Vis), both on their way to London and as they droned along the south coast towards Portsmouth and Southampton. Only small patches of beach were accessible because of the rusting relics of the defences against a German invasion in 1940. Skulled and crossboned signs on the tempting dunes warned us to 'BEWARE MINES'.

The buzz-bombs excited more interest than fear. They flared through the clear summer sky, like big cigars with smaller, lit ones clamped to their backs. As long as the smoke and exhaust spurted from their horizontal chimneys, the missiles could be objects of contemplation; they became dangerous only after their engines cut out. This timely warning was said to occur because of a design fault: as they burned more fuel, the tail became lighter and the nose – where the explosive charge was mounted – dropped down, thus interrupting the fuel supply. This precipitated the ominous silence as they dived. Even if the buzz-bomb was directly overhead, it was safe to watch it. The reason was, as Delamain would have said, elementary: it could never plunge vertically to the ground. Whoever was going to get hurt was at least several hundred yards further down the track.

The RAF sometimes sent out Typhoons to tilt any Vis flying parallel to the shore into the sea before they reached their targets. The pilots had to fly alongside the sinister cigars, on the landward side, and then flip them off course with their wing tips. I am not sure that I ever actually saw this being done, but I do recall a Vi plunging into the Channel in front of our eyes and exploding in a cheerful plume of spray.

One fine September day, not long before I was due to

return to north Devon, the morning air was full of droning planes. We looked up at a sky ruled by neat lines of bombers and gliders and escorting fighters. It reminded me of the blue pages which Mr Workman handed out to be filled with copperplate writing if someone committed a misdemeanour meriting an imposition (impot.). The powerless gliders were latched by dark hyphens of cable to their throbbing leaders. Each was marked with triple white bands on their wings, like sergeants of the sky. When the moment came, they would be unhooked and their hitherto impotent pilots would guide them down into a clear space and crash land. One of those pilots was my mother's kid cousin, Irvin Weintraub.

Irene was still in her early thirties. Her beauty and smartness, even during the war, were an easy source of pride. She had kept all her triple-A I. Miller shoes from the days when we went to buy them at Saks; her wardrobe was no less stylishly stocked from the days before rationing and patriotic austerity. I never doubted her love; nor did it occur to me that she might be bored, day after day, with my seaside company. Did she have any notion that Irvin might be flying over our heads that September day, when the gliders were on their way to Arnhem? To me, a grand and invulnerable fleet was on its way to an undoubted victory. Did I ever imagine the fear, or the blood, or the deaths on our side?

Twenty-three-year-old Lieutenant Irvin Weintraub crash landed his glider, and its cargo of airborne soldiers, in the assigned area of north Holland. They had been told that they would encounter trivial resistance. Through inaccurate reading of the reconnaissance photographs, Intelligence had failed to detect the presence of a strong reserve force of *Panzers*. As soon as Irvin's glider hit the ground it was surrounded by heavily armed SS men. The troops inside had no chance even to unship their equipment. They, and the crew, were forced to come out with their hands up. The Germans herded them together and then shot them all.

I do not know how soon my mother heard the news of Irvin's death, nor did I ever see her uncontrollably distressed by it. Perhaps it did not suit me to observe that she cared for someone else as much as she did for me. Irvin's photograph is still on the table in her living room. He looks younger every time I see it. Irene sometimes goes to Holland and visits the village whose inhabitants remember the hopeless sacrifice of the young Americans who died there. I have never been.

By the Christmas of 1944, the war was clearly won, but it did not end. One day I was walking alone in Green Park, perhaps on my way to Charing Cross Road where Mr Howard had recommended the second-hand bookshops. I found myself trailing a group of American soldiers, who were kidding around in the usual way of young males. Suddenly there was a very large explosion, followed instantly by the whooshing sound of the V2 rocket which had delivered it. The soldiers reacted with alarm: they scattered and one or two of them threw themselves flat on the grass. Soon they were laughing sheepishly at their fear, or pretending that they had been kidding. Yet their alarm had been palpable enough. Ignorantly innocent of what bombs could actually do to people, I had remained calm while soldiers took fright. There was nothing courageous in my response. I observed it quite as if it were someone else's: I had been fearless while adults had not. And that was that.

The Germans mounted sporadic, but violent raids on London during a last spasm of Luftwaffe activity before the Allies achieved complete mastery of the skies (how triumphant the clichés had become!). One night, despairing of an 85 or a 93 bus, my parents and I had started walking up Putney Hill, when the darkness was scissored by searchlights and badged by loud yellowy orange anti-aircraft fire. As we ran to the nearest shelter, in Lytton Grove – a block of less luxurious flats across the road from the pavement on which we had been walking – I saw one bomber in the X of intersecting searchlights. I was running and I had my hand on the top of my school cap, but I had time to wonder what it must be like to be laced like that between the trembling pincers of light, like one of Preston's frail moths spread for spearing.

When we dodged into Lytton Grove and down the stairs into the shelter, we were received with tea and chocolate biscuits by the residents. My mother remarked on how sweet it had been that I ran along with my hand on top of my head, as if that would protect me from the bombs. 'It wasn't that,' I said. 'I was afraid it would fall off and Daddy would make me go back for it.'

I had no reason for such fear. I may have wished draconian sternness on my father, but he had never done anything cruel to me. Only his grim-eyed, straight-lipped coldness made him occasionally fearful to me. Nothing alarmed me more than a quietly spoken request that we 'have a word'. I would go into the bathroom while he shaved, in underpants and vest, and listen in silence to whatever he felt had to be, as he put it, discussed. For the rest, he was patient with my sulks and did his best to teach me the various skills, not least the tango, which might be useful to an English future.

In the evenings my parents would play contract rummy with me, which I assumed they enjoyed. The requirements for going down became more elaborate with each hand. Ten cards were dealt and, at first, you needed only two lots of three, to which you could add further triplets until you went out. The final contract was for a sequence of seven *and* three of a kind, so that the other players were left suddenly with a full hand to be totted up against them. I suspect that we brought this form of rummy from America. I have never met anyone else who played it.

On Saturday nights, when there was no manifest air raid, my parents and four of their neighbours had a regular poker game. When it was at our house, which it seemed frequently to be, and I was on holiday, I would sit and watch, just as I had the bridge games in my grandparents' flat in Dorset House. My mother would bring out the racks of chips which, once again, had come with us from New York. Less than a decade later, I would borrow these chips as props in a musical comedy for which I wrote the book at Cambridge. I had promised to return them, but they were lost when the sets were dismantled. I am still ashamed of my shrugging confession of their disappearance.

The Sulises and the Heaths and my parents played six-penny raises. My mother kept a running tally of purchases of fresh chips from the bank. Did I sometimes play banker? I certainly played nothing else. As with bridge, I learned the game before I held a card. They played all kinds of variations in order to while away the long evenings: stud; seven-card low; high low; and the rest. There were no regular winners or losers. The game was always friendly with gossip and half-time refreshments.

I have never wanted to play poker in later life. Is it because it needs more nerve than bridge? Certainly not because it is less skilful. Or is it because, in poker, you are responsible for your own unpartnered fate? Unlike my father, I lack the gambler's sangfroid: I cannot lose without showing regret, or rage; I lack the mathematical agility to keep re-assessing the odds, the means by which a good poker player adds logic to luck. Precise odds are no less significant to the great bridge player, but even the average hacker can remember the more usual probabilities, such as that of six cards in a suit breaking 3–3 rather than 4–2 (the latter is slightly more likely); in poker, the chances change as each card is revealed. I remember playing for (spent) matchsticks in north Devon, but only a few times.

In my last year at Copthorne, however, we did have quite a regular bridge four. The certainty of an Allied victory meant that some of those who had been evacuated to the US and Canada at the beginning of the war returned to England. One, who came to Copthorne, was Richard Bird, a dark-haired boy with the beginnings of an adolescent beard. We established a bridge partnership. The greatest of our successes, which I reported to my father, came when I doubled our vulnerable opponents and Richard redoubled. 'They went down 3,400,' I said. It was galling to learn that the same side could not both double and redouble.

By the spring of 1945, preparations were in hand to return to Sussex for the summer term, which would also be my last. Richard Bird and I were to try for Winchester scholarships that summer. During the war, public schools registered their examination papers to the candidates' headmasters, who then invigilated their completion in the hermetic silence of a room where the candidate(s) worked in timed diligence. Such was the assumed integrity of prep-school headmasters that it seems never to have occurred to anyone that an unscrupulous usher might put a thumb on the scales, by whispering illicit advice, in order to tilt things in his charges' favour. Bird and I were to be in the first wave of candidates once again to go to Winchester to take our papers.

Before we left the Lee Bay Hotel for the last time, we (I and some forgotten others, perhaps Delamain and Preston among them) prepared a final 'First Form Bomb'. This was a puppet show, contrived and scripted by the happy few. Ours was a slapstick comedy along the lines of Punch and Judy. We took great trouble with miniature lights (procured for us by Mr McGaw) and with the elaborate sets in which our handmade, funny-voiced glove puppets did their knockabout stuff.

The Lee Bay Hotel had housed me between the ages of nine and thirteen. It had not seemed odd to be there; it was not odd to leave. I felt no nostalgia for the place, though I did go back years later and found it boarded up and abandoned. Fuchsias still flowered by the verdigrised *porte-cochère*. The things I learned in wartime seclusion served me well in all the scholarships and examinations which I took in subsequent years. My mind was unforgettably stuffed with what a generation or two later would be for ever dismissed (from *dimitto, dimittere, dimisi, dimissum*) as useless: I knew more tenses, indicative and subjunctive, active and passive and middle than any modern student is asked to master, not to mention more pronouns and conjunctions, expletives and enclitics of the Greek variety: *ge, dee, men and de, alla, meta, kata, ana, pros*; and the Latin: *cum, quin, quinetiam, -que, -ve quid and quod, seu and seu etcetera.*

I had also had to learn a number of exemplary sentences which alerted the student to idiomatic usage such as *Occurrit quidam notus mihi nomine tantum* (a certain person comes up to me whom I know only by name) and *Non cuivis homini contingit adire Corinthum* (not any old person has the luck to go to Corinth). Mr Workman would not have dreamed of disclosing why you were lucky to go to Corinth: before its alleged levelling* by the Roman general Mummius in 146 BC, the city was renowned for the beauty and expertise of its courtesans.

School seemed to be an almost arbitrary matter of learning whatever was likely to lead to scholarships. The Classics were the heart of the curriculum. French was hardly less arcane than Latin or Greek, but earned fewer marks; logarithms furnished a supposedly quicker form of multiplication, though it required referring to a booklet of dazzling figures of 'logs' and 'anti-logs'; history was calibrated according to the reigns of English sovereigns and the dates of English victories: Agincourt, Crécy, Poitiers. The mystery of how the Hundred Years War was finally lost, when the French never managed, it seemed, to win a battle, was never broached. Castillon-la-

---

*Recent archaeology suggests that the destruction was limited.

Bataille? *Connais pas!* The righteous benevolence of the British, in all European and imperial actions, was unquestionable. So was the truth of the Christianity which it was the British mission to spread, along with justice, to those 'without the law'. Dominion over palm and pine was a Kiplingesque duty, without profit but demanding sterling character and steadiness under fire. If the Gatling jammed, and the Colonel was dead, we might any one of us be required to encourage the men to play up and play the game. Life was at once earnest and not to be taken too seriously.

My ambition to go to Dartmouth was whittled away both by my father (who considered the Navy an unrewarding post-war career) and by Mr Workman, who had other, civilian laurels in mind. I continued, however, to find British achievements at sea more exciting than the redcoats' triumph at Oudenarde and Malplaquet and Blenheim; Badajoz and Ciudad Rodriguo and Coruna (where 'his [Sir John Moore's] corpse to the ramparts we hurried') could not compare with the Nile, Copenhagen, Quiberon Bay and, of course, Trafalgar. Britannia's rule over the waves was never in doubt, despite Van Tromp and his broom. He jolly soon learned his lesson. What patriotic master would dare to mention what Beattie had said at Jutland ('There's something wrong with our bloody ships today')? In no case was the wickedness of the enemy in doubt; still less did anyone wonder whether another's patriotism or defence of his country might be justified.

The ancient Romans retrojected upon their greedy history the same affectations of virtue which dignified our imperial past. The historian Livy observed, with smug irony, that Rome had acquired its empire 'in self-defence'. What difference was there, *mutatis mutandis*, between Pax Romana and Pax Britannica, save that the British *imperium* would neither decline nor fall? The Samnites like the Scots, the Numidians like the Zulus, the Gauls like the Germans, should have known better than to stand in the way of civilisation. According to our textbooks, the British conquest of Africa and subjugation of India were undertaken for the benefit of the natives, who had languished under tyrants and suffered arbitrary barbarism. Because I was, to some degree, a stranger to the British ethos, I was more easily convinced than those who had known no other: the convert takes pains to be credulous.

Our teachers, and their textbooks, left small room for scepticism about the God-given virtues of the imperial mission. Since Britain was at war, scepticism would be tantamount to treason. The memory of the Abdication, and of the all-too-human character of the once-venerated Prince of Wales, had been effaced by the dutiful gallantry of George VI, who was to be seen in the Gaumont British or Pathé News clambering through ruined parts of London displaying the common touch in the uniform of a field marshal. His Christmas broadcasts, during which he struggled to enunciate the nastier consonants, were listened to as if his laborious diction confirmed its oracular significance.

No vestige of derision was visited, to my naive knowledge, on a single member of the government. One knew their names, and offices, as Catholics did the saints, all the way down to Sir Archibald Sinclair (Lib., Sec. of State for Air). Even the somewhat disgraced Edward VIII, who had stepped down to mere Duke of Windsor, had rallied to the flag and pluckily undertaken the onerous duty of governing the Bahamas. The coalition government proved how unnecessary party politics really were. If ordinary people could combine to defeat Hitler, why should our betters fall out when the chance recurred to 'win the peace'? Yet by the time we were due to return to Sussex, for the summer term of 1945, both Richard Bird and I (now the self-appointed first-form intellectual elite) were strong for Labour in the General Election which, once the Germans had been defeated, could not long be postponed.

I was at home on VE Day. Manor Fields was not given to Bacchanalian display. There was no communal manifestation of joy. That evening, my parents went out with friends to celebrate, perhaps in the newly lit West End (Hatchett's, near the Berkeley Hotel in Piccadilly, was their favourite place to go dancing). I was thirteen (and three quarters), but it did not occur to them that I might go with them; I should not enjoy what they were going to do. I cannot say how long I had known the little girl, of my own age, who lived a few entrances away from us, in Somerville House, but Dorothy Tutin and I had played tennis together on the Manor Fields courts (which roofed the garage where we had sheltered during the mini-blitz) and found ourselves equally abandoned by our parents on the evening of 8 May. Did they imagine that we should have more fun with each other than being jostled by drunken crowds? They did not, of course, mean by that that we should, as young Americans might have, settle to an evening's necking, still less to petting. It was assumed that, like Toots, the dachshund, when left alone with the broken-legged chicken, I should respect Dorothy, and that she would cluck in alarm should I forget myself. Alas, I knew no worse. I was a timid early teenager; a kiss on the cheek was a wild erotic fantasy.

Dorothy was a pretty, precisely spoken dark-haired girl, whose theatrical ambitions were being fostered by her stagey mother, Adie. Her father (who served at tennis with a strange dabbing motion) designed the propeller of the Queen Mary. Falling on hard times, he used the writing room of the Piccadilly Hotel as his rent-free office. No one questioned his presence, or his access to the writing paper.

I smoked my first cigarette (Player's No. 3) with Dorothy, in the tennis court toilet. As for kisses, I neither dared nor, strangely enough, desired to kiss Dorothy. Our sexual timidity was at odds with what we did on VE night. We sat side by side on the couch in my parents' flat reading the parts of

Elyot and Amanda in Noël Coward's *Private Lives*, which I had found in a handsome Literary Guild compendium, *Play Parade*. Coward's skimpy text alerted me to the fact that renown was much more easily acquired by writing plays rather than books. *Private Lives* was less than a hundred pages long and many of the speeches were markedly laconic. Dotty and I exchanged Coward's sophisticated dialogue quite as if we were familiar with the passions first enacted by him and Gertie Lawrence, whose real life love for each other was more frantic than mine for Dotty, if no more vigorously expressed. The Tutins owned a stack of mildly risqué records, of which my favourite was 'She Had to Go and Lose it at the Astor ...'.

Dorothy was to train as a flautist, under the conductor of the Metropolitan Police band, before she went to RADA. She often said that she never wanted to be an actress. This did not prevent her from being 'destined for the stage', even if Adie had not pushed her on to it. I often imagined writing a play for her, but I never did more than find her a too-small part in a radio feature. Her clear, yet husky, voice lent charm to everything she said. There was something woeful in her lovely smile, long before she was diagnosed with the leukaemia from which she died not long ago. When I knew her, she too was an only child, but she had had an older brother, Eric, who died when he was ten and she was five. Knowledge of pain always underlay her levity. 'Sunt lacrimae rerum,' as we used to quote, 'mentem mortalia tangunt.'

Copthorne School was restored to Sussex in the calm summer of 1945. It promptly recaptured its pre-war allure. The tractor cut its wide swathes in the cricket field which, remarkably, had escaped the plough. The RAF must have used it for recreation. The swimming pool was filled; we bathed naked in its healthily cold water (Macintosh displayed a remarkable pubic bush). Mr McGaw resumed his yellowing Nomads sweater and, although Mr Crowe was no longer there to insist on it, I again took up my right-handed stance, quite as if four summers had not lapsed without an opportunity to keep a straight bat.

Richard Bird and I must have been quite complacent about our chances at Winchester. We found time to start a magazine, *The New Spectator*, which was, of course, handwritten. It affected the humour, and certainly the Augustan elegance, not to say stiltedness, of Addison and Steele's original essays. The silly pattern in the unrolling carpet of my life could be said to have revealed an ominously proleptic stitch in the selection of those two literati as models. Both were Old Carthusians.

Having reached the top of the school, and of the top form, I was less anxious about how I was regarded by my fellows. Tall for my age, and not a weed, I probably appeared more overbearing than anxious. Richard and I had quick tongues and the intellectual smugness of Winchester postulants. Mr Workman prepared us like Aeschylus's 'corn-fed trace horses': when the time came, he accompanied us to Winchester with an attaché case primed with an energetic hoard of chocolate and sustaining snacks (sausage rolls, apples and cold chicken).

We were to take something like a dozen three-hour papers, two a day with only a couple of hours between them. After the morning session, we picnicked with Skete on a bench in Winchester College's grounds, while other candidates jostled for lunch in some crowded hall. He not only calmed us with encouraging words, he also made sure that we had two hours of fresh air before we went into the Great Hall for the next event in our unrelenting calendar.

The examinations were conducted in two stages. For the first, all applicants took a series of papers which were marked before the second stage. Only candidates who 'made the cut' were eligible for the final round. After that, there was an interview with the headmaster, the Reverend Dr Spencer Leeson. The marks for the first stage were added up and a list displayed in the bottle-glassed bow window of Wells the bookshop. These preliminary rankings took no account of the candidates' ages. The final list, on the other hand, which would determine who was to be admitted to College in the following September, would be adjusted to give 'weight for age'. Since my birthday is in August, and candidates had, a priori, to be under fourteen, I was among the oldest of them. Who was I to question the fairness of the traditional handicap? It might be wondered, however, whether it made much sense in effect to penalise a boy for the date of his birth, when only a matter of months distinguished the oldest from the youngest. The policy may have fostered the prodigy, but – can sour grapes affect the vision? – I still see little virtue in advancing those who might, potentially, excel their semi-peers at the expense of those who had already proved their ability. Those were the rules, however. It needs small wit to see that they afforded ample opportunity for manipulative discretion.

I cannot remember where we stayed while we waited for the semi-final tallies to be posted, but it must have been a tense day or two. Richard and I were rivals with no wish to efface each other; when we compared notes, we were glad to have given similar or identical answers. My dreams are still haunted by one particular maths question about what happened when a squiggle of string on a plane was moved until it was affected by two fixed pins. I did not know what the question was asking of me, and I still do not; it did not seem crucial, but perhaps it was. For the rest, I was like a clock-work toy, wound up and set to go for three-hour spells without stopping.

When the first lists were posted, I was the fourth highest, a few places above Richard, who was some months younger than I. Since there were to be twelve new scholars, I appeared at least as well placed as he. Despite the posterior protests of Wykhamist archivists, I remain convinced that, had I not been a Jew, I should have been admitted to College. Did we have to do further three-hour papers in the second stage? I cannot remember; but if we did, I am unlikely to have done worse in them than in the preceding ones.

I recall with obstinate clarity the Reverend Doctor's testy courtesy in the crucial interview. He pressed me to say whether, if I came to Winchester, I should object to going to chapel. Did nervousness make me seem duplicitous when I answered, with artless candour, that I had been going to chapel, and church, for the last five years? I omitted mention of my secret recusance in failing to bow at the mention of Jesus in the Creed. May Leeson, like the Grand Inquisitor, have guessed at some atavistic inward reservations? In fact, Judaism meant so little to me as a religion that I should have found it more difficult to explain its tenets than those of Christianity. The issue seemed more irrelevant, by far, than the use of *ei* (or indeed *eithe*) with the optative or the role of the accusative case in Latin 'exclamations': '*me miserum!*' (woe is me!) was a standard opening to hexameters and pentameters alike (automatic memory supplies a line that continued '... *quantis increscunt aequora ponti*').

Anxiety may have led me to reveal with too little caution how eager I was to charm the Headmaster (and please Mr Workman and my father). Did I make the mistake of smiling, or even of making a wry joke in Cedric's style? Can I have been ill-advised enough to try to beguile Leeson with the story of my father's ruse when he asked not to have to eat bacon on Wimbledon Common? I was dismissed courteously enough, but I was not told that anyone looked forward to seeing me again.

When the final list of accepted scholars was posted in the bookshop window, Raphael, F.M., had sunk – *me miserum!* – to thirteenth place; Bird, R., had risen to third or fourth. My disappointment was soon allayed by Mr Workman. I had told him that my father could not afford for me to go to Winchester as a 'commoner', and so, I daresay, had Cedric. I was promised that not everyone offered an award necessarily took it, and that, in any case, my gross total of marks had been so good that, given Copthorne's close association with Winchester, some kind of arrangement could almost certainly be made. We travelled back to Sussex in modest triumph. Richard and I would, it seemed, go in tandem to the best school in England (M.M.G.P. Slot had been elected a King's Scholar at Eton, but how great an intellectual achievement was that, since he came well below us in class?).

Within a few days, however, it became clear that my thirteenth place was indeed unfortunate: no one above me had decided to go elsewhere, or to forego the honour. My only hope was that Something Might Happen before September. It may be that I was offered an exhibition and that I am deluded in my intimate, and abiding, conviction that anyone but a Jew would have been accommodated, if only by having his age weighed more lightly. There is the piquant, if uncorroborating, fact that in 1945, after the murder of six million Jews in Europe, Eton College instituted a covert *numerus clausus*, lest the place be swamped by hordes of slick, surviving Hebrews. Only after Freddie Ayer, the Oxford philosopher and himself a *quondam* King's Scholar, threatened to publicise this iniquitous measure did Eton retract it, at least officially. Winchester can, no doubt, advertise many Jewish Wykhamists and, had my father been a Rothschild, I might have been among them. As it was, I had to be told that Richard Bird was to be a Wykhamist and I was not.

My reaction was not brave: I wept, though not so uncontrollably as I had five years earlier when I realised that I was to be separated from my mother. My tears were more of shame than of regret. What was Winchester to me that I should weep for it? It meant more, at least, than any of the schools whose scholarship exams were held subsequent to Winchester's and for which, if Mr Workman acted quickly, I still might enter. Charterhouse was, I was told, the most prestigious: Mr McGaw had been there. I had no idea where it was, or even whether it played rugger or soccer, but a few days later I was sitting in a quiet room at Copthorne, still sniffing a few tears, doing a set of scholarship papers for entry to this unknown establishment. The corn-fed trace horse was degraded into entering a point-to-point; Mr Workman did not comfort me with apples, let alone with chicken. The Charterhouse examination involved no travel to a historical town, nor any visit to 'non licet' gate. Alone in a classroom with some supervising teacher, I was quarantined but not privileged. I had, however, been well trained. I responded to the usual questions with the usual answers. Did resentment give me a cooler head than ambition? I finished the papers without caring much what the result might be. I clung all the while to the dwindling hope of good news from Winchester. It came from Charterhouse, Godalming (wherever that might be): I was declared to be fourth (I think it was) in the list and had won a junior scholarship of one hundred pounds a year. I felt no exhilaration and derived small pleasure from Mr McGaw's promise that I should not regret my relegation (not that he called it that).

I was now only a few weeks away from the 'leaving jaw' from Mr Workman about which there had been so many whispers down the years. Whatever he said to those who were going on to their public schools (only Niman, a Jew, had sloped off to Manchester Grammar School), it was never, never divulged by those who had been made privy to it. The prospect of this *rite de passage* was both alarming and exciting: would we be embarrassed or horrified? What could the solemn message be? When Richard Bird and I and whoever else was leaving that summer (when the war in the Far East was still unfinished) went into Mr Workman's study, he delivered a slightly cryptic, conventional and unfoolish warning against being too easily impressed, or coerced, by older boys into certain acts, which we might later regret, when we went to our new schools. He did not go into any details of what they might propose; we were simply, and inexplicitly, advised to have nothing to do with it. In those prudish times, when the English took the lid off, there was usually another lid underneath.

I left Copthorne with the first-form prize: a modest blue, leather-bound edition of Robert Louis Stevenson's *Travels with a Donkey in the Cévennes*, inscribed in Mr Workman's elegant hand.

The Charterhouse school tweed was available only at Harrods. It was unthinkable to arrive in anything else. We had to have both white and blue shirts for football (at least they played soccer) and long socks and short socks, boots and plimsolls and indoor and outdoor shoes and some regulation number of handkerchiefs, pants, vests and the rest. I was informed that I had been allocated to Lockites, a boarding house whose tie (it had to be ordered from the school outfitters in Godalming) was black with 'apple-green' stripes. I had to be wearing it when I arrived for the Oration Quarter. Carthusians divided the year into three quarters. The OQ began in mid-September and would last till latish December.

I may have been apprehensive as I caught the train from Waterloo to Godalming. I was certainly not excited. Unlike Winchester, and Eton, Charterhouse did not sequester its scholars in an exclusive forcing house. They were distributed through the school, in order at once to leaven the lump and abate their vanity. It was no great credit to a Carthusian to be a scholar. To my disappointment we did not even wear gowns, as Winchester Collegers did. The slang term for a scholar was 'hash-pro': a hyphenate compounded of 'hash' meaning schoolwork, and 'pro' as in professional. Since there was something disreputable about working at all, especially for money, Charterhouse scholars were doubly damned. Deprived of arrogant segregation, they formed a caste, but never a clan.

Charterhouse is built on a Surrey hill, which is quite steep as you come up from Godalming. It flattens out at the summit into a plain where the main buildings, in the Victorian Gothic style, sit nicely among broad playing fields, each of which had a distinct title: Green, Broom and Leas, Lessington, Nomads and Big Ground (which was quite small, but had goalposts with nets, where the first eleven played).

The school had originally been sited in urban Southwark, where it was founded, in 1611, by one Thomas Sutton, a hard-faced man who had done well enough out of trade to want to save his soul by an ostentatious benefaction. The school motto, 'Deo dante dedi' (God giving, I gave), was sweetly alliterative, but poor Latin: a present participle ablative absolute with a verb in the past tense was not quite the thing, though appropriately flash for an arriviste. Since the old Charterhouse had been more or less derelict since Henry VIII emptied the monasteries, cynics suspected that Sutton had acquired it, and the hope of celestial preferment, rather cheaply. 'Sixty poor scholars' were to be accommodated as well as a number of 'impotent old gentlemen' to be taken care of in their toothless last days. The pupils were not drawn, then or later, from the grand families who preferred Eton or Winchester; I cannot have been the first person to remark that Charterhouse was a school designed for the fathers of gentlemen.

In 1872, William Haig Brown, the Headmaster who was to become the 'Second Founder', decided that the foul streets of south London were too constricted both for his pupils and

ABOVE LEFT: My father with Teddy Slesinger, the friend and surgeon who inadvertently ruined his health.

ABOVE: Six weeks old with my nanny, Sadie in St Louis, 1931.

LEFT: Myself with Cedric and Irene in St Louis, Missouri, March 1932.

ABOVE: Me, 4 years old on the
S.S. *Georgic* on route to England,
1935.

RIGHT: The American Freddie
who went over to England, on
board the S.S. *Georgic*.

RIGHT: The English Freddie who
returned to America, on board
the M.V. *Britannic*.

ABOVE: Reading with my mother, aged 5. New York City 1936.

LEFT: In New York, Central Park, with my American grandparents, Max and Fanny Mauser.

Cedric Raphael.
New York City 1935.

Irene Raphael.
New York City 1937.

ABOVE: Jones Beach, Long Island 1937 aged 6, with my grandmother, Fanny, Irene and Cedric.

RIGHT: With my mother on Putney Heath, Spring 1939.

BELOW: Sussex 1939. Playing cricket with John Slesinger at their country home near East Grinstead.

ABOVE: Copthorne School on the beach at Lee Bay, 1942.

BELOW: Martin, myself, John and Billy. Martin with the bad accent is on the left with me next to him.

RIGHT: At Charterhouse,
wearing a Lockite House
tie, 1945.

BELOW: Copthorne School
at Lee Bay Hotel, 1943.

ABOVE: Charterhouse, Lockite House
hockey XI team, spring 1948.

BELOW: Charterhouse, Lockite House
photo, summer 1949.

for his own ambitions. In a bold stroke, he removed the school to the open country above Godalming, where Gothic revival buildings were constructed to give the school the ivied venerability it was eager to parade. The impotent old gentlemen remained in the smoke. Fee-paying scholars were now drawn largely from the nurseries of the middle classes. Some were more scholarly than others. During the grand years of the Empire, a fat proportion of Carthusians were in the Army Class, which was suppressed only after the Great War. More remarkable for beef than for brains, they went on, not to the university, but – if they could – to military colleges.

The War Memorial Cloister was near the Sixth Form room and adjacent to Saunderites, where the Headmaster, Robert Birley, was also Housemaster. The walls were inscribed – like a miniature Menin Gate – with the many names of Carthusians who had 'given their lives for their country'. The cloister had been built to commemorate Carthusians who died in the Boer War, but it included names from the wars that followed. Among them was one who had died fighting for the Kaiser. He was not distinguished from other OCs, save by his rank and by the Teutonic style of his regiment.

The cloister also enclosed a noticeboard where school teams were posted. Were 'school beatings' – public cere-monies to be attended by all School Monitors – also adver-tised there? These rare and solemn punishments were reserved for those who had seriously transgressed the Carthusian code, but did not quite merit expulsion.

Since they belonged to the HM's House, Saunderites were honoured by another instance of the narcissism of small dif-ferences which created gradations of vanity in every aspect of school life: all other Carthusians had the initial letter of their House printed next to their names in the School List, but Saunderites were distinct by remaining immaculately blank.

Lockites (designated by an L) were lodged in a steep brick

barrack almost at the top of the road that descended to Godalming. There was a gravel-led entrance, through formal gates, to the 'Private Side', where H.A. ('Ham') March, the Housemaster, lived. A narrower, meaner opening led to the 'Fag Entrance'. In practice, not only fags made their way through this door; it admitted Lockites of all estates, including the monitors responsible for in-house discipline. The Head Monitor was an august figure, whose name, when I arrived, was F.E. MacWilliam. His shy speech and personal diffidence, even physical pallor, somewhat resembled that of the king-emperor; on all silver coins, George VI was still FID.DEF.IND.IMP. during my first quarters at the school. After Indian independence, IND.IMP. was amputated from his milled dignity.

MacWilliam was not only *primus inter pares*, he was also (*ex officio*) a School Monitor. This senatorial status entitled him to privileges throughout the school. He could, for instance, parade down the middle of 'Bridge' – the road leading into the main school buildings – with his jacket unbuttoned. He was permitted, if he wished, and if nature supplied the means, to grow a moustache. Only one boy, a Girdlestoneite, ever did so during my time at Charterhouse. School Monitors also figured in the rota of those who, as the bell tolled, shut the door of Chapel at nine in the morning and had then to march the full length of the Giles Gilbert Scott War Memorial Chapel, between observant rows of the rest of the school, to their privileged stall close to the altar.

For many, this solitary parade was a penitential privilege: they were obliged to a long, echoing, self-conscious progress during which some were scarcely able to swing their arms and work their feet in easy combination. Swank and fear led to a variety of postures and paces; few were able to walk without affectation or distress. If you were late for chapel, you were officially in trouble, but such absences were rarely remarked and seldom sanctioned. People ran to get in all the same; it was hells rude to God not to get to His house on time.

The new boy was immediately alerted to a fantasticated hierarchy of privileges. Opportunities for their display increased as people progressed through the school. It was part of the new boy's immediate duty to learn the full regis ter of them, none of which, of course, was yet to be enjoyed, not even the wearing of the school scarf, which could not be wrapped round your neck until you had survived your first quarter.

When, much later, I learned the term 'serialisation', which Jean-Paul Sartre used to describe the cunning of the Nazis in creating artificial divisions between those who might otherwise have made common cause against them, I realised that the way in which Carthusians were recruited to police, and to despise, each other had long preceded the German use of kapos. The Nazis granted trivial privileges in order to maintain discipline by affecting to offer exemptions from what, in the case of the Jews, would turn out to be a common doom. The creation of slave-police economised in manpower by offering the oppressed a chance, seldom refused, to replicate their oppressors.

Lockites had fallen empty during the war, either because of a paucity of pupils or for economic reasons. It had been reconstituted only in the Summer Quarter preceding my arrival. A posse of volunteers from other houses had been impressed to furnish a top dressing of older boys so that when we, the new and pristine Lockites, presented ourselves, we could be supervised by seniors who knew the ropes and, so to say, how to wield them. These pioneers had to forswear fidelity to their previous houses; none, it seemed, had more difficulty in switching horses than I had had when I ceased to be American and became English. People always overesti-mate the problem of what motivates people to redirect their enthusiasms; given the right uniforms, slogans and privileges, the mass of men can be recruited to almost any cause. The lure of Fascism was, and is, crass: it graces nastiness with a mission and officiousness with a doctrine. Arthur Koestler once pointed out that the human capacity for fatuous, or vile, wholeheartedness is more alarming than any scepticism. How many people's favourite disciple is Doubting Thomas?

As a result of Lockites' recent resuscitation, it contained more new boys than any of the established houses. However, since there were eleven houses in which to lodge ten new scholars, I was, in one evident respect, a marked man. The school distributed a printed white booklet of its full establishment, in which stars and daggers distinguished both scholars and exhibitioners, as well as monitorial office holders. I was thus able to discover that Lockites contained only two other scholars, both senior to me: Atkinson, J.J.W., and Randall, B.S.C.G., who was starred not daggered, since he was a senior scholar. In my own year, there was only an exhibitioner, Jordan, J.F.R..

Atkinson was in the previous year and already belonged to 'Top Table', a court of summary jurisdiction, whose troika of older boys presided, in hoop-backed chairs, often with self-important feet on the table, over 'Long Room'. This loud common room was on the ground floor, down a concrete passage from the Fag Entrance. It was home to the milling, noisy mass of New Bugs who played, and did their 'banco' (prep), at ink-stained refectory tables with backless benches.

If Top Table was the lowest rung on the *cursus honorum*, its occupants gloried in their petty powers: they could not put your name in 'the Book',* as monitors could, nor set you

---

*Ten such entries in the same half-quarter, or in the whole of the Long (Easter) Quarter, which was the shortest, led automatically to a beating.

essays (of varying number of pages, according to the gravity of your alleged offence), but they had a non-commissioned authority which made it unwise to cross them. At the limit, they could 'show you up' (report you to a Monitor), though an unwritten rule deplored unduly officious delation. In order to intimidate neophytes, Atkinson ('Atty' to some) preferred to rely on tersely enunciated sarcasm learned, I daresay, from his naval officer father.

J.J.W.A. was a mathematician, but he appeared to recognise an articulate affinity with me. My confidence in his fellowship was breached when I heard him remark that the new intake seemed to contain an unwarranted tally of 'Hebrews and folk of that order'. He uttered this pronouncement, *ex cathedra*, seated on a fat grey radiator, which might lead to piles, but was enviable all the same. He was reading the previous day's newspaper which I had brought to him, not because I was trying to 'groise', but because a notice pinned by the Fag Entrance announced that I had been appointed 'library fag'. Among my duties was the circulation of the Housemaster's old newspapers from 'Hall' – a distant sanctuary where monitors and other seniors took refuge from the common crowd – to Long Room, a name originally given to a vast communal classroom in Southwark, from which Haig Brown had delivered us. As abject offices went, Library Fag was a lofty one: its tenant was exempt from answering 'fag calls' which – after a fortnight's period of grace – were a loud and frequent menace to the junior boys' peace of mind. Fag calls supplied a cross between an air-raid warning and action stations. As soon as one of the Monitors, whose studies were high up the stone stairs that also led to the dormitories, let loose his cry of 'Feeeeayayayay', all those of 'running fag' status had to rush from Long Room, or anywhere else within earshot, and clatter up the stairs in instant response. The design of the concrete steps took into account the danger of collisions or falls. The 'bannisters' were iron poles which ran, uninterrupted, from the ground to the top floor of the house. No one could fall down the well, since there was none. The worst that could happen was to tumble as far as the nearest landing, but you could always grab a steel pole. Those in a hurry to get downstairs learned to swing and land, swing and land, like monkeys.

The last fag to arrive was given whatever task the Monitor might designate. Being excused such Gadarene rushes, my main, undemanding job was to make sure that the newspapers and magazines (*The Illustrated London News*, *Punch* and others) were duly rotated; I also had to sweep out Hall on Sunday mornings, before chapel. House Lib. did not, to my knowledge, have any books in it, but it had an extraterritorial aura: many articles were said to be House Lib. property. Whoever damaged or appropriated them was committing a sin against the community, similar to Stalinism's anti-state activity. Even the antique footballs, mud-black and heavy as cannonballs, which could be borrowed for kickabouts, fell into this improbable category.

Official duties required me to visit Hall daily. I had to knock on the door and wait for someone to say 'Come' before going, obsequiously, in. As a result of my pampered slavery, I became familiar with senior members of the House rather sooner than the running fags who simply belted up and down the stairs trying to get ahead of each other. My scholarly status did not impress the members of Hall, but I enjoyed their condescensions and did my best to entertain them with my muted 'festivity' (insolence). Cheek was, in other circumstances, severely sanctioned. If it was dangerous to be 'festive', it remained tempting to be precocious. It was a form of chaste flirting; although public morality might disapprove of drawing attention to oneself, social advancement depended on it.

Jeremy Atkinson soon conceded, sighingly, that he and I were more intelligent than other people in Long Room, including his fellow triumvirs on Top Table: Upfill-Brown might be decent but was manifestly not quick and 'Veg' (V.J.P.D. Marot, whose surname was, indeed, pronounced like the mature courgette he somewhat resembled, even though he was in the fourth eleven football) was a cheerful rascal, popular enough for his French origins never to be investigated. Fourth eleven footballers were entitled to wear 'blue cuts' (shorts) in any game in which they were playing, although it could never be for the fourth eleven which, like the fourth estate, had no palpable existence. Since it played no matches, it existed only for the purpose of creating yet another caste.

Although F.E. MacWilliam was an exhibitioner, and a member of the Classical Sixth, the sole monitorial scholar in Lockites was B.S.C.G. Randall. He not only had four initials but was also a member of the school first eleven soccer. This entitled him to a flourish of privileges. Despite clothes rationing, Bloods had socks and sweaters and scarves which, however diffident they themselves might be, flagged their fame. The dissident French master, Harry Iredale, called this colourful wardrobe 'hab-er-dash-ery'. His staccato delivery hyphenated the word into four, ridiculous, components.

Randall had been a Verite in his pre-Lockite life, but he had lit out bravely for the colonies, so to say. He was also captain of the House team and declared who should play in the various Lockite elevens. Newcomers were graded, after summary inspection in House Games – pick-up games between any Lockites who chose to turn up – into 'yearlings' and 'second 'tics'. The apostrophe denoted the slangy suppression of 'peripate(t)—'. The House Captain's initials, B.S.C.G., stood for Brough Stuart Churchill Gurney. He let it be known that his family was entitled to be called Gurney-Randall, but had abandoned its hyphen with democratic tact. Not a markedly modest youth, he had a Grecian profile, with an enviably straight nose, blue eyes, fair hair and an hauteur which I longed to imitate, and was no less quick to satirise (every recipe for satire contains a fat pinch of deference to what it derides).

Randall was a modern linguist. His affectation was not only to use a dip pen – not uncommon in those days – but also to carry it clenched between his teeth, like some unlit cigarette holder, as he strode, with open-coated, bloody arrogance, up the steps on his way to the middle of the road across Bridge. When, in my more senior years, I read Harold Nicolson's *Some People*, it was as if B.S.C.G.R. had sat for his portrait in the character of J.D. Marstock. How I wished that I could match what Harry Iredale might well have called his *morgue*! As it was, I did walk around for a while with a wooden pen-holder clenched between my teeth. I abandoned the practice when it gave me mouth ulcers.

After a fortnight's grace, all of the new intake lined up to take the New Bugs' Exam. This took place in Hall. One after another, we were called into the presence of the seniors, who required us to stand on the table before asking us tricky or recondite questions on Carthusian lore. This ritual had something of the warranted sadism of the *bizoutage* that is traditional in French Grandes Ecoles, or of 'hazing' in American colleges. It was not, in truth, very exacting. I was asked what the 'buttery hop''s nickname was ('Mad Eric') and where to find 'Crown'. It was the tuck shop – never known by that oikish name – facing Green, where the first eleven cricket played. My personal inquisition was disappointingly tame. There were stories of stammering boys being forced to dance and sing songs to atone for their nervous memories. I escaped anything like that, thanks to my keenness to shine in examinations, whatever they were.

This desire was not a function of virtue. At the onset of puberty, I was impelled by some dark ambition to shuck the reputation for being good which had dignified me at

Copthorne. Was there something seductive in the range of punishments which might be visited on the Carthusian delinquent and something glamorous in risking them? Every penal code procures the delinquencies it promises to punish. To be bright and a little wicked had a Byronic glamour. The frequency with which flogging was mentioned in schoolboy literature, not only in *The Fifth Form at St Dominic's*, but also in the naval novels of Captain Marryatt and of C.S. Forrester (whose spare prose style gave his work exemplary allure), lent a sort of ritual grace to corporal punishment. I have to say that when I allowed Strangways to be sponged by Mr Workman for our joint offence – the details of which were too trivial, rather than too heinous, for me to remember – it was, apart from cowardice, due to the fact that it was a grown up who would do the beating. At Charterhouse – for all but the direst of crimes – Head Monitors were *ex officio* Lord High Executioners.

The nuance – which surely accounted for the charm of the ceremony – was that flogging was not only a punishment inflicted by one boy (of seventeen or eighteen) on another (of fourteen or fifteen), but also a relationship between them. If there was no conscious affinity, or sexual bond, between beater and beaten, only a bonehead or a hypocrite could deny the ritual piquancy of the occasion itself. The victim was promoted in the eyes not only of those of his own caste (who became connoisseurs in assessing the degree of the pain he had endured, by inspecting the depth and texture of the marks) but also in those of the seniors, who had attended or got to hear of his conduct during punishment. It was essential not to cry out; as long as the culprit endured in dry-eyed silence, and conducted himself with unintimidated dignity, he emerged as a kind of initiate. No stigma attached to anything but tears or pleas for mercy.

Scholars began their ascent to the Sixth Form by being assigned to the Remove, a class halfway up the scholastic ladder, which began with the dunces' form, Shell.* Until specialisation began, after School Certificate (a negligible test, taken only because the government insisted on it), all scholars and exhibitioners, and a very few promising others, were under Mr Arrowsmith's aegis. Not even modern linguists and mathematicians escaped Latin for the two years before they were sixteen. The top of the Remove was composed of all the best Classicists: Cotterell, B.S.C.; Rennie, J.D.; Simpson, D.A.J.; and Raphael, F.M.. Arrowsmith had a lupine smile, a booming voice, a swinging limp and an exquisitely neat Greek script. His florid complexion and hawkish nose gave a confused impression of bonhomie and menace; he was capable of both. 'You're supposed to be *professionals,*' was a favourite, drawled reproach to those who failed to prepare their Sallust or their Sophocles (the first Greek tragedy we read was the *Ajax*). 'Ah my dear sir!' was a milder objection to laughable incompetences. I had the impression that 'the Arrow' quite liked me; he seemed to make his little jokes somewhat in my direction and I was quick to prove that I understood them.** He combined rigour and indulgence. He took us for English as well as for Latin and Greek. Quite soon in that first quarter, he set us an essay on 'Humour'. Since Oxford scholarship essays were notoriously set on a single word topic of that kind, it was never too soon to get into practice.

My Copthorne composition of *The New Spectator* had given

---

*During my time at the school, only one boy who began in Shell gained a university award. He was a Girdlestonite (white striped tie) called Ogle. I never told my father, a 'Shell man' for forty years, what being 'in Shell' implied in Carthusian usage.
**Terence Rattigan's *The Browning Version* has a curmudgeonly Classics master who is acidly gratified when a rare small boy appreciates his wit. His line, 'You laughed at my little joke, Taplow', catches perfectly the tone which the Arrow might have matched, had he been a trifle more desiccated.

me a certain belief, however spurious, in my ability to parody a variety of styles (the Classical education was, in part, a solemn version of the same thing). Rather than write (or crib) a single unsmiling treatise on humour, I elected to present my essay in the form of a series of letters from humorists of various epochs, discussing what they thought amusing, and why. Bold, but not impudent, I preferred the pleasure of impersonation to the drudgery of formal composition. When it came to marking, the Arrow announced that I had chosen a dangerous course. In doing something entirely unexpected, by composing what was not formally an essay at all, I had run a serious risk of receiving no marks whatever. His only alternative, since mine was the only offering he had enjoyed reading, was to give me the top mark.

With a dark smile of complicity, he declared that he had elected to take the latter course. I was advised, however, not to take indulgence for licence ('No, sir, I won't, sir'). My success, he warned me, fell into the category of 'six and out', a term used in games of Tip and Run, when the batsman put more beef into his shot than the occasion merited. Bob Arrowsmith was addicted both to cricket (he was later to be the official chronicler of the Kent CCC) and to Carthusian history.

As a fervent OC, he was said not only to wear pyjamas striped with the school's lurid colours (pink, dark blue and rose) but also to sport an I Zingari nightcap. Our sources did not reveal how this information was acquired. The passage in Homer where Odysseus responds to Thersites' oikish insolence by whacking him with his staff reminded the Arrow of an occasion when he was at the school and a boy was being beaten in his monitorial presence. The victim affected to faint in the middle of his punishment and fell realistically off the chair over which he was bent. The Head Monitor was somewhat alarmed until some 'bilge spee' (biology specialist) with medical affectations recalled that a genuine faint was accompanied by a loss of colour. The recumbent criminal was still healthily flushed, so 'we propped him up and went on to give an extra three for festivity'. It was a moot point whether the Arrow admired the unfortunate boy's Odyssean ruse or despised his want of guts.

Arrowsmith's wooden (?) leg – I never knew the exact nature or cause of his lameness – made him only a flat-capped spectator of winter games, but he was in charge of the training of the first eleven cricket. In due course, I should watch him whacking steeplers into the sky over Green where the club-sweatered members and apprentices of the school side assembled for fielding practice. With a gleam of regular malice, he observed the steadiness under fire of those whose feet stuttered on the grass as they positioned themselves to receive the sagittarian volley between their hot palms. The Arrow was equally adept at sending the ball skidding across the turf at high speed, to be gathered and returned in one sweet gesture. 'Ah my dear sir!' had its uses here too. Then came the slip cradle, a slatted device, like a sagging bench, into which the ball was flicked and from which it emerged on the far side, somehow accelerated, to fly at unpredictable angles to the waiting practicants. The Arrow's genial sadism made boys alarmedly eager to please him. I should have wor-shipped him more unreservedly had he not had the Carthusian habit of alluding to Jews and 'jewing', albeit in so routine a fashion that, even as I winced, I could sense that it entailed nothing concerning his personal feelings about Jews, or at least about me. It was a way of staying one of the boys. Even Lord Byron, who was the author of the proto-Zionist *Hebrew Melodies*, and whose favourite author was Isaac d'Israeli (Benjamin's father) referred disparagingly to 'the Jews', when speaking of money-lenders. This was a generic rather than a racial sneer, since many of those who lent money to his Lordship (and had great difficulty in recovering it) were not Jewish by origin. Byron's servant and travelling companion, Fletcher, whose prejudices were trenchantly anti-European, later became Benjamin Disraeli's valet (and perhaps the model for Dickens's Sam Weller).

I have little doubt that the Arrow's bachelor passion for cricket, and for its schoolboy exponents was, like Byron's Harrovian crush on the Duke of Dorset, both intense and 'chaste'. In his pastoral world, cricket was never out of season. He must have told every Remove he taught how a certain wicket-keeper resembled the Ancient Mariner ('He stoppeth one in three'). Even in the darkness of the Surrey winter, the Arrow alerted us to the genius of the youngest batsman in the previous summer's side. May, P.B.H. (Saunderites), was only fifteen when he made his first runs for Charterhouse. The school professional, George Gearey (Leicestershire and England), had already confessed that there was nothing more he could teach the boy. If May was a manifest prodigy, I suspect that another member of the eleven, Raven, S.A.N., was dearer to the Arrow's heart, though the latter was an organ he never wore on his sleeve. However, he made no comment when, not many weeks into my first quarter, the true rumour spread that Raven major (Saunderites) had been expelled. Simon was not only an amusing member of the cricket eleven but a Classical scholar with a talent for impious opinions and elegant verses. I am prepared to bet that some of his pentameters ended in three-syllable words; he was that kind of a Silver Age, going on post-Classical Classicist.

The details of Raven major's crime were too delicious to be spelt out. Those outside senior circles heard only that Simon, whose swagger had already made him remarkable, had been 'sacked for the usual thing'. Despite Mr Workman's judicious warnings, I had no precise notion, still less experience, of what was usual in public-school circles. It was, however, something of a Carthusian tradition: an earlier headmaster had confessed, with complacent regret, that 'My boys are amorous but never erotic.' He had reckoned without Raven, S.A.N..

Although he was mortified to be deprived of another season in the cricket eleven, Simon's dismissal was mitigated not only by the fact that King's College, Cambridge, where he had already obtained an open scholarship, agreed to turn a blind eye to his offence, but also by an unofficial assurance that he would not be disqualified from joining the OC club. This concession may well have been sponsored by the Arrow, who occupied a vice-presidential position in the OC club.

As for King's, even in the 1940s, it would have been the height of humbug for the college to take a solemn view of Simon's pleasures. The Provost, J.T. Sheppard, was a renowned pederast; one of the college's most honoured alumni, and benefactors, was Maynard Keynes, whose late conversion to conjugal life did nothing to apologise for other pleasures to which Bloomsbury's hedonism had no objection, whatever the bedint laws of England might say. 'Bedint' was an adjectival code word used by Harold Nicolson to his wife – the often lesbian Vita Sackville-West – for what would later be termed, in a best-selling 1956 book by Nancy Mitford and a Professor S.C. Ross, the 'non-U' (Not Upper Class) world, in which, for example, sitting rooms were 'lounges', writing paper 'stationery' and lavatories 'toilets'.

Simon always believed that he (and his lover) had been 'shown up' – he preferred the Latinate term 'delated' – by the officious William Rees-Mogg. The latter's treachery, so Simon alleged (wrongly, assuming recent researches to be conclusive), had been primed by the hope of political advancement. Ancient Romans with ignoble ambitions were often tempted to report the misdemeanours, real or trumped up, of those from whose defenestration they hoped to profit one way or another, or both. Since Rees-Mogg had indeed been appointed head of the school at the beginning of the quarter, *post hoc ergo propter hoc* was a tempting tag to tie to what was, I have no doubt, a coincidence. Raven the cad took it out on the Mogg, but Raven the sportsman did not whine at being given out. He maintained only that he had been unfairly sanctioned: as the offence – which neither of the amorous participants had found offensive at the time – was committed during the summer holidays, why should school rules apply to it?

Simon was an unsentimental Byron. If he paid small attention to morals, he claimed to honour a certain romantic code: chaps might indeed bugger each other (though he did not favour the literal form of this activity), but they neither let each other down nor subscribed to the pusillanimous guilts of middle-class morality. *Carpe diem* was the synecdochic Raven motto (implying also *carpe noctem*, even though it did not scan). Simon was eminently middle-class in his egocentricity; he held that anarchic appetites did not justify bad manners. An unchivalrous Lancelot, for whom Tennyson might have devised the tag 'His honour rooted in dishonour stood/And faith unfaithful kept him falsely true', Raven ma. treasured the obsolete mystique of the society he defied, and defiled. Like Sir Walter Ralegh, he might have taken pride in saying to his executioner 'Strike, man, what do you fear?'. As for being expelled, it was no time for lamentation, nor much more cause. A louche version of Milton's Samson, Simon quitted himself like Simon, less by pulling down the temple than by making a virtue of his vices. Later, by becoming a novelist, he also made a living out of them.

'Bags' Birley, on the other hand, had done what he conceived to be his duty with self-denying regret. By his own act, he was deprived of Simon's spicy conversation at the luncheon table; Peter May might have better strokes on the cricket field, but he sloughed his genius with his pads. Some said that Simon's fall bruised Robert Birley more than it did the accused. Bags was a tall, not very old man with a baleful expression. His nickname alluded to the bags under his eyes, which were attributed, even by the naughtiest tongues, less to masturbation (the putative cause) than to his unremitting sense of duty. On the morning that Simon packed his bags – or, more probably, got some fag to do it for him – and took the taxi to Godalming station, it is said that 'Bags' discovered that his hair had turned white overnight.

In due course, Simon took slow and salacious pleasure in depicting William Rees-Mogg, who was tall, spotty, bespectacled and egregiously elderly, even in his youth, in a luridly unflattering fictitious light in the 1960s novel sequence *Alms for Oblivion*. The character of Somerset Lloyd-James, the sententious editor of the magazine *Strix* who comes to a scandalously bad end, was so patently *à clef* that it took little wit to turn the key. The Mogg never complained about the revenge taken, justly or unjustly, on him. Would Simon, in similar circumstances, have refrained from issuing a writ for libel? He would, of course, have been motivated to go to law less by indignation or *amour-propre* than by the hope of a few tax-free bob.

Simon, like the Arrow, and many generations of Carthusians, alluded to Jews and 'jewiness' with a trite scorn that, in his case at least, implied no lack of affection – if that emotion can be attributed to a hedonistic solipsist – for his Jewish friends (whom he contrived to lampoon both pitilessly and, in Anthony Blond's case at least, with graceless gratitude). Simon aimed more to scandalise the bourgeois – and to get them to buy his books, not least by alleging that his novels were much too good for them – than to advertise any considered social programme. In this he had something in common with his model, Evelyn Waugh, who displayed similar toadying insolence when it came to toffs. They wore old Etonian prejudices as con-men do the tie.

Simon was never more than an amiable acquaintance, but I miss him as a lunchtime fellow Classicist. I remain slightly irked that he never touched me for money, as he did so many of his friends: it smacks of discrimination. My connection with him, such as it was, began only at Cambridge. He came to my rooms in Third Court, St John's, one Sunday morning, during my first year. I was still in bed. He announced that he was the secretary of the Cambridge Old Carthusians and that he had come to recruit me. I replied that I had no wish to have anything whatever to do with Charterhouse or with Carthusians. 'I expect you're quite right,' he said, and departed at once.

We never met again at Cambridge, from which he contrived to be sent down, despite all the indulgences which King's had offered him, but he reviewed one of my early novels with measured generosity and we began the habit of irregular lunches together. At the last of them, about a year before he died, I also invited Jim Cellan-Jones, the television and film director, an old Lockite, for whom Simon had adapted Trollope's *The Pallisers*. Simon was a Dorian Gray whose pitiless portrait he himself had painted (as the disfigured 'Fielding Gray') in *Alms for Oblivion*. He had the brave effrontery, and squalid decency, to abide by his code of unrepentant sybaritism until the end. Suffering, aptly enough, from Crohn's Disease, he remained cheerful and, as he hobbled to the loo, observed what a comfort it was that all three of us were still as delectable as we had been in our youth.

Simon was, in some ways, an English recension of that naughty boy who pissed on his mother's carpet with conscienceless pleasure in St Louis. At that last lunch, he told us that he had recently become a resident of Charterhouse in Southwark, the home for 'impotent old gentlemen' which Thomas Sutton had founded and from which William Haig Brown had removed the school. Was Simon unique in having been both expelled from Charterhouse and welcomed back as its pensioner? He enjoyed his own (regularly cleaned) room, telephone, cooked breakfast and evening meal for a minimal rent. I wonder if he died still owing it.*

Among the obligations of the new boy was to be auditioned for the choir by Dr Thatcher, the head music master. My father may have been a champion ballroom dancer, but no one could call him musical: dancers cared about the beat, not the tune. Neither he nor my mother sang; they rarely, if ever, went to concerts. We neither owned a gramophone nor ever listened to serious music on the radio. I had every reason to absent myself from the humiliation of not knowing – or even hearing – the difference between B flat and E major, but I was so indoctrinated with docility that I presented myself in Chapel. As soon as I attempted to match the sound made by my dry throat to the note tapped out on the piano by the soon-disenchanted Dr Thatcher, I was designated a non-singer, a classification which not even I can ascribe to prejudice.

Mr Howard's dismissal of my acting ability, when I was at Copthorne, remained less easy to accept. When word was posted of a House Play Competition, I was prompt to inscribe myself. It was typical of Charterhouse that even the arts should be pursued in teams: the only tolerated ambition was that of bringing glory to The House, or The School. In the Play Competition, kudos was to be won by putting on a better one-act show than Hodgsonites or Daviesites or Bodeites or even bloody Saunderites.

Having heard that B.S.C.G. Randall was to be in charge of the Lockite production, I auditioned with nervous keenness. Though I have found it useful to be tall, I have never had any

*For a less indulgent reading of Simon, under the pseudonym 'Crowman', see the story 'Seniority', in my Think of England.

reliable vanity about my personal appearance. Perhaps because my mother, in a moment of irritation, once called me 'thick lips', I took myself to be innately displeasing to look at. If there is such a thing as negative narcissism, then I confess to its defining symptom: self-regard without self-admiration. I have a keen memory for what is said about me, as long as it is disparaging; grievance, not fame, is the novelist's keenest spur, though one must never, of course, *appear* aggrieved.

The stage in Hall was wide and well equipped. Acting was part of the school tradition. When the blue-uniformed 'Sergeant' showed visitors round the school, he always cited C. Aubrey Smith and 'Stinker' Murdoch, Kenneth Horne's partner and a well-known radio comedian of the day, among the famous Old Carthusians, who included William Thackeray, Max Beerbohm, Ralph Vaughan Williams, John Wesley and Osbert Lancaster, the *Daily Express* cartoonist. It was hardly a roster that batted all the way down to number eleven.

The Sergeant was a glorified gatekeeper, from whose lodge one could, if armed with a suitable chit from one's House Man, make emergency telephone calls. It was the only way to gain access to a telephone, except by going to 'Godge' (uninventive Carthusian slang for Godalming). In order to do that, however, one needed another chit from, in Lockites' case, 'HAM' March, since to get to the town one had to cross a railway line. Without 'per.', it was a literal transgression to be discovered on the wrong side of the tracks. A signed chit was a *laissez-passer* which, in theory, allowed us to cycle all the way to Land's End, or Inverness. The preferred destination was Guildford, where the more raffish young Lockites (Tony Trafford *en tête*) were soon claiming to have talked to girls, and to have had them talk back. This seemed improbable, if not decadent.

I was as uncertain an actor as I was ambitious but, since

the competition was not unduly eloquent, I was immediately cast – in a one-act play by George Bernard Shaw – as Gurney-Randall's wife. I was given a chit to phone my mother to ask for one of her evening dresses, and some costume jewellery, and a pair of her triple-A shoes, which she supplied without overt demur. There was no question of females being allowed to act with Carthusians, even though Nurse Monk, from the San., was said to be quite a keen performer. In a strictly monastic environment, the Housemaster of Daviesites, W.C. Sellar, was alone of a heterodox disposition; he allowed his boys to invite the girls of Priorsfield School to their annual Christmas dance. Sellar was the history master who, with Yeatman (deceased), had co-authored 1066 and All That, one of the few funny books which live up to their reputations. It may be that notoriety, and his royalties, encouraged a measure of independence. However, a certain eccentricity was in the Carthusian tradition. The original, and enterprising, Mr Lock and Mr Davies and the others had founded their boarding houses outside the school limits, though with easy access to it. Like the boarding-house landlords which they indeed were, they could post their own laws. Their foundations were federated, as it were, only during the last century. Mr Sellar's daring was not challenged, but he was advised – by the Headmistress of Priorsfield perhaps – that it would be prudent to rope off the corners of the room in which the dance was held.

If I were writing a novel, how could I resist making some plotted use of the hot excitement with which my fourteen-year-old 'hero' puts on his female clothes and acts out the décolleté fantasy of being Randall's Shavian playmate? It is almost sad to report that I cannot recall the smallest wink of amorous contact between us. Since the play itself was a mere skit, and Shaw no great enthusiast for sexual repartee, my lines were limited to cries of uxorious alarm or skittish silliness. I wore a black twenties'-style dress, with several ropes of jet beads, clip-on Diamond Lil (paste) earrings and high-heeled shoes. For all my Clara Bow make-up, I was neither a hit nor a miss. Only two lines from the play remain in my mind: 'Is the gazogene full?' (for some reason, a soda syphon played a crucial part in the action) and, after a police-man – played by Cellan-Jones, C.J.G.? – had been felled in a thunderstorm, 'The copper attracted the lightning.'

I emerged from the play without the smallest subsequent temptation to wear female clothes, or to play the girl's part, in any sense. My performance as Randall's wife left no mark on me, or on him. Was the play well or badly received? I have no idea. The only effect of my brief encounter with his work is that I cannot stomach the plays, or the playfulness, or anything else about George Bernard Shaw, including his vegetarian eyebrows.

The war was over, but its effects, and style, persisted. Food was still rationed, conscription was in force, and we were soon warned of impending trouble by Churchill's 'Iron Curtain' speech. This was delivered in Fulton, Missouri, not far from Kansas City, where Max and Fanny had their now thriving delicatessen. They still sent us bulging CARE pack-ages; the tinned butter was no good at all, but the Hormel hams and Hershey bars were luxuries in basic England. The Labour government had been elected to honour Lord Beveridge's scheme for a welfare state, but paradise did not seem imminent. Like the rest of the nation, Carthusians were torn by conflicting notions of what the world was, or should become. Officially, Britain was still a great power; her stand-ing was enhanced, though her Reserves (whatever they were) had been depleted, by her victory. There was some-thing anomalous, yet presumed progressive, in a govern-ment which proposed to change the social system within Great Britain, to the punitive detriment of the rich and the titled, while maintaining its plumed authority overseas.

Presumptions of superiority, deplored at home, were freely paraded abroad.

One Old Carthusian with no conflict of feeling whatever, Sir Waldron Smithers (Con. Orpington, Kent) was also an Old Lockite. Giving the perpetual impression of being a demobbed Colonel Blimp, he regarded 'Bags' Birley as a Bolshevik anti-Christ. He pursued his vendetta against this rabid liberal at Question Time in the House of Commons. When Bags went to purify German education, and had to resign his headmastership, Sir Waldron boomed his delight.

Sir Hartley Shawcross, the Labour Attorney General, had informed the opposition, when parliament reassembled after the Labour landslide, that 'we are the masters now', but he had done so in the style of a smooth-toned barrister of implacable vanity. When a chance came to prove their rupture with obsolete paternalism, after Mr Attlee deposed the king of Basutoland for having the nerve to marry a white woman, neither Labour's Oxbridge toffs nor their oikish fellow ministers would find any principled reason to resign. On the other hand, none doubted that Attlee was right to proceed with giving India its independence. Since it would remain within the Commonwealth, it seemed more a matter of changing the tiger's spots than of releasing it from the menagerie. The massacres that followed Britain's hasty disengagement were of nameless hordes who had demanded to be free and who could scarcely blame others for the mutual slaughter which they insisted on enacting. Such conduct proved only that some people would be wise to hasten slowly to be shot of Britain's just supervision.

One of my fellow Lockites was called Sinha. The son of the only Indian peer in the House of Lords, he had something of the aura both of Ranjitsinghji, the princely Edwardian cricketer, and of a dusky, but well-born, and highly articulate Indian character in the Billy Bunter novels. Since Sinha was 'spoey' (good at sport, not least at boxing), and full of

Roger-of-the-Raj plumminess of diction – 'Hit him, some-body!' was one of his favourite cries – he never, to my knowledge, provoked the smallest expression of racial preju-dice. More British than the British, and reportedly half as rich as Croesus, he was unmistakably our kind of wog. When Mahatma Gandhi was assassinated, he wore a woefully sub-continental expression for a day or two (even his skin looked darker), but he soon got over it.

Anxiety about my own implicit pariahdom, added to the tenuousness of my belief that I was at home among these English middle-class children, led me to look at my fellow Carthusians through two different sets of lenses. Through one, I saw the majority of them as mentally clumsy and physically intimidating. I observed their individual peculiari-ties with the wary malice of the outsider who feared that he might one day need to know how precisely, and most tellingly, to get back at them. Through a second set of lenses, I scrutinised myself, pitilessly, for symptoms of distinction which I could smooth away or hide before I could be abused and isolated on account of them.

Mimicry, of which I had become a minor master, allowed me to match the accent and imitate the social attitudes which would best homogenise me. If I showed dissent, my hetero-doxy was nicely phrased. Was not stylishness as much part of the English (radical) tradition as conformity? My efforts to be accurately invisible mirrored that of the chameleon, who can be loyal to any background on which he happens to find himself. Alert mutability concealed my true colours, even from myself. I was a *sincere* chameleon who genuinely cheered for Charterhouse when I turned up to watch Randall and Peter May – a mere mortal on the football field, but still good enough to be in the first eleven – as they and the other muddied oafs played their straightforward Corinthian-style game (back-passing was girlish) against Westminster or Bradfield, Shrewsbury or Eton.

My critical eye, and ear, noted the difference between the gaits and accents of 'Tubby' Gladstone and 'Jagger' Jordan, 'Fatty' Ashworth — whose father was an important figure in the Yorkshire Penny Bank — and Cellan-Jones, who required people to pronounce his Cellan 'Kethlan'. I realised soon enough that H.J.M. Bury, the smiley Second Monitor, had a more relaxed manner of keeping order than Gurney-Randall, whose narcissism avoided benign creases, and I knew that Carson was a rascal (he wore a felt hat on exeats) and must have something to do with Ireland, just as Weber was unequivocally American (which disinclined me to make friends with him).

Weber may well have been Jewish as well as American, which made him doubly alarming. He had short dark curls and a big behind and a want of shame in being whatever he was (his father, I was later to discover, had money). He had never played soccer before, but in a House game which was being played at a leisurely pace he raised a huge laugh (derision and appreciation rolled into one) by suddenly calling out, 'Come on, guys, let's get the lead out!' He was a keen cyclist, an enthusiasm he shared with Leach and a contemporary of mine from another House called McIlwraith, who quit Charterhouse at the age of seventeen and went to California, where he became a lawyer and tax expert. When I met him not long ago, I had the envious feeling that he had been much more enterprising than I, when he got on his bike and pedalled away for good. Maybe Weber showed him the way. So reluctant was I to reveal anything in common with the latter that I cannot remember how long he stayed in Lockites, nor the circumstances of his departure.

All the social gracelessness which I detected in my fellows was put in the repository of foibles that might discomfit or — if self-defence required it — render them ridiculous. At the same time, my other set of lenses saw almost all the other boys as my social superiors. I took them to come from homes with servants and ancestral estates and big motor cars, with fathers who were company directors or senior officers and unredeemed gentlemen. For all my keen attention to detail, I got the whole picture comically out of focus. In that apprehensive mood, my fellow Carthusians became a homogeneous band which hunted in a cohesive, Aryan pack. Their likeliest prey was a Jew and an outsider.

The fact that I was circumcised did not, as it had Jews in Nazi Germany, render me immediately detectable, but it gave me small appetite for the communal tub. Although keen on sport, at which my energetic mediocrity avoided attention, I made a habit of solitude. Was that the only reason that I was never tempted to the homosexuality which, it seemed, was a common *pis aller* for randy adolescents? Intimacy would lead to revelations, and revelation to rejection. I was friendly, but I made no close friends. In my first years, I spent much time in the Library (less because I was bookish than because it was very warm, thanks to an ingenious double central fireplace) and in Studio, a chill loft in the Old Stinks Block, where there were pots of poster paint and liberal supplies of cartridge paper. I began to paint because it could be done in an atmosphere of freedom: boys of different ages, from different Houses, mixed more easily, and more affably, in Studio than anywhere else in the school. Art had no privileged ranks; it therefore conferred no status either.

In the Remove, the scholars were more colleagues than friends. Jostling together in fractious emulation, we were Achillean swots, vying for personal glory on the scholastic battlefield. I felt no nervousness in class, either about shining when I could (Cottrell and Rennie were both diligent and very bright) or about being revealed, or reviled, as a Jew. Academic dignity trumped all distinctions, it seemed: the world of the intelligent had a purity, I thought, in which no right answer was ever dusty and excellence procured admiration and advancement. It was another sweet misreading.

Attendance in Chapel did not strike me, or my parents, as hypocritical. It was implicit in going to a good school that one should abide by its rules. Chapel was compulsory at Charterhouse, a matter of discipline, not of personal belief. Those of an enthusiastic Christian disposition could advertise their piety by applying to the House Man for permission to go to the Friday evening service. This was conducted by the more ardent (and junior) of the two chaplains, a man with an egregiously pious Adam's apple. It took place, with a faint whiff of incense, near the War Memorial Cloister, in Haig Brown's original chapel, which had been rendered obsolete by the huge, austere, modern War Memorial Chapel where we all had to go for morning service. Was Sir Waldron Smithers alone in regarding Giles Gilbert Scott's edifice with distaste? A high, towerless brick building, nicknamed 'the Zeppelin Shed', it was lit by a series of slim, unstained glass windows going almost to the roof. A huge gilt cross hung over the altar, but it was bare of other decoration. John Wesley, OC, would have found the tone unadornedly low and un-Popish. Oliver Cromwell, on the other hand, would not have appreciated the occasion when the chaplain and Under Sixth master, Henry Bettenson, alluded – on the beheaded sovereign's birthday – to 'Charles the First, King and Martyr'. It evoked a roundheaded murmur among some of the assembled Carthusians.

Going regularly to chapel did not for one second incline me to Christianity. Had I been a better singer, might I have been recruited more harmoniously to Christian fellowship? As it was, I never had the smallest symptom of credulity, any more than I did of adhering to Judaism, which was barely a scintilla more plausible, though it did avoid the benign Cerberus of a 'Three-in-One and One-in-Three' supreme Divinity. *Credo quia impossibile* was never my idea of a likely story. Proximity did, however, leave me with a useful knowledge of the King James Bible.

If, once or twice, I asked for per. to go to the Friday evening service, my motives were not spiritual: I may have hoped to convince 'Tubby' Gladstone and others of – to put it as ignominiously as the case probably deserved – my unexceptional piety. I was also curious about what was preached to the voluntary elect on such occasions (Publius Clodius gatecrashed the ceremonies of the *Bona Dea* for similar reasons). When, a mere ten years after I left the school, I depicted Charterhouse under the permeable disguise of Greyfriars in the novel *The Limits of Love*, I declared, quite falsely, that the chaplain had, 'with much working of the Adam's apple', warned us against the evils of masturbation. He might as well have preached against the moon.

Do I exaggerate the anti-Semitic tendencies of my fellow Carthusians? Exaggeration is a tenable charge, advanced recently by John Gross, in his insipid memoir of an English Jewish childhood in which he shone with so amiable and unexceptional a light that he never attracted the smallest hostility. Gross's ascent from the East End to High Table and thence to the high chair of editorship of the *Times Literary Supplement* was evidence, to him at least, that Jews in post-war England incurred only what their individual qualities, or want of them, deserved. Those who encountered prejudice must, he declared, have provoked it; he did not. Gross was clever, or bland, enough to escape treatment which he takes to be the consequence of individual want of civility. Of his merits I have hardly more doubt than he, but he was a day boy: he had no need to dissemble, still less to disavow, the Judaism which he showed no marked signs of embracing. He has continued to manifest the ability, in both his literary and his theatrical criticism, to procure the admiration of those he himself has elected to admire and whose favours he has, accordingly, enjoyed.

I should be more ashamed of confessing my dreads and dissimulations, and my petty wounds, were it not easily verifiable that other Jews at Charterhouse had experiences not unlike mine. My contemporary and now close friend Brian Glanville suffered from savage anti-Semitism in Bodeites, from which he emerged bruised but notably unbowed. Even at school, he realised his wish to be a football journalist. He wrote in *The Carthusian* with precocious derision about the first eleven's witless tactics and mediocre achievements. Does Brian's abiding refusal to compromise, even when diplomacy (or John Gross) might advise it, not derive from pride born of excellent judgement and puerile pariahdom? Damned if we do and damned if we don't, we damned well might as well tell the truth as we see it.

If my purpose here were to recruit sympathy for my young self, I could probably offer a more charming portrait of the artist as a young crawler (albeit with a vestigial sting in his low-slung tail) than I have chosen to paint. I was not, I hope, unduly Shylockian in my expectations of, or response to, Christian malice. My gabardine was, of necessity, of the regulation school tweed; and my sufferance owed less to cowardice than to the want of any plausible alternative. Anti-Semitism was so natural to my companions, and to Brian's, whose housemates formed an entirely different cast, though they acted out more or less the same script, that it flatters him and me to suggest that our personal qualities did anything much to affect, or sponsor, the performance.

Although convinced that the English middle classes, or those who aspired to them, were united in self-elevating prejudices of all kinds, I am suspicious of the cant which makes all anti-Semitism derive from the same virus. Even the mildest jest or jibe can be deemed, by root-and-branchers, to be proof of embryonic Nazism. This view is as silly as the gross notion that nobody is visited by prejudice unless he or she behaves unbecomingly. That 'Jew' and 'jewing' had (and have?) inescapable meanings in the traditional vernacular cannot derive from the spontaneous discovery, by successive

182

generations of fair-minded, fair-headed schoolboys, of Jewish meanness or greed. Such usage comes from parents, and from the osmotic influence of Christian culture. The comedy of prejudice is that their best friends often announce it by exempting particular Jews from their anathemas. Anti-Semitism was at once the regimental tie and the crease in the trousers of genteel uniformity: it gave mundane flannel its edge. The young did not merely inherit the prejudices of their elders; they were admitted to them.

Nevertheless, golf club stories about the Jew and the Scotsman are not of a piece with the Jew-baiting of Julius Streicher or even with that of Hilaire Belloc. Jewish humour itself often sacrifices tolerance to the incautious desire to get a laugh, even by means of a kind of self-admiring anti-Semitism. Of the first category, the chestnuttiest (often, but not too often, told by my father) concerns an ethical dilemma. A Jew and a Scotsman, all square as they come to the eighteenth green, are looking for the latter's ball in the rough. Just as his lost ball is about to cost him the match, the Scot declares that he has found it. He takes his shot and not only puts it on the green but, to the Jew's horror (there is a sixpenny bet involved), sees it roll into the hole. The ethical dilemma is this: what should the Jew do when he knows that the Scot has dropped and played a new ball only because he himself still has his foot on the Scotsman's original shot?

Of the anti-Jewish (and 'anti-black') Jewish jokes, the best is of the (American) Jew and the black man who die and arrive at the pearly gates almost simultaneously. St Peter assures them that heaven is now multicultural and that they have nothing to fear from discrimination. In fact, every new-comer can ask for a welcome gift of anything he wants. Since the black man died a split second before the Jew, he is given priority. As the Jew waits out of earshot, the black man asks for 'all the money in the world'. He is directed to the little booth where payment will be made. When the Jew steps forward, he too asks for all the money in the world. Peter explains that even in heaven the rules of logic apply: the black man has pre-empted the world's wealth. So what else would the Jew like? 'Give me ten bucks worth of junk jewellery,' the Jew says, 'and ten minutes with the black guy.'

Talleyrand used to observe that no one who did not experience life under the *Ancien Régime* – as a pampered aristocrat, *bien entendu* – could have any idea of the real meaning of *douceur de vivre*. Similarly, but not very, no Jew who first came to consciousness after 1948, and the foundation of the vexed state of Israel, can have any notion of the apparently incurable alienation of even the most sedentary, and sedate, Wandering Jew. Although Zionism was, in central Europe at least, a political and social answer to The Jewish Question, nothing appealed less to my father's family, or to my parents, than unalloyed Jewish company. What could be more cramping or less seductive? To be assimilated was evidence less of cowardice or of trimming than of civilisation. If one wished to be tolerated (and tolerance was the most civil of virtues), one subscribed to the general rule. To be unashamedly what one was, and yet to be as British as the next man, was to follow the example set by Benjamin Disraeli. He had, it was true, to be baptised before he could be Prime Minister, but he was sage, and bold, enough to flaunt his Jewishness before others could reproach him with it. Since Jews could enter the modern House of Commons without apostasy, my dual citizenship made me a legal candidate both for the premiership of Great Britain and for the presidency of the United States. What nobler duplicity could there be?

Not the least of my puerile *naïvetés* was the defective syllogism which argued that, since Hitler had been an enemy of the Jews, and the British had been the enemies of Hitler, the British were friends of the Jews. It was not even accepted that Jews formed a specific section of Europe's brutalised peoples;

after all, they had no national anthem. The refusal of the (rapidly disaggregating) Allies to distinguish them from other unfortunates was not due solely to malice. Jews who were citizens of pre-war nation states had themselves insisted that they did not want to be singled out. After Napoleon had initiated their assimilation, had they not proved their emancipation by displaying a patriotic willingness to kill each other in the uniforms of France, Germany, England or Austria?

What looked like Balfour's philo-Semitism was based on calculation, or rather on miscalculation: if he and the British government of 1917 had not had a grossly inflated notion of the strength of Jewish International Finance, would it have sanctioned so magnanimous, and eventually disastrous, a policy? A similar over-estimation provoked Hitler, a quarter of a century later, to exterminate European Jewry.

Nazi policy towards the Jews was less an outrage, more an embarrassment, to the British. Anthony Eden had done his best, during the war, to block any means by which any Jews who escaped their murderers might reach their Promised Land. Within a few months of VE Day, the new socialist Foreign Secretary, Ernest Bevin, rejected claims for preferential treatment. His assertion that he wasn't "aving the Jews pushing to the front of the queue' may not have been delivered with mandarin diction, but it echoed mandarin thinking. The common, unspoken sentiment was that if Hitler had to launch his war of annihilation against the Jews, it might have been better if he had seen it through. How movingly the walruses and carpenters of the United Nations might then have elided their sobs and their sighs of relief! All the crocodiles of Europe would have been in tears. As it was, Bevin embarrassed more English Jews than dared to challenge him. How careful my parents had been to have nothing to do with the black market, so as not to lend substance to rumours of Jewish malpractice!

In Palestine, a typical British combination of unrealistic *realpolitik* had deepened the antagonism between Jews and Arabs, long before Hitler. The necessity of the British presence in the 'Near East' was vindicated by turf wars which their own geographers had contrived to sponsor. At Versailles they had not only divided in order to rule, they had also used an arbitrary ruler to mark the divisions. States such as Iraq and Jordan had been established by fiat from London, just as Syria and Lebanon had from Paris. Only since 1919 have these fabricated nationalities, and the interests of their two-faced princes and tyrannical presidents, persuaded or, more often, conscripted their citizens to defend and die for arbitrarily defined borders.* By making things difficult for the selfless administrators of Palestine – a territorial entity which had, in unspoken fact, been 'south Syria', until the British printed the atlas – the Zionists were proving, once again, that the Jews were their own worst enemies.

If I dwell on the hypocrisy of British policy, it is because, as a callow youth, I had little doubt about its rightness, or righteousness. What did I or anyone else get told about Auschwitz? Who dared to admit that the efficiency of the slaughter was thanks, in large part, to clever 'non-political' Germans who were promptly reinstated, in many cases, in key positions? 'Bags' Birley – to whom Carthusians were unaccountably devoted – shocked the school, not long after my arrival by agreeing to be seconded to the British zone of Germany in order to preside over the moral regeneration of German education. H.C. Iredale, who taught French to the Remove, murmured in his primly wicked way, that 'Sir Robert' (Birley was still plain Mr) was doing his 'pat-ri-ot-ic

---

*Elie Kedourie's *The Chatham House Version* is a thoroughly documented, heartlessly fair-minded analysis of the follies of British Middle Eastern policy as promulgated by Arnold Toynbee and others, after the unnecessary dismantling of the Ottoman Empire. See also Jon Kimche's *Seven Fallen Pillars* (of pseudo-wisdom).

um duty'. Bags may have been shrewd in assessing the morals, and predicting the future, of English schoolboys; he proved markedly inept in detecting who had or had not been – or still remained – Nazi sympathisers, among the German scholastic community. Impressed by those who most resembled the kind of gentlemen with whom one might choose to dine, he was no less dismissive of any whose grievances and accusations smacked of special pleading. The former, no doubt, smelt more dainty.

Birley discharged his task with despatch and with results that did not displease those who appointed, and soon knighted, him. Shortly afterwards, Charterhouse was appalled, and betrayed, by his appointment as Headmaster of Eton, to which he transferred with all haste. I had met him only once, when invited, as a new junior scholar, to breakfast in his House. Austerity had not prepared me for the full box of cornflakes in each place. When Bags tilted his packet into his bowl with uninhibited appetite, we all followed his example. There was also toast in racks, and butter in pimpled balls. A Birley teenage daughter was present, without make-up

The tragedy of the Jews was neither applauded nor lamented in England. Its small claim on public attention was ensured by the indifference of newspaper editors – what human interest could there be in Jews? – and by Fleet Street's deference to what was passed off as the National Interest.

I felt little sympathy for the Zionist cause. I merely dreaded the hostility which it might provoke. To keep one's head down and not make waves was the inglorious advice which Jews had often given each other when they faced overwhelming power. The only alternative was to invite martyrdom. When the waves were of Jewish – or Zionist – making, I watched them with more alarm than solidarity. The news of the concentration camps did less to make Carthusians think better of the Jews than to furnish them with a new idiom. There was a scrawny boy in Lockites called Maxwell, C.J.M., who was not particularly 'spoey', but turned up for House football games. On one occasion, in the winter of 1945, he was running awkwardly down the wing when 'Veg' Marot (who was sporting his blue fourth eleven cuts, of course) called out to his scrawny team-mate, 'Come on, Belsen, get a move on!' The loudness of the resulting laugh was proof both that people had heard about the camps and that they were glad to rephrase the unspeakable in terms of the comic.

Despite the outbreak of peace, England remained on a war footing. If the shiny cheapness of the 'demob suit' – issued to soldiers on their return to Civvy Street – was one of the earliest targets of snobbish derision, fifty-shilling-tailored 1945 Britain gave small impression of disarmed revelry. As a Fabian step towards classlessness, what had, before the war, been the Officers' Training Corps was now tactfully retitled the Junior Training Corps (JTC). However, no Carthusian doubted that, when the time came, he was likely to be commissioned as of right.

The Corps paraded on Tuesday afternoons. It was run, like so much of school life, on House lines: each House had its own platoon and House Commander. There was a Drill Competition in the Oration Quarter and a more practical demonstration of martial skills in the summer, when the platoons of various stripes competed for the Arthur Webber Cup. Professional umpires from Southern Command awarded marks, in December, for the keenness with which the school square was bashed, and in midsummer for the efficiency with which the boy-soldiers stormed enemy machine-gun nests or brought their (blank) fire to bear on bushy-topped trees and other military targets while they themselves were safely sprawled in Dead Ground.

During my first year, I watched the skimpy Lockite House Platoon without interest. It paraded in hairy uniforms, blancoed gaiters and webbing belts and more or less polished brasses on the slope of gravel outside the Fag Entrance, before marching off to the Drill Hall (behind Lessington) to be issued with antique .303 rifles. Men scarcely much older than ourselves had been involved in the real thing not six months earlier. No one knew when we might have to man the front line ourselves, which kept all of our faces appropriately straight.

Since new boys did not participate, the Lockite ranks contained only those who, a term before, had been seconded from other Houses. I have a notion that H.J.M. Bury was the House Commander. He took a more relaxed view of his khaki duties than was conducive to good order and discipline. The Lockite House Platoon was a notorious shower. Saunderites drilled like guardsmen and Robinites were not far behind; Lockites brought up the rear.

I and other new boys were inducted into the gentler arts of scouting. Since Robert Baden-Powell, 'the hero of Mafeking' and the founder of the Scout Movement, was an OC, the Charterhouse Troop was expected to be especially keen when it came to tracking wildlife and pitching tents. The local Eagle Scout was the chief chaplain. The suitably toggled and badged Reverend George Snow (who soon left to be Headmaster of Ardingly, whatever that might be), sat us around him in a wet circle on the grass and taught knots. It was said that it was possible to light a fire by rubbing two sticks together (there was whisper of a ribald variation of this Promethean pursuit, of which I understood nothing), but I never managed to excite the smallest spark.

'Jagger' Jordan, the only other Lockite in the Remove, declined even to join the Scouts, apparently from a scrupulous reluctance to do anything so warlike as to 'Be Prepared'. He opted for Estate Work, which smacked of being a conchie. On the other hand, he was not unwilling to box for Lockites, less from belligerence or House spirit than because he was a fervent fight fan. He owned a fat history of the Square Ring. From it I learned of the prowess of such second-order figures as 'Slapsy Maxie' Rosenbloom and Ted 'Kid' Berg, both of them recent mutations of Jew Mendoza, the bare-knuckled Regency pugilist who figured in one of Conan Doyle's historical novels.

Jordan boxed in deference to the traditions of the Noble Art of Self-Defence. Punctual use of the straight left kept the other man at a distance. He was out to establish his virility, not to demolish his opponent. Buchan-Hepburn was far more dangerous, though less correct. He had been the only new boy of my year to arrive wearing shorts. I remember his raw, embarrassed knees. Once he had displayed the effectiveness of his right hook, however, no one found his costume in any way ridiculous. Although of an unassuming disposition and inclined to keep himself to himself, he was strong enough to be indifferent to the herd. Even he, however, concealed the unshameful fact that his first name was Alistair; he preferred to let it be known that his Christian name was John. Scots had some reason to fear condescension, if nothing worse (provided they had a knock-out punch), from their southern cousins.

The boxing ring was in the gymnasium, in a field behind Robinites. The gym had a purple corrugated-iron roof and was the domain of an ex-sergeant major, a trim, balls-of-the-feet man, dapper in workout trousers, roll-top sweater and plimsolls. Vaselined hair *en brosse*, he could talk and climb a rope, swiftly, at the same time. I had had quite enough of boxing after my bumping bouts with Mackinnon. If I entered the ring at all, it was only to spar with Jordan and Sinha and Armitage. I declined to be considered for the inter-House competitions. My nose was getting bigger.

At the beginning of each quarter, we returned to find the new 'house seniority' pinned on a baized board near the Fag

Entrance. This notified the upper crust of any appointments to monitorship or Top Table; the *thetes* – as the Arrow, in Attic mode, once called the lower scholastic orders – could read of reshuffles in the disposition of their servility. In January 1946, I was deputed to become the Head Monitor's study fag. Since MacWilliam was in the Classical Sixth, my duties gave me access to his bulky (but coverless) Liddell and Scott *Greek Lexicon*, and a chance to peruse the dusty obscurity of the texts which it helped him to translate. MacWilliam was an undemanding Fag Master. He asked little more of me than that I clean his smallish window, dust his books, empty his wagger-pagger basket, and shake his carpet; no demanding task, since even the grandest grandee's study had floorspace for scarcely more than a hearth-rug. Among his peers, Macwilliam was a blushing adolescent, whom I overheard confessing to having a 'popsy' at home. His authority depended more on the kudos attached to his office than on any forceful exercise of it. Being a clever small boy, with smaller prudence, I had an early sense that, despite his possession of Liddell and Scott (and of Lewis and Short's *Latin Dictionary*), MacWilliam was not in the first rank of scholars; he was vulnerable to artless questions about things which he should have known, and I often did; I pretended ignorance the better to discover his. Clever folly was compounded by the idea that, by teasing flatteries, I was ingratiating myself with the Head Mo. If MacWilliam was tolerant of my quizzing, he can be excused for not welcoming it. Too amiable to charge me with 'festivity', he did not find it implausible for other monitors to do so.

During our first quarter, new boys might sometimes have been chided, but they were rarely punished. With the right to wind our C'house scarves around our throats came full subjection to the disciplinary machine. I was less inhibited by the fear of punishment than tempted, by some savage urge, to sail closer and closer to the wind. My recklessness was purely verbal, but it was, I think, a symptom of the absurdity of my situation: I was at this particular school, just as I was in the English social system, by mere chance. The urge to conform (which always implies apprehensions of not truly belonging) made me diligent in games and eager to shine in class. But the ethos of the school itself was as alien as it was arbitrary. If I wished upon the other boys a social assurance and homogeneity which their variety of accents and personal circumstances manifestly belied, I also despised the lame intelligence of the vast majority. Such an attitude was unwise, but not unusual among the scholarly elite. Despised by the mass, and rarely favoured even by the beaks, swotting was an activity to be practised in secret. Brains were dubious assets; brawn was what counted. Oh to be hells beefy!

If games were the way to general admiration, brief tribute was paid to those who won major Oxbridge scholarships. On the day of his election, the laurelled scholar took a card, signed by the Headmaster, announcing an extra half-holiday, from classroom to classroom, thus embracing the whole school in his lap of honour. His progress was applauded more for the idleness it procured than for the wit to which it testified. What honest Carthusian would not sooner have been entitled to first eleven socks and a gaudily striped 'hasher' (slang for sweater)?

The school elevens continued to play soccer in the Long Quarter, but the rest of us were recruited to hockey, which I had never played before. The House Lib. cricket balls were painted white (though they were soon rouged again by the stick they took). We played in the same rigid boots, fortified with strips of leather and shod with shin-piercing studs, and on the same lumpy fields of Broom and Lees, as we used for football. The unevenness of the ground made sure that finesse obtained no sly advantage over loutish endeavour. Although Sinha was far more adroit in his stickwork, I discovered that I was quite good at the game, which never had the glamour of soccer or cricket. Hockey players, even in the first eleven, were not regarded as full-blooded Bloods. My contemporary David Berkeley made the shrewd decision to volunteer for the unwanted position of goalkeeper. Rigged in outsize cricket pads, discreetly protected by a 'box' and disfigured by a sort of fencing mask, he had so little competition for his unglamorous post that in almost no time he was playing for the school.

The humblest sporting decoration was to win your house colours. I was puzzled in my early weeks by a notice pinned up on the board in the Lockites dining room which announced that, after the match against another House, this or that grandee had 'received Houseteams'. I had some fatuous notion that this denoted having hosted a social reception, for which H.J.M. Bury or 'Veg' Marot had supplied the refreshments. It turned out to mean no more than that the nominee had been awarded his House colours.

This misunderstanding is another small indication of the sense I had, and tried to conceal, of having fallen among a tribe of savages whose social rites and language were both bizarre and beyond easy comprehension. It would be vanity to claim that I was alone in this; it is more likely that a majority of Carthusians were furtively afraid that they were unworthy of so apparently grand an establishment. As if designed by some impersonal calculation, the proliferation of rituals and grades was guaranteed to mystify and intimidate. However arbitrary a society may be in its morals, if it has the means and kudos both to reward the submissive and to coerce the rebellious, its contradictions will be declared to be mysteriously consistent and its absurdities conducive to traditional virtues. What makes no sense will be venerated as part of a sublime scheme which heretics must be too perverse or too self-centred to understand.

Having abandoned metaphysics along with Popery, the

English had made their society, rather than their faith, the opiate of the people: so enviably grand were its grandees, so subtly calibrated their privileges, so menacing their sticks and so juicy their carrots, that salvation could be achieved this side of the grave, provided one accepted the rules of England's sublime and quirky game. Marx and Engels agreed that the English working class had been lost to The Revolution: even the abused proletariat subscribed so credulously to the myth of empire and so revelled in delusions of innate superiority that they could never be expected to turn, as a class, on those who offered them the opportunity to parade as the vigilant, and smartly uniformed, sentries of the very system which underpaid and exploited them.

What was still true in society at large was especially true at Charterhouse in the twilight years of the *imperium Britannicum*: salvation and advancement were to be gained not by understanding the system, still less by the intelligent dissection of any part of its workings, but through patriotic acceptance of its fatuous necessity. The faith of the English middle class was not vested in creeds, but in institutions. The Reformation had given Thomas Sutton the chance to create a school where there had once been a monastery; the Charterhouse of the 1940s was still (of course) monastic, but in this, and in almost every other aspect of its mystique, there was no religious vestige: chastity was a matter of rules, not of morals, or rather of moralising rules, the speciality of all our houses.

Post-war Britain had elected to be governed in accordance with a mundane, undogmatic version of Christian socialism. Its improbably popular paragon was the Chancellor of the Exchequer, Sir Stafford Cripps. An owlish and emaciated ex-Chancery QC, allegedly of rare legal astuteness, he had renounced a profitable practice in order to become an evangelical socialist politician. If he had put on a hair shirt, his sermons were still silky. Having eschewed wealth for himself, Cripps found self-denial to be a virtue of which no taxpayer should be deprived. Prodigal with inverted generosity, there was almost nothing that his Christian budgets were not designed to take away. He practised what he preached to such an extent that he became anorexic *avant la lettre* and starved himself to death. This literal mortification won him a reputation which sanctified the folly of his political judgement. When British ambassador in wartime Moscow, he had treated J.V. Stalin as a sort of Fabian-in-a-hurry: Uncle Joe might be setting a somewhat faster pace for socialist advancement, but we were all headed for the same promised land. As Attlee's Chancellor, Cripps's prescriptions for the post-war economy were a spiritual medicine which his renown at the Bar was taken to validate as a panacea. If they did no more practical good than bleeding an already anaemic patient, they left the voter's soul in a healthy condition.

No one was more credulous of the merits of all the mutually embarrassing formulae of post-war England than Raphael, F.M.; nor was anyone less sure of his place in the future which they advertised. Since the Labour government seemed to have been irreversibly endorsed by the electorate, there was nothing heterodox in assuming that there was justice in its utility-furnished purposes. On the other hand, since I had been sent to Charterhouse to be educated in the British way of middle-class life (that is, life which aped what it took to be upper class), I had every incitement to the gullibility with which I deferred to antique caprice. How odd, how very odd, that never once did it occur to me to regret that I was not still the American child I had been seven years before!

During the Long (short, spring) Quarter of 1946, I honoured the rules by their regular breach. Some undefined rage to be other than reputation made me, or to have another reputation, made me reckless in my sarcasm to those in a position to punish me. Nothing convinces me more of the futility of severity than the appetite it gave me for further provocations. I did not hate authority; in some sense, I doted on it. The three-, four- and five-page essays which Randall and others imposed on me were opportunities no less than punishments. In what was a form of servile journalism, I scribbled pages and pages on all sorts of randomly enforced subjects. I took more trouble over their composition than other convicts and I handed them in with a flourish; my only true punishment was when a Monitor counted the required tally of pages and threw them away unread. That really hurt.

There was a dark charm about the ritual of being beaten by the Head Monitor. Bumming gave the victim, especially before the event, something of the singular sanctity of the Tarot's Hanged Man. The most solemn moment in the English criminal calendar was less the execution of a murderer than the judge's donning of his black cap when pronouncing sentence. The seriousness of British justice was established by the existence of the supreme penalty from which no one was exempt. Imagine the condemned cell! How good were the warders at chess, which murderers allegedly liked to play during their last hours? How hard did they try? Morbidity and justice went on the beat together.

The abolition of the death penalty became a righteous cause in the 1950s, for which few to the left of Lord Goddard, the Lord Chief Justice, whom they held to be a modern Judge Jeffries, failed to campaign. Since there was no evidence that hanging was a deterrent, and since the procedure itself involved such deliberate and macabre barbarity, what rational man could argue for it? The dark truth remained that capital punishment was somehow (ah somehow!) integral to a certain gravity in English society. It could not be *argued* for, since argument implies a retinue of plausible reasons, but its existence implied that certain things were beyond negotiation; society, as encapsulated in the Crown, had powers which it was almost treasonous to dispute. The deterrence of murder was not the heart of the matter; the sterling symbolism of the law as an implacable force, never to be taken lightly, had capital punishment as its hallmark.

British conceit concerning their institutions had as much to do with the exact means by which they enforced their rules as with the benefits that they were alleged to secure. The seedy allure which made Graham Greene's 1938 novel *Brighton Rock* so popular lay less in its Catholicism than in the perverse relish with which Greene depicted Pinky's appetite for damnation. God's Englishness lay not least in his impersonation of the ultimate hanging judge. The Catholic hell was, and remains, an almost pornographic variant of what happened on the scaffold: the miscreant was, as it were, continually being killed, eternally subject to the supreme penalty. The infinite extension of the sinner's agony was part of its seductive thrill: Christianity itself led us into temptation. Pinky's zeal for damnation endorsed the system that would roast him in penal fire. He would, Greene led his readers to believe, have been scandalised by any well-meaning attempt to wake him from his sweet nightmare of an inevitable hell. Reprieve rather than property was the Catholic idea of theft. The sinner was valued because he *craved* the truth – the crueller the better – of what others, with more squeamish metaphysics, preferred to question.

By the same token, in a petty way, the bad boy, in going out of his way to seek punishment, demonstrated how great a claim the penal system had on his erotic imagination. I cannot say quite how, still less exactly why, I was seduced, above all by the existence of corporal punishment, into the delinquency of my second and third quarters at Charterhouse. I was not bullied; I was no more unhappy than many others, and much less than, for sad instance, the wretched boy who wet his bed and whose reeking sheets had to be displayed over the wooden partition of his cubicle each morning ('A

wet sheet and a flowing sea/And a wind that follows fast'
was the cruelly prompt quotation from the *Golden Treasury*).
No, I was expressing more respect than scorn for the law by
my breaches of it. Not the least of my motives was curiosity.
Was the greatest of them a certain desire to be the centre of
attention, as condemned men always were?

Carthusian beatings were seldom as savage as at Eton,
where flogging was almost a sport, and often a pleasure
(Quintin Hogg never ceased to gloat over the fact that he had
caned Freddie Ayer, who deserved it for being a bit of a Jew
and too clever by half). In its bureaucratic niceties, there was
something typically middle class about Carthusian flagella-
tion. Once a boy had had his name 'put in the book' ten
times, he had, in a phrase that deserves analysis, 'asked for it'
(the promise 'I'll teach you to misbehave' comes in the same
sweet basket of ambiguities). The Head Monitor was then
required to go to the House Man for permission to use one
(or more) of the canes which – like footballs, blanco, and
fives gloves – were officially House Lib. property and kept in
some discreet place.

Once this permission had been granted, a particular night
was appointed for the ceremony. Everyone went to bed
knowing that sooner or later footsteps would be heard on the
stone stairs and then on the polished planks of the dorm, that
they would stop outside the condemned man's 'cube' and
that the voice of the Junior Monitor (the newly elevated
Chrissie Raeburn, né – though, luckily for him, no one knew
it – Ravensberg) would command him to put on his dressing
gown and trousers and come down to Hall.

I cannot remember which or how many boys had preceded me in being the recipient of this instruction, but a
curious and unbreachable silence always followed the slip-
pered departure of the condemned man and his silent, shod
escort. Who can deny that the erotic imagination of everyone
in the dorm was excited by visualising the ritual of the

victim's walk down the dark stairs, through the faintly lit dining room and then his entry into the brightly lit Hall where the Head Monitor, doubling as governor of the prison and Pierrepoint, the executioner, would ask him, politely, to take off his dressing gown and 'bend over that chair'? The other Monitors, gravely unsmiling, stood with folded arms – there was something dignified in such a pose, which also took care of the bad actor's problem of what to do with his hands – and watched the proceedings. It was part of their duty not to flinch or look away; showing no emotion was an obligation common to all concerned. It was, you might say, a rehearsal for attending executions. For whatever unspoken reason, no one was beaten on his bare buttocks. This was probably less to avoid inflicting undue pain on the culprit than to deprive the spectators of undue pleasure. The result was that a certain kind of juicy spectacle was promised and *almost* enacted, but that something was withheld.

Such prudish prurience was of a piece with the censoriousness of the Lord Chamberlain who, in those days, determined what could or could not be seen in the theatre. Older boys told tales of standing in the queue for the Windmill Theatre, in Soho, whose boast, 'We Never Closed', derived from the fact that it had never shut its doors during the worst of the Blitz. Since the Windmill's speciality was naked girls, 'We Never Clothed' was its unsurprising unofficial motto. Men in mackintoshes stood patiently in line at the box office for hours on end. Since the show was continuous, with no embarrassingly lit intervals in which to be recognised by a friend, once inside there was no obligation to leave one's seat.

The girls were only apparently naked, for although they flaunted their breasts, they were forbidden by law to show any signs of life and were obliged to wear what were called 'fleshings', the deliberately charmless term for skin-coloured, and skin-tight coverings for their nether regions.

Immobility was enjoined upon the girls, by law, at all times. Men waited not only to get into the theatre but also to advance, when vacancies occurred, into the front rows, where close inspection was possible of the almost literally breathless beauties. The customers knew, even when in the queue, that they were going to be deprived a sight of genuine nakedness: even the girls' nipples were capped with stars. Once again, *more Britannorum*, when the lid was taken off, there was another lid underneath.

The success of the first post-war Picasso exhibition at the Tate in 1946, to which my mother took me, is often attributed to a solemn zeal for art, created by wartime isolation. The reproach of the Calvinist preacher when Byron giggled during one of his Aberdeen sermons – 'No hope for them as laughs!' – might have been the slogan of 1940s novelists and intellectuals in general: life was not a laughing matter. Even Evelyn Waugh had become a sourpuss to whom being in England was, he said, 'like living in an occupied country'. However, the crowds that jostled among the Picassos in such large numbers came, I suspect, not only to be reassured, as the English like to be from time to time, of the trashiness of what they did not – or chose not to – understand, but also because, in those censorious times, art alone could not be prevented from depicting the underlying truth of things, not least (to my hungry adolescent self) that females could have, *did* have, pubic hair. Picasso's wanton flourish of black curlicues in the groin of at least one of his two-nosed, boss-eyed ladies was not only art, it was also a liberation. Art gave nudity a good name. What shame could there be in taking an appreciable time over what the artist saw in his model? How fortunately different art was from the photographs which I had found once fluttering on the barbed wire! Yet the sacrosanct and the obscene were tantalisingly adjacent. Today, it could be argued, they have come to overlap.

The novel was soon to be no less important than art as a means of learning what grown-ups did after dark. The more that the cinema and journalism tend towards pornography, the less urgent grows the appeal of art and literature. Can the latter outlast the century in any traditional, stylish form? Writers will soon only report, not create; if they respond copiously to commissioning editors, how many will ever aspire to be among Shelley's unacknowledged, and often unrewarded, legislators?

I daresay there was, in the later 1940s, a busy underworld (and – though the reticent gossip columns gave small hint of it – overworld) where sex was not a mystery and frustration not a problem, but the huge majority of English men and women yearned guiltily for pleasure and resigned themselves to rectitude. Their shame was so natural that they agreed, uncomplainingly, to be teased by the pier-end machine which promised, if you inserted a penny, to show you the Nudist Colony. On reading the advertisement, you could scarcely believe your naive luck, but when you paid your copper (as I once did on Bognor Pier), you had a brief glimpse of, yes, completely naked, incarcerated... ants. That would teach you. Being cheated, and jolly well deserving it, was part of the English price for sexual appetites of any kind. Neither the masochistic junior Carthusian nor the sadistic senior – who might gloat officiously as he put you in the book for the clinching tenth time, knowing that it meant that the culprit would be beaten – received full satisfaction.

I scarcely remember, and have no inclination to recount, the details of my own experience. I was neither a cry-baby nor was I required to be brave. I was, in some sense, present only as an observer: certain sensations, like surgical operations and ceremonial rituals – circumcision or flogging – seem to take place with the victim's ego in a state of interested detachment. May even death come in this way? One is permitted to hope. I watched myself playing the part of the condemned man, but I felt little fear and, in the event, an embarrassing want of pain.

MacWilliam went through the motions of severity without being severe. When I inspected the marks before going back to my cube, I was scarcely even pink. This led me to refuse, as if for reasons of modesty, to display myself, in the traditional way, to the rest of the dorm. MacWilliam's leniency had another, possibly interesting, effect: I was disappointed that I had affected so manful a silence when, in fact, I was hardly pinked. As a result, I had a distinct feeling of contempt for my Fag Master and an unappeased desire to endure something more testing. His squeamishness created an appetite for measuring myself against authority in a less half-hearted mood. If capital punishment could be – *per impossibile* – undergone several times, who can doubt that the mixture of frisson and morbid attention which he earned on the first occasion would lead the murderer to kill again as soon as he had the chance? The hanged man's notorious terminal orgasm was the very instance of the natural – or God-given – convergence of the supreme penalty and the supreme pleasure. If released from adamantine chains and penal fire, would Pinky ever resist the dreadful thrill of having them reimposed?

The sense of not belonging at Charterhouse did not declare itself consistently. Although aware of what was in the newspapers about Palestine, I felt small sympathy for the survivors from Hitler's camps as they tried to scramble ashore where 'we' did not want them. The philosophy of tolerance, by which my father set such store, had its craven aspect; replacing Shylock's sufferance with deference, modern English Jews did not have to crawl but they were careful not to antagonise the dominant culture. I lacked both the conviction and the muscle to confront, and challenge, what had demeaned me. My emotions matched my opinions in being so imprecise that, even when I knew what I should feel, I remained incapable of feeling it. Prophylactic anaesthesia rendered me insensitive to anything that might have a genuine claim on me. Only what was alien was enticing. Where the vocabulary of prejudice was not applicable to me, I was not slow to use it: if I never talked about 'jewing' people, or even about 'groising' or being 'oily', I was prompt enough to talk about 'oiks' (the standard term for the lower classes).

My sense of having fallen among barbarians was camouflaged, sincerely so to speak, by an eagerness to take part in organised sport or to play pingpong, if only because it meant proposing a game to another boy, or being proposed to. There was a House Lib. 'pingers' table in the centre of Long Room. The sustained, yet intermittent, tock-tock, tock-tock, tock-TOCK of the ball deterred any attempt to read or do anything which required concentration. 'Tubby' Gladstone was the improbable pingpong ace, though Robin Jordan – with his personal Victor Barna bat – could run him close. In his glittering glasses, Tubby moved with neat-footed agility and delivered smashes of conclusive ferocity. He claimed to be a direct descendant of the great William Ewart (his own names were Robin Ewart). It may be that he had something of his great-grandfather's anti-Disraelian animus, though he did not yet express it. Not a scholar, nor was he a fool; he was a modern linguist – hence one of Harry March's pupils in Upper Four (a) – and he had a tart tongue. In order to assist his agility, he took to wearing gym shoes to play pingers. Their slight squeak on the Long Room floor was the nimble sign of his will to win. He combined the smile of the fat boy with the menace of the conspirator. He and his friends left the pingpong table only, it seemed, to go to the Music Room, at the top of the house and the end of one of the dormitories. If you went in there, you felt that you were interrupting something malign, as well as Benjamino Gigli.

Robin Jordan and I often went to the same classroom, although he did peel off for French, with Harry March, or German, with 'Alfie T.' – Alfred Tressler – when the Remove did Greek. If I had trusted him, he would have been my confidant. He had a certain appetite for intimacy, or at least for some kind of hold over other people, which was gained by the appearance of attentive sympathy. Robin may well have been less calculating than nervous of his own place in the school. We shared a scepticism about the regimented enthusiasms which, in many respects, we also honoured: he was a goodish footballer and would prove a better cricketer, but his refusal to join even the Scouts seemed like an act of impressive rebellion, which I could hardly match, save by my habit of goading senior boys with my unwise wit.

Robin was a smiler; he wished to be liked by everybody, while giving the furtive impression that he was shamming with them but in earnest with you. He could even suggest, without ever alluding directly to it, that he might have some Jewish, or at least un-English, blood. This possibility was encouraged by there being a Saunderite called (Tony) Jordan in the Classical Fifth, a year ahead of us, who looked undoubtedly Jewish. About Cohen, in Weekites, or Judah in Saunderites, there was no doubt at all, while Hodgsonites – where 'Sniffy' Russell was Housemaster – was known as 'the ghetto', for its alleged high proportion of Jews, to none of whom I ever spoke.

Jordan, J.F.R., was evasively forthcoming about his family, in which divorces and half-brothers seem to abound; he hinted that one of the latter was a delinquent, or at least a prodigal, of some kind. The family businesses seemed to include the ownership of a seaside pier. When I came to read *Brighton Rock*, I associated Robin's errant (but admired) Heathcliffian 'brother' with Graham Greene's Pinky. 'Jagger J' – as he rather liked to be called – created intimacy without warmth; or did I find it easier to accept the first than to offer the second? He seemed somehow to know me, and to insinuate that we had something unadmitted in common. Although without the slightest sexual overtones, we imitated exclusivity in a way that convinced both of us of a certain superiority. When we were higher in the school, we wrote a joint letter to *The Carthusian*, advocating certain reforms to the system of discipline and privilege. Our letter mixed caution and boldness in a sadly liberal way: its elderly tone was calculated both to affront and to appease. If we said that we were 'inveighing' against obsolete customs, our very vocabularly deferred to them. Certain OCs were rewardingly indignant, but the system did not change. Robin and I did, however, make sure – against no loudly dissenting voices – that during our senior period no small boy was beaten in Lockites. If we were scarcely revolutionaries, we were – in Karl Popper's phrase – Piecemeal Social Engineers, on a very modest scale.

I might, I suppose, have found kindred spirits (and other Jews) elsewhere in the school, but the Carthusian ethos deplored friendships with boys in other Houses, though one might salute classmates without arousing suspicion of extramural affections. I was once pursued by a Weekite whom I did not know but who, when he caught me up, asked knowingly whether I minded going to chapel. His name was Clive Marks and he was, as they say, an unapologetic Jew. If he hoped that I was, he hoped in vain: I took his approach to be more accusatory than friendly. As I brushed him off, I told myself that I was being a loyal Lockite, rather than a disloyal Jew. Since that encounter, I have always had a shameful sympathy for Flavius Josephus, who saved his bacon, so to say, during the disastrous Jewish revolt of AD 66. By deserting to the Romans, he survived to defend and dignify the cause which he had, to a degree, betrayed. After all, had he died at Masada, what should we know of its heroic defence? If the defenders had not fought only to the penultimate man

(Josephus himself, who ducked out of the corporate suicide pact) their bravery would have passed unrecorded. Josephus turned his coat the better to celebrate those who did not.

The early months of 1946 were extremely cold. Chilbains were so much a part of daily expectations that their size became a matter of grotesque pride. They first itched and then they split, which was painful but excited little attention from 'the Hag', Miss Kellett, who dispensed rudimentary medicaments from a warm snuggery on the first landing. There was no point in complaining of colds, since there was no treatment for them: no temperature, no reprieve from school. The Fag Entrance door was open all day, so that fresh (and refrigerated) air circulated freely and drove the warmth up towards the studies of the senior boys. Brough Stuart Churchill Gurney Randall devised a punishment whereby the penitent had to carry buckets filled with cold water up and down Lockite steps, which mounted steeply from the Fag Entrance, in easy sight of his study, towards Bridge. When he had been heroically ballocked in a House match, and limped home with his laurels, I was heard to remark that 'the wreck of the Hesperus' had made port. As a result I was both 'put in the book' and ordered to carry two full buckets of icy water, without gloves, up and down Lockite steps six times before breakfast. B.S.C.G.R. watched me through his closed, frost-starred window. I continued to regard him with insolent admiration.

Such was the privileged life to which, in the post-war climate of creeping egalitarianism, a few oiks now craved, and obtained, admission. Thanks to a liberal scheme initiated by Robert Birley shortly before he departed to assume the headmastership of the most exclusive and snobbish school in the world, selected council school boys were given admission to Charterhouse. We were instructed that these assisted pupils were to be treated just like everyone else. This sounded more welcoming than it was likely to prove. The only Lockite of this character was called Knight. I do not know exactly when he arrived, but we could tell him to be of oikish provenance because he wore a pen and pencils in his (non-regulation tweed) front top pocket. He is another of those dramatis personae who appear in one scene and then, though he may have remained in the cast for two or three years, play no further part in my memory-theatre. That I remember him at all is because of an incident which is both despicable and symptomatic of the confusions of my schoolboy life.

In accordance with Kiplingesque principle, I accorded Knight the tolerant condescension recommended towards lesser breeds. Was I protective because I hoped for praise from above? I was not quite as genial, or as creepy, as that; it could be that I simply thought I ought to be nice, if only so that God should have cause to think well of me, if I needed Him. When at Copthorne, such attempts to curry favour with the Almighty were markedly more frequent after I had lost my current penknife. It seems to me even now that the hillsides and lanes of north Devon must be plated with rusting penknives, so many of them did I buy from Mr McGaw, and so regularly did I lose them. I hate losing things and am worse at finding them.

It was, I daresay, because I had lost my pencil that, one day, I asked Knight whether I could borrow one of those he kept in his top pocket. I had not befriended him to cadge a favour, nor did I mean to keep the pencil for long. But then, as was not unusual, I lost it. I did not steal it; I did not keep it; I lost it. What would it have cost me to buy him another? It was a propelling pencil, with a dry little rattle from the spare leads kept in its belly, but it was not nearly as expensive as, for ostentatious instance, 'Tubby' Gladstone's biro, which – whenever it was bought – had cost him, or his father, two pounds ten shillings, which was almost half the national average weekly wage. However, I did lose Knight's pencil and, when I could not find it, I began to avoid him. He pursued me and, eventually, with justice, threatened to 'go to somebody'. Such a threat provoked the humbugging moralist which Carthusian lore had taught me to be: I warned the little oik that we did not 'show up' our friends. Enduring 'hard cheese', like chilblains, was part of being a Lockite. Did I recall with what craven stoicism I had failed to complain at the theft of that beautiful compendium of games which I took to Copthorne in 1939? I did not bully Knight, or consider that I had stolen anything from him, but I may have persuaded myself that, by not restoring his loss I was proving that I was not to be pushed around, at least by a manifest oik.

Another of my inalienable characteristics is to leave certain things – sometimes as trivial as an unreturned library book or an unanswered letter – until they pass some strange inner frontier and become, very nearly, a source of unpurged anxiety so obstinate that the postponement of dealing with them, and the hope that they will simply evaporate, renders me incapable of the simple act – returning the book, writing the letter, buying a new pencil – which would dissipate my guilty distress. To the banal question 'Why not just do it?', the answer has to be either a schoolboy's terse 'Dunno' or some Proustian attempt to arrive at the *fond des choses*, even if it risks requiring a complete autobiography.

I did not find Knight's pen and I was damned if I should buy another. Had people not lost, or stolen, my things and not replaced them? I cannot swear that I did not tell myself, and perhaps Knight himself, that this kind of thing was part of the Carthusian education which he was so privileged to be offered. If he couldn't accept that, he was proving only what an irredeemable outsider he was. Knight did not take my lessons with gentlemanly meekness: he told his father, in a letter, who exactly had taken his pencil and failed to return it. His father – very decently, I now realise – wrote to me rather than to HAM or to the Headmaster and warned me that, if I did not make proper recompense to his son, he would go to the Authorities.

My tendency to ignore communications which distressed me did not assert itself on this occasion. I might despise the lined Basildon Bond on which Knight *père* had penned his board-schooled lines, but the threat was the more convincing for coming from someone unbothered by what I thought of his stationery. I bought a new propelling pencil from the school bookshop and – with a contemptuous 'Here!' – thrust it at the little oik. He pocketed it without thanks or apology. I never spoke to him again. I only hope that I did not speak ill of him to other people.

As crimes go, my offence scarcely ranks. Yet shame, not only at taking something and not returning it, but also at excusing myself to myself by reflecting that Knight wasn't really a proper Carthusian, more a charity patient, may have contributed to an upsurge in my continued and incautious defiance of monitorial authority.

In class, I was eager to earn good marks and, on the whole, I did so, though H.C. Iredale managed, within a year, to abort my previous competence in French, not only by the dullness of his set books – how I hate Alphonse Daudet's *Lettres de Mon Moulin*, a sort of literate, home-grown prototype of Peter Mayle's Provençal publicity! – but also because he clearly favoured prettier company than mine. I associate him always with his bicycle, though never on it; he put on his clips outside the classroom (facing Green) and then wheeled his 'grid' slowly towards Brooke Hall, accompanied by a toadying coterie, Cottrell, Robson and Burton-Brown *en tête*. They smirked at his carefully cadenced sarcasms and rattled off the prescribed lists of irregularities learned from our boring French grammar. '*Bail, cail, corail, email, ventrail, vitrail, soupirail*' (a basement window, generally with bars, and – can it be ? –

one suitable for sighing at) do remain in my mind; I shall never make a mistake in their plural form (always in -*aux*), though I have yet to find occasion to use any of them. H.C.I. was at once dissident and typical of a certain kind of Carthusian beak: he might not subscribe to the whole ethos, as the Arrow did, but his snide allusions to 'haberdashery', like his want of respect for 'Bags', would have had no savour outside the system. As with so many English radicals, his eccentricity emphasised how dependent he was on what he toyed with undermining. Did my want of the blonde charms that graced his Daviesite favourites, 'Bubbles' and 'Cuddles', disincline Harry Iredale from welcoming my company? Or did he find greater pleasure in scandalising more manifest conformists with his sibilant and subversive staccato?

Hindsight colours my schooldays with portents and darkens them with the shadow of what was to come. I should distort even what I believe to be the case if I pretended to endless dread or unmitigated alienation. Before the Summer Quarter, my father was generous, and keen, enough to give me a course of cricket coaching at the indoor school which Alf Gover, the Surrey fast bowler, had opened on Wandsworth Hill. I could easily cycle there from Putney on my new second-hand, three-speed 'grid'. Alf's partner was Andy Sandham, the ex-Surrey, and occasionally English wicket-keeper, who once scored a double century as an opening batsman. Gover – a gangling, genial man who gained a handful of England caps, the last at the Oval against the Indians in 1946, when he took one for plenty – persuaded me that I too could bowl quickies.

Returning to Charterhouse full of emulous enthusiasm, I was mortified when B.S.C.G.R. (*toujours lui*, as H.C.I. might have said) did not even pick me for yearlings. I was relegated to second 'tics, as I had been for football. It meant that, as the Arrow put it, I was classed among the 'ferrets'. Why 'ferrets'? Because – wait for it! – 'they go in after rabbits'. I endured relegation for a week or two, but one day after I had made twenty-five not out in a ferrets' match, I happened to be standing near Randall while he was composing the yearlings list. Very untypically, I dared to ask him why he never put me down for a game with them. Since he was probably having difficulty in remembering eleven suitable names, he instantly added mine to the team, in which I then became a permanent member. It was an instance of another English lesson I never managed to learn: those who want to get on among the Anglo-Saxons are ill-advised to hide their light under a bushel. Unfortunately, my father had warned me that it was unwise to push oneself forward in 'Christian' company; you should work and play hard, and unobtrusively, and wait for people to 'beat a path to your door'. Was more impractical, anachronistic or laming advice ever given to anyone who wanted to succeed in the post-war world? 'Keep your head down', when hitting a ball, was an eternal verity by contrast.

In the first full post-war season of county cricket, Edrich, W.J., and Compton, D.C.S., were already hitting runs without limit, it seemed, for Middlesex; I made a few, painstakingly head down, for yearlings. In the long summer days, there was early school: the first period started before breakfast, at 6.30 a.m., so that we might have three long afternoons a week free for cricket. The House 'butler', Mr Lockhart, came clanging through the dorms at 6.15, rousing the usual groans and detonating a few loud, clever farts.

Through a series of wilful provocations which I have entirely forgotten, I managed once again to qualify for a beating in the Summer Quarter of 1946. My delinquencies were never important breaches of rules. I was, and am, a cautious transgressor. It was all a matter of attention-seeking. I doubt if I had any single motive for asking for it yet again, but the same ritual was duly enacted. This time (it may have been on HAM March's advice, or as a result of his own exasperation, or even for my supposed good) MacWilliam was more energetic with the cane. He may have taken a run even, though he scarcely matched Charles Laughton's prescription to the bo'sun, in *Mutiny on the Bounty*, 'Lay on with a will.' He hurt me all right and I had the necessary satisfaction of enduring in silence.

When it was over, I stood up, my usual rosy (facial) cheeks no doubt a little rosier, and looked at the spectators with a sort of contempt which did not exclude a certain expectation of approval. I had not embarrassed them or myself. I was in no hurry to leave the bright lights of Hall.

MacWilliam said, 'You can go now.'

I looked at them again – Bury, Randall, Lethbridge, Raeburn – and then I said, 'Goodnight.'

After a moment, they were obliged to say it back, a small victory for the uses of courtesy.

That second time, I had some marks to show, and showed them, with rueful pride. I have never had the smallest wish to go through anything like that again, although I have not lost my appetite for making provocative remarks, often in the fatuous hope that those whom they wound will appreciate, even perhaps anthologise, my barbs. In an odd way, I had offered a belated apology to Strangways, for letting Mr Workman punish him alone for what we had both done. Perhaps I had also atoned for my conduct towards Knight. I never sought punishment again. I cannot even recall being put in the book after that summer.

Because puberty was so empty of amorous – never mind erotic – adventures, it leaves few flags in the landscape of my memory. I played tennis with Dorothy Tutin on the Manor Fields courts (she had a fluent forehand), but I did not try to kiss her any more than I did the other local girls to whom I was introduced. As for asking them out, I lacked both the nerve and the means (which often supply the nerve).

It cost ninepence to go to the Globe Cinema in the Upper Richmond Road and it always gave me a thumping migraine. I went alone, knowing the pain that was to come, because it was two hours of anonymous peace. It was in that fleapit that I saw *Odd Man Out*, the masterpiece which primed my enthusiasm for telling stories in dialogue and pictures. I never dared to ask girls to come with me, because I had very little pocket money and would not have known when, or how, to get my arm around them.

My father did his best to cure my clumsiness on the dance floor by sending me to the school run by Phyllis Haylor, his ex-partner in the tango, and her carnationed and Brylcreemed colleague, Norman, who looked as if he had been cashiered by Fortnum and Mason, but allowed to keep the black coat and striped trousers. The school was in a basement to be reached by walking down Raphael Street, a brief and ill-favoured tributary of Knightsbridge. I did my best with the chassis-reverse and the various counts – *one*-two-three (the waltz), one-two-three-*four* (the rumba) – and I understood in principle that the tango was the only ballroom dance which allowed – nay, demanded – that one take a patent-leathered foot off the floor, but my practice remained knock-kneed and arhythmic (oh that alpha privative, what a lot of exercise it has had in my life!).

My parents took me to St Leonard's for a week's summer holiday. The hotel was like a static liner: every evening we dined adjacent to the dance floor and every evening, happily partnerless, I watched Irene and Cedric dance. During the day, he and I played French cricket. Only on the next to last night, fuelled maybe by a glass of Gewurtztraminer (his favourite wine), did I respond when my father suggested, again, that I make some use of the dance floor.

I said, 'I'm afraid everybody will look at me.'

My father's reply was as crushing as it was true. 'Nobody,' he said, 'looks for very long at a bad dancer.'

In his personal habits, Cedric combined a British regularity with sudden caprices, almost always connected with being Jewish. One year, he would ignore 'high days and holy days' and the next, since he maintained membership in the Liberal Jewish synagogue, he would have an excess of piety and insist on attending a Pesach or Yom Kippur or Day of Atonement service. I dreaded such occasions; the approach to the synagogue, along St John's Wood Road, was furtive with the fear of seeing another Carthusian, who would – whether Jew or Gentile – then know for certain What I Really Was. The services themselves were of protracted tedium and unrelieved by the kind of thumpingly familiar tunes which even I managed to sing in Charterhouse Chapel ('For all the saints, who from their labours rest' etcetera). Not the smallest feeling of election, still less of belief, enlightened my spirit or fortified my alleged 'faith'. We did not belong to the north London Jewish community and made no friends by our attendance.

During the summer holidays of 1946, my father told me that, since, at fourteen, I was a 'man' by Orthodox standards, I should already have been bar mitzvah-ed. It was easier, by far, to feel at home with the passive pluperfect of Latin verbs, or to reel off the provisions of the Sullan constitution (the key element was the relegation of the Tribunate from a popular step to the consulship to a dead end in the cursus honorum), than to feel any vocation for the laws or lore of Judaism. What was Ezekiel to me or I to Ezekiel? However, the time had come – as times did so punctually and yet unpredictably in what the sociologist David Riesman would soon term my 'other-directed' life – for me to learn the rudiments of my religion, that is, the Ancestral Faith that had been wished upon me.

If bar mitzvahs smacked of side-locked orthodoxy, then confirmation – which the Liberal synagogues had instituted – had a nicely English ring to it. My father enrolled me in the correspondence class that would qualify me to be confirmed, by Rabbi Mattuck, if he had not retired, in a year's time. Once a fortnight I should receive my 'student's exercise' and be required to learn about key biblical figures: Ezekiel, and Hosea, and Nehemiah, whom – had they been in Weekites – I should have done all I could to avoid. I had then to reply to questions at the end of the Roneoed pages. The dates were not given as BC (which would have acknowledged Christ's advent) but as 'BCE'. It meant the same thing but stood, non-committally, for 'Before the Common Era'.

I lacked the will to reject or the piety to enjoy the prospect of additional fortnightly, epistolary banco. I already had a burdensome scholarly load. Lockites' mail was put out on a table for collection (can it have been by the library fag?) and I was mortified to see that the brown envelope from the synagogue was not only rubber-stamped with its return address but also, hardly less shaming, it was declared to contain a 'student's exercise'. Can anyone today believe that I was as mortified to be labelled a student as to be proclaimed a Jew? Since the oikish connotations of being a student have now been effaced by egalitarian practice, it must seem exaggerated, if not crazy, to confess that no 1940s Carthusian would *ever* admit to being a student, nor wish to be anything but an undergraduate. Students went to polytechnics or demonstrated in Cairo.

The only acceptable use of 'student' was that current at Christ Church, Oxford, where certain dons, among them Hugh Trevor-Roper OC, bore that archaic title. Someone called Holford Hewitt had endowed a 'closed' scholarship from Charterhouse to the House (as my father called it), which meant that each year selected Sixth Formers sat for automatic admission to Oxford. The lucky victor secured the right to a scholar's (longer) gown and a hundred pounds a year for four years, though he did not, I think, earn the school a half-holiday by his easy achievement.

The threat of the fortnightly arrival of my student's

exercise, and the fear of curious eyes, led me to volunteer to collect the post and arrange it for general collection. In that way, I was able to subtract my beastly brown envelope before anyone knew it had arrived. Because my father had decided that it was something that had to be done, I was powerless to resign from the course, but my determination to conceal its substance from other Lockites led me to postpone even looking at it (as one sometimes does, even today, with tax demands, solicitors' letters and reviews by critics with high standards). Since no sanction could be visited on me, procrastination led to lies (claims to have posted my replies) and recriminations during the holidays. I came to hate Nehemiah and still cannot distinguish between the reproaches of Ezra and those of Jeremiah. I did not believe either that Elijah had defeated the followers of Baal in a fair firefight, so to say, or that he ascended into heaven in a fiery chariot (a route to paradise later taken, it is alleged, by the Prophet). Elisha – after whom my grandfather was named – was clearly a pale copy of Elijah, but with fewer improbable achievements to his name.

As for the dietary rules, these were boringly irrelevant, since no Liberal Jew was expected to 'keep kosher' and my mother certainly did not. Not a single aspect of Judaism appealed to my spiritual, social or literary self. Jesus's injunction 'Consider the lilies of the field; they toil not, neither do they spin, yet I say unto you, Solomon in all his glory was not arrayed like one of these' seemed a much more commanding text, and excused close attention to Solomon's glorious achievements (though those concubines did have their charms).

Should I have come clean and told my father and the synagogue that I was unable to prepare for confirmation on moral grounds? I lacked the bottle. I preferred – if preference ever came into it – to skimp the exercises and bluff my way through. During the holidays, there were classes at the synagogue. I should be overdoing it to pretend that they were attended by any candidates for concubinage, or anyone remotely reminiscent of the Queen of Sheba, but there were indeed girls. One or two of them were very pretty. The one with the biggest breasts was called Mona.

There were important changes in the Charterhouse Classics department at the beginning of OQ 1946. The most famous Sixth Form master of the generation before mine, A.L. 'the Uncle' Irvine, retired, making way for Ivor Gibson and 'Sniffy' Russell, who had previously commanded the Under Sixth. Among the Uncle's pupils had been not only Simon Raven but also George Engel, Dick Taverne (who pronounced his final e – of Dutch origin – in those days before he became a Labour MP) and Peter Green. Engel, whose father was a colleague of my father's in Shell, had won an Oxford scholarship with so much time to spare that the Uncle had authorised him to skip routine Sixth Form lessons and find an arcane speciality. As a result, he became a schoolboy authority on Corinthian – can it have been? – pottery, a sort of Godalming version of Sir John Beazley, then the great expert. Engel's achievement was such that, although a Jew, he had to be named Head of the School.

However, the most remarkable, and durable, scholar fostered by the Uncle was, and is, Peter Green, who has been my friend for almost fifty years. By virtue of his learning, his polyvalent industry and his originality, Peter should have become a Regius professor, unless the last of these qualities is the least in demand in Oxbridge professorial chairs. If I have none of his scholarship, he may have shown something of my impertinence in being 'festive' to those whose suffrages, when appointments to the Faculty were being voted, would have been useful to him. Had he conducted himself in a more serpentine fashion, he might have spent a lifetime in the Fens instead of living in Mytilene, Athens, Texas and now

Iowa where, in his latish seventies, he continues both to teach and to sprig the Classical landscape with voluminous milestones and pungent markers. Simon Raven always maintained that Peter, who had little time for Simon's journalistic dilettantism, had been ostracised by Cambridge's Classical faculty because he had not only been in the RAF during his National Service but had also, and more crucially, declined to be considered for a commission, even in that unfashionable galère. This allegation has always seemed quite dotty to me, but that hardly proves that it was without foundation.

Despite his informed insolence, Peter's manifest academic superiority could not be wholly ignored; it won him the Craven scholarship when he was up at Trinity, Cambridge. The Uncle came up to a feast and sat next to Green, P.M., soon after the award had been announced. Legend promises that he turned to Peter and said, 'I understand that you are to be congratulated. In which event, congratulations.' After which he did not address another word to his most brilliant pupil.

My new Form Master was W.O. Dickens, a man of ponderous humour and small wit. He was a respectable Classicist, more at ease with ancient history than with grammatical niceties. I remember little of what he taught us, except for an extra-curricular dilemma which had confronted him when running an RAF station during the war. There had been an outbreak of thefts of plugs from the ablutions. By stealing a plug, the thief was able to be sure of prompt access to one of the vandalised basins, since he alone had the means to fill it. 'WOD''s dilemma was this: should he replace the plugs as often, and as soon, as they were pilfered, thus making their purloined possession no sort of an advantage, or should he remove all the plugs, thus making it prima facie evidence of larceny to be found at a basin which possessed one? Since the first expedient would require, in theory, an infinite supply of plugs while the second needed none, it was no great surprise that the latter was adopted. This, however, required a permanent guard on the ablutions in order to catch villainous other ranks in flagrante delicto, plug in hand. Other beaks – for instance the linguist Lieutenant Colonel Rowan-Robinson – probably had braver war stories but it would, of course, have been immodest to make them known.

My only sight of the recently (perhaps reluctantly) retired Uncle was during his voluntary art lectures. Irvine was a wildly white-haired man with a lisping delivery and a capacious, Bohemian style of dress, as if he were standing in for W.B. Yeats. His sets of slides and other illustrations were projected by a large, hot machine called – with an eruditely accurate duo of prefixed Greek prepositions – an epidiascope. They retrieved a Europe, and in particular an Italy, unblemished by bombs and artillery. The Uncle never mentioned the war as he relived his *amours de voyage*. 'Of all the places I have ever visited,' he told us, 'the one to which I should most care to return is San Gimignano.' It was the first Tuscan town I headed for when I went to Italy in 1952. I found it stark, jaundiced with cheesy stonework, and – *pace* the Benozzo Gozzolis – charmless, despite those famously contentious towers.

However, the Uncle's enthusiasm for Classical art, and for the Mediterranean, primed nostalgia for a world I had yet to visit. There were, it established, more interesting places to spend European holidays than Knokke-le-Zoute. One of Irvine's memorable asides, when it came to Hellas, was the suggestion that the fluting of Greek columns was a formalisation of the draped folds in the long skirts of archaic statues. Was this his own notion or did it derive from some now obsolete or discredited textbook? Peter Green will know.

So far as House life goes, my year in the Fifth Form leaves little trace. I was still in Long Room, but exempt from fagging. If I was taller and stronger, and hairier, I remained, in my own eyes at least, a mere schoolboy. There were more dirty jokes, but small joy in incipient sexuality. The jokes were meant to scandalise rather than amuse. They also tested how much, or little, one knew of the mechanics of forbidden pleasures. The punchline of one, which I disdain to repeat in full, was 'Who's chucking custard around?'; another told of a commercial traveller – such people did seem to have all the fun – who is allowed to share the bed of an innkeeper's glamorous daughter as long as they keep a red blanket between them. Years later – some pundits may guess – the same traveller calls at the same inn. The door is opened by a weedy youth with red hair who can't even lift the traveller's suitcase. When the traveller remarks on how feeble he is, the boy replies, 'So would you be if you'd been strained through a red blanket.' It was as near the gutter as a middle-class education could bring one.

I remember going to 'Baths', where we all swam naked, and seeing a Robinite, whose name was Thompson, standing dolefully by the pool with a very raw-looking erection. It was as if he had been ambushed by some unpredictable affliction which he did his best to ignore. I do not think that he had been excited by the naked flesh of the swimmers; he had simply been visited by one of adolescence's more un-subtle symptoms. Sex was an affliction whose most regular symptom, after erections, was 'balls-itch'; masturbation cured one, if temporarily; 'pocket-billiards' the other.

Because both School Certificate and – much more conse-quential – the senior scholarship exams came at the end of the school year, those of us in the intellectual *peloton de tête* (H.C. Iredale had alerted us to the curious French obsession with bicycle races) became more urgently studious when it came to Euripides' *Rhesus* – a strange choice of set book, since the noto-riously corrupt text is not even certainly the work of the great tragedian and, if it is, is one of his weakest – and Cicero's *Verrines*. The elaborate scorn of Tully's rhetoric, in which suave-ness and savagery were blended, made an art, and a career, of invective. Cicero was the only manifest civilian ever to dominate, however briefly, the militaristic society of Rome; his tongue was his sharpest – if sometimes trembling – weapon. I neglected to note that Tully ended up with his throat cut by people who did not appreciate his jokes. His tongue was torn out and nailed up, with his hands (did he talk with them too?), in the forum. The Roman Bar was never as safe as the Inner Temple, where my father hoped I might be enrolled.

My appetite for the Navy had waned with the Allied victory, but I had little choice, and exercised none, when the time came for me to join the House Platoon. I was measured for very rough khaki at the Armoury, handed a pair of thick-soled, scarcely pliable boots, belt and gaiters, and became a once-a-week soldier boy. We marched around the Surrey countryside, or rehearsed for the Drill Comp. until it was time to di-is-miss! Right turn, two, three; salute, two, three; down, two, three; and bugger off. The ineffective, because genial, House Commander was a biologist called Barnard. He died young, in Malaya.

Although I regarded Corps as a waste of time, I had no moral objection to playing soldiers. We all expected to be called up properly in three years' time; why not get 'Cert A' and so be well placed for a commission? We learned the essentials of military lore, such as never saluting an officer without having a forage cap on; only Yanks did that. I slouched about on Tuesday afternoons with an antique rifle on my shoulder and watched, yawning, while the Bren was stripped and reassembled. I had no ambition to do it blindfold, as corps-fiends allegedly could. Although I blancoed my webbing and polished my brasses and used the handle of an old tooth-brush to rub polish into my boots in a parody of keenness, I was, like the rest of the Lockite platoon, going through the motions of militarism; we none of us wished ourselves, for a second, back in the Army Class. In the event, however, the Corps was to play a crucial part in my Carthusian life.

When I arrived for OQ 1946, at the start of my second year, I was without my ration book. This was scarcely a crime, but since bread rationing was literally on the cards, HAM March told me, quite civilly, that I must send at once for the missing coupons. For some reason, if reason was involved, I could not bring myself to write to my parents and ask them to do as HAM, and routine, required. The same odd reluctance showed itself which, in various forms, has dogged me all my life: despite a usually ardent determination to meet deadlines there is often some trivial duty – a form to fill in, a licence to renew – which I fail to perform before neglect has become an embarrassment, if not a crime.

HAM was a tall, gaunt, nervous, lip-licking, tip-of-the-tongue-between-the-teeth, acolyte of 'Bags' Birley, whose House Tutor (second-in-command) he had been in Saunderites. In a significant move up the *cursus honorum*, Bags chose him as the pioneer governor when Lockites was re-instituted. Even after Birley had departed for Eton, it was as if those baleful eyes were still fixed on Harry March. His ambition was to be a headmaster, as Bags was, but his autonomy was lamed by indecision. Even his severity was not far from servility to his now remote model; the harder he tried to emulate Birley, the more irremediably did he remain, in point of fact (as he would say), HAM.

When my ration book failed to arrive again and again, and my protestations of having asked my mother – *twice*, sir – ceased to convince him, HAM ordered me to go to the Sergeant's lodge with a chit and telephone for my coupons and then to do twenty hours of penal service under the Lockites gardener, who hoed and planted a wide allotment on the far side of Big Ground. The vegetables which he grew supplemented the house's rations; hence it was only, as it were, fitting that I should assist him. HAM's tongue snaked for a moment between his teeth. 'Now off you go.'

The gardener wore a green baize apron, with useful

pockets, and spectacles which glinted, in my resentful eyes, like Heinrich Himmler's. I attributed more malice to him than he deserved, although he did seem gloatingly glad of a pair of extra hands, and feet. I hoed and I dug and I looked at my watch and I dug and I hoed some more. As the afternoon wore on, the lowering sun glittered on the steel frames of his silly glasses.

It seemed as though my every spare hour was spent working out my sentence. I regarded HAM forever afterwards with patient loathing; since it was likely to have damaged my chances of advancement in the House seniority, I never forgave him for my stupidity. Why did I fail simply to write for my ration book before I fell into disfavour? Who knows, or cares? The result of my outdoor peonage is that – although I like gardens – one of the hobbies to which I confess in Who's Who is 'having gardened'.

As far as 'hash' was concerned, I must have worked efficiently: though I gained one fewer distinction in School Certificate than Bryce Cottrell (later a stockbroker) or James Rennie (later a parliamentary draughtsman), I took third place, after them, among the six new senior scholars. Henceforth I should have a star appended to my entry in the school list. Those who had failed to convert their junior scholarships had their unfulfilled promise stigmatised by still carrying only a dagger attached to their printed names.

MacWilliam and Randall and the other titans of my first year had departed to Oxbridge, and with them any urge on my part to play the naughty boy (instead of a tip, MacWilliam had given me his coverless Liddell and Scott and a clutch of Oxford texts). He proposed to read architecture at Oxford.

If festive squits continued to be beaten, as I am sure they did, I was not among them. I did not suffer fools much more gladly, however. Quick to emulate the sarcastic Cicero at their expense, I preferred to seek smarter, older company. As an

223

only child, I was always limited, in the evenings when I was at home, to adult society. The alternative, which I often chose, was to read in my room. Having no radio, still less a television, of my own, what else was there to do? If I no longer played with Dinky toys, I missed the three-dimensional dramas of my confected world. Even in Manor Fields, I was less my natural self, whatever that might have been, than a facsimile of a precocious, but inexperienced, adult. I tried to be the kind of boy that my parents and their friends thought boys should try to be. The Heaths and the Sulises still came every Saturday evening to play poker. I counted out the chips; I watched; no one dreamed of suggesting that I play. I was a spectator of the grown-up world who lacked a world of his own.

Dread of the mass of my fellow Lockites was far greater than any other feeling towards them; I envied the footballing agility of some, and Buchan-Hepburn's left hook, and Sinha's stickwork, and Nicol's fast outswinger. I was so nervous when I was put on to bowl, even in minor matches, that I never realised the ability which Alf Gover declared would take me into the school first eleven, for which Peter May made a century at every home match. Robin Jordan and I watched him as we sprawled on the grass and supplemented our rationed meals (no Copthorne-style soup for Lockites!) with double and treble scoops of chocolate ice-cream, bars of Fry's Sandwich – alternate layers of milk and plain chocolate – and jam-filled doughnuts from Crown, where 'Bloods' had their own pre-emptive queue; scholars never had such priority, however many school half-holidays they might procure.

My confirmation took place either in the spring or in the summer of 1947. The Jews in Palestine were still fighting, by whatever means they could contrive, to be rid of the British and to fend off the Arabs and to establish their own state. I regarded their activities, out of the corner of my eye, only with disquiet. As even Men of Goodwill conceded, terrorist tactics were dissipating whatever sympathy the English might have had, briefly, for the victims of Nazism. Had the bloody Americans and the bloody Russians, for nefarious reasons of their own, not continued to support the idea of a Jewish state, the Foreign Office would gladly have welshed on Balfour and let the courtly (and literally oily) Arabs have their way. If they pushed the bloody Jews into the sea from which, alas, all too many of them had come, illegally, as you might expect, the Jews would have only themselves to blame, and not for the first time: had they not said 'His blood be on our heads, and on our children's'? *Mutatis mutandis*, if you knew what the FO meant; and everyone did.

The only joy I derived from being confirmed was the knowledge that, once the ceremony had taken place, no more brown envelopes would arrive at Lockites from the synagogue. The tradition in Orthodox Judaism was for the bar mitzvah boy to read a passage from the Torah, following the text as it was pointed out by the Rabbi. After he had complied with this ritual, he was welcomed as a full member of the community. Being too well educated to have time to learn Hebrew, I could only compose and read out a prayer in English. Since the composition of texts, in Latin and Greek, was what 'hash-pros' did – as the Arrow would say – 'for a living', I mimicked anglicised Hebraic imprecations with no greater difficulty, or sincerity, than I had Cicero, Sophocles or Ovid. I can only hope – pray, indeed – that the few sanctimonious paragraphs which secured my admission to a community with which I had little affinity have been lost to posterity. It was yet another exercise in style without content, the mark of the examined life of a middle-class 1940s schoolboy.

Before the ceremony, my father took me to Adamson's in Sackville Street to be measured for my first 'proper' suit. This secular initiation into bourgeois uniform was hardly less alienating than confirmation, or than being beaten with a cane. Rimbaud's *'Je est un autre'* has been quoted too often to keep its edge; my feeling, yet again, was more *'Je est un absent'*. God, Simone Weil claimed, is a 'present absence'; scarcely divine, I was, in my adolescence, more an absent presence, capable of doing things in the world in which I had been placed, but not of *being* in it: *Autenticité? Connais pas!*

Material was chosen and held up and a dark blue, woollen chalk-stripe finally selected, quite as if it had not been decided on from the beginning. The style of buttons on the waistcoat – bone or covered – was discussed, but not by me; measurements were taken; and dates made for fittings. Although money was not mentioned in front of me, the suit would cost my father thirty-five pounds, a fat proportion of his weekly salary. He paid it without demur; it was the entrance fee into respectability, a presage of the office wear – no department-store label sewn on the inside pocket – which awaited me further down, or up, the obligatory professional track.

When we went for the fitting, there was my suit on a stiff mannequin. After it was transferred to me, I felt no more real than the mannequin. The head tailor made chalk marks here and there; he and my father looked at me from the back, at length; more chalk marks were made and then, to my unsur-prised amazement (why should anything that happened in England make sense?), the head tailor ripped the lapels from the jacket, jerked off the sleeves and left me, in shirt and underpants, to resume my Carthusian clothes. The suit would be ready for a final fitting within the week.

The only thing about my confirmation that was not fraud-ulent or fake was what I was at pains to conceal: my erec-tions when I was near Hilary Phillips. They were not provoked solely by her (far from it), but her exceptionally pretty and intermittently encouraging proximity meant that what Hilary excited was particularly reluctant to decline.

Mona had bigger breasts, but she lacked Hilary's vivacity and flirtatiousness. Having switched my attentions, I was amazed at how responsive Hilary was to my gauche, and chaste, advances. They took the form only of 'clever' remarks and jejune innuendo. I could not imagine how such a beauty would ever condescend to have her hand held, let alone allow her lips to be kissed.

To say that England was not yet eroticised is to say nothing of the shame and repression which covered every aspect of life below the belt or between the sheets. It is impossible to prove a direct link between Britain's idea of itself in the world, its self-infatuated notion of its imperial importance, and the public prudery of its vocabulary and culture. However, as long as England stood on the pedestal of its own dignity, its leaders had the power, and the will, to make decorum a national obsession. Sex, and even affection, disrupted discipline and made for dissidence; soldiers were trained to 'keep their dressing'. Being uniform in style, and habits, demands unnatural and impersonal conduct. The human body does few favours to ageing leaders; those who wished to retain their aura of potency depended on plumes and high horses, on big cars and big cigars. Hitler had taken care never to appear in a bathing suit; he regarded the notorious films of the Tsar's family bathing naked while on holiday as having contributed to their loss of public respect and thence to The Revolution; their pudenda proved that they were like everyone else, which is never what everyone else wants. England's era of censorious propriety ended less because of the triumph of liberal ideas than because the sexual revolution was preceded by the collapse of global mastery, as was the loss of authority by the Church.

Meanwhile, to the preachers in Charterhouse chapel, sex was a sin outside marriage and a mystery, of which the least said the better, and the more mysterious, within it. It was akin to treason to suggest that members of the royal family did that kind of thing, least of all for fun; when Edward VIII had wanted to, he had had to abdicate. 1066 and All That and our purposefully skewed view of the history and morals of modern England had much in common.

Like a number of other keenly anthropological households, my parents for a while had a subscription to The National Geographic Magazine, which sometimes featured natives in grass skirts and uncovered breasts, but it was still only in Lilliput and Men Only that a white female could be seen naked in any sort of erotic pose. There was an under-the-mattress magazine called Health and Efficiency which, in its affectations of conducting a virtuous black-and-white crusade for nudism, depicted nice-looking young women playing with a beach ball or preparing a picnic in a state of nature, though always with their lower parts either cropped by editorial scissors or fortuitously concealed by (leafy) bushes or sausage-topped primus stoves. Even a frustrated adolescent had to pump hard to be stimulated by their robust activities. To possess a copy of Health and Efficiency was, of course, an offence in Lockites. I should, in any case, never have had the nerve to buy a copy.

In the winter term of 1947, I had just turned sixteen. Not only was I a senior scholar, and a member of the Classical Under Sixth, but I was entitled to a study. My parents gave me an apple-green flexible anglepoise lamp and a thin cotton rug. The school supplied bookshelves, a desk and a chair. There was scarcely room for an (armless) easy chair, but I squeezed one in. My private cell, eight feet by four, was a heavenly elevation after the noise and promiscuity of Long Room. Promotion also entailed being a member of Hall. The sole privilege of this group of seniors was to congregate, with the Monitors, in the very room over one of whose chairs I had bent to be beaten not that many months before, and in which I was now authorised to sit and read today's newspapers.

Hall was between the dining room and the Private Side. HAM, and the strutting little nose-wrinkling House Tutor Mr White, who later committed suicide, came down a narrow staircase at lunchtime and in through a door between panels incised with the names of Monitors of past years (Head and School Monitors were emphasised in red) and out through a further door into the dining room, where the rest of us were standing. The Monitors said grace in rotation. Then we all sat down to see what the hell we were going to get to eat this time.

Although being in Hall meant that we mixed socially with the Monitors, there were limits to our familiarity with them. We might share newspapers and *Picture Post* and *The Illustrated London News* (with its dramatically fanciful line drawings of topical, and often tropical, events) and we had shelved lockers – containing our butter and jam rations – adjacent to theirs, but we never called Monitors by their first names, as they did each other. 'Tubby' Gladstone, Robin Jordan, David Berkeley and I sometimes still went into Long Room to play pingers. We were not slow to pull rank with the fag class and we no longer had to defer to Top Table, which consisted of a trio of our superannuated contemporaries who had failed, or were not yet eligible to take, School Certificate.

My senior scholarship did little to increase my kudos, except among other scholars. Jeremy Atkinson (now a Monitor) and I might have a mutual admiration society, but no one else craved membership. Had I been in the fourth eleven football, or boxed for the school, as Sinha did, I should have been thoroughly venerated, but my new dignity did more to isolate than to earn me respect in the House. Fellow Lockites might fear my wit; they did not fear me. Individually, none had displayed any hostility, which might have warned me of what was in store. I was physically too large to be attacked with impunity, and my tongue too sharp. I was to be ambushed without warning.

In the Upper Sixth, it was easy for witty retorts to make friends, of a kind; the Classics sponsored piercing polemic, provided there was a Golden Age precedent for it, Cicero or Demosthenes, for preference. A.E. Housman's prefaces and *obiter dicta* are serrated with sarcasms and well-turned malice towards other scholars. Richard Bentley's suavely snide reaction to Alexander Pope's translation of the *Iliad* – 'It's a pretty poem, Mr Pope, but you must not call it Homer' – had a trenchancy that the Arrow commended, and emulated. 'Flyting' was an admired aspect of Theocritus's *Eclogues* (which were written in just the kind of abstruse and mock-bucolic Greek that I most feared in unseens).

At sixteen, I was full of desires but without access to the satisfaction even of my mildest curiosity: were there girls who liked to be kissed? Was Hilary possibly among them? I had held her elbow while crossing Baker Street, but that was the height of my sexual achievements. I caressed my solitary pillow with more fervour, much, than I had ever dared display to her. On New Year's Eve 1947–8, she agreed to come to a dance at the Manor Fields restaurant. It was hardly a location in which caution was likely to be thrown to the winds. The strict tempo quartet played standard tunes at standard tempi. I chassis-reversed as best I might (I often danced in retreat, since it made it less likely that I should crush my partner's toes). My champion father cut a more confident dash on the dance floor than I. Hilary and he made a fine couple. There were others in our party, whose identity I forget, and we all repaired to 12 Balliol House to see in the New Year. I seem to remember that someone (a Scot, or someone who had served in a Scottish regiment) was deputed to play the 'first foot' who crossed the threshold with a sooty face and – was it? – some fresh bread and salt. Had I yet read enough Herodotus to know that when the Persian ambassadors demanded those things of the Spartans, in evidence of their submission, they were thrown into a well? I certainly knew more of Ovid's *Amores* than I had had any experience of my own. Soon after midnight, I was alone in the narrow kitchen with Hilary. She managed somehow to bump her elbow and made quite a fuss about it. I was apologetic, but she said, 'Why don't you kiss it better?'. I bent, eagerly, to do so, but found her lips between me and her elbow. Poor girl, she must have despaired of my ever making a bold move. Once she had contrived the occasion, however, I was eager to repeat it, often, and for longer. We went into my room, while the adults chatted in the living room, and made up for lost time and opportunities. God, what bliss it was when her lips parted slightly and our teeth clicked! She was so pretty and so, if briefly, willing. I did not touch her breast or slide any Casanovan hand between her legs (I doubt if I even dreamed of doing so), but our kissing was Catullan in its repeated urgency.

She stayed the night in our spare room. I made no brave early-morning foray, but I did go into her room to say that breakfast was ready. In her pale blue-green pyjamas, without make-up and slightly astigmatic, she looked more peachy than ever. Her breast fell plumply, and as if by mistake, into the V of her pyjama jacket and then my mother was wondering whether we were ever coming to breakfast.

I went back to Charterhouse for the Long Quarter of 1948 imagining what Hilary might next permit, or even want, me to do with her. I was, I thought, some kind of a man and less of a monastic schoolboy. Did my vanity make me more careless of what I said and with what asperity? Maybe. I waited for the post, and the blue-enveloped letters which it would bring from my Baker Street Lesbia. Schoolboy society was, I thought, beneath me.

One night, after exercising my new privilege to work late in my study (the habit of meeting deadlines, but only just, began early), I went alone, and in the darkness, into 'senior cubes'. The long creaking walk, shoes in hand, down the parquet was enough, no doubt, to alert the rest of them as I felt for the door of my cubicle. Suddenly, a cascade of coins fell on the floor. Why? I could not imagine. Then there was another. And I knew. How did I know – after a few moments of nausea and disbelief – that the falling shekels were the signal that everyone had turned, as one, against me? I recognised the symbolism of money easily enough; avaricious Jews and shekels (otherwise known as 'monnith', uttered in a Shylockian lisp*) were integral to the language of malice. I undressed and lay in the darkness, dreading the day, too old for tears and too young to smile.

The usual small noises warned me that day was coming, and then that it had arrived. Lockhart, the butler (whose leather belt was never through its loops), rang his bell. 'Wikey, wikey, rise and shine.' I did neither. I waited till the others had washed, if they did, and I dressed only as the five-minute bell rang: vest, shirt, sweater all in one. When I opened the cube door, they had all gone down to '*Adsum*'. Might the previous night's episode have been a joke '*sans lendemain*', as Harry Iredale would say? I wish that I had cut a less abject figure as I took my place in the dining room in time to answer to my name. In fact, I wilted utterly under a petty persecution which, for no more than a week or two, reminded me that I had no reliable friends. I was never physically bullied, or even harassed. One of my early novels, The Limits of Love, contains a brief, but candid, account of how my hero, Paul Riesman (named for the author of The Lonely Crowd) endures a Jew-bait at Benedict's, my fictional version of Charterhouse. Written only a dozen years after the events it dramatises, my novel somewhat understates the venom of my enemies, as it does the abjectness of their victim. All the

---

*How nice that Venetians are notorious for their subtle lisp!

jokes which were cited against my sorry hero were certainly current at the time (for instance, 'Did you hear the one about the man who went to sleep on the steps of a synagogue and woke up in the morning with a heavy djew on him?'). Such remarks were made as if I were not there; no one spoke to me, no one answered me. My presence was an absence in which I could be abused but never addressed directly. I was 'he'.

In class, nothing changed. No one in the Under Sixth was in my House. Among the clever, I could continue to shine, as best I might. I spent the day in Library or the Studio, but I dreaded the evenings. Locking Up Time was six o'clock; I had to be in Lockites from then on. I sat in my study, with the door locked, and pretended to work. There was a reproduction of Van Gogh's *Bridge at Arles*, in a *passe-partout* frame, on my wall, proof of defiant avant-gardisme. I dreaded anyone coming to my door, and I wished someone would. I looked up words in F.E. MacWilliam's Lewis and Short and wrote them in above the text of Sallust's history of the Jugurthine wars. When finally defeated and taken to Rome to be paraded, in chains, behind Marius's triumphal chariot, Jugurtha was thrust into a pit which served as a condemned cell. 'How cold this bath of yours is!' Sallust reported him to have said.

Many worse things happen to people than to be persecuted, verbally, and shunned, for a few long days. Countless public schoolboys, of all kinds, endured humiliation and fear and wanted to run away. So, God knows, did those in humbler, bleaker circumstances. Are such things worth remembering half a century later? I have small wish to pick old scabs or to rehearse antique grievances. Shame no less than tact forbids a full account of the sullen dejection, with no redeeming show of defiance, with which I suffered the gleeful fools and sly clowns who took pleasure in my fall, and in needling my prostration. I had attained no great height, God knows, but I fell as heavily as if I had. However, no single event in my life was more determining of my future career, in which careerism – with its dependence on procuring the goodwill of others – would, I liked to think, play no part.

The most ignominious symptom of despair was what I wrote to my father:

Dear Dad,

I did not want to write this letter. I write because I must talk to someone, because unless I can speak, I need not exist. Here I do not exist. For days no one has spoken to me. I am the Yid. I never thought I would write like this. It was never my intention. A few days ago, I would never have dreamt of writing. In spite of occasional things, I have never really suffered till now. All my friends, or those I thought my friends, have turned against me. I have no one. They mimic Jews all day and mimic me too. I sit here and shiver. I am powerless. I do not know what I have done or why God has treated me like this. I do not know why there are Jews or why I must be here. I would sooner be dead. Perhaps I soon shall be. I can't hit them, since they do nothing directly. I am not a person. I am a thing: the Yid. It's true, isn't it? I am the Yid. I did not want to write, but I must talk to someone. Don't worry about this, I simply had to write for someone to see, or I should explode.

Poor Cedric! I can reprint this lamentation verbatim only because the text was preserved in an old cutting from the *Evening Standard* which I found among his papers. He had sent my letter to Rebecca West, who had been writing a series of articles about the resurgence of Oswald Mosley and his postwar version of Fascism, which wore the lineaments (as Hitler's did) of pan-Europeanism. She quoted it, *in toto*, in the paper; it was the first time that words of mine ever appeared in print. Many years later, when she had adapted her novel, *The Fountain Overflows*, for television, Rebecca insisted that the

Radio Times send me to interview her. I imagined that she had always remembered my piteous *cri de coeur*. It turned out that she had no idea that I had written anything except a eulogy of Somerset Maugham of whom she too had friendly memories. Willie was a lot nicer to a lot of people than the majority of them cared to recall.

As I reread my letter, and wince, I see, in its stilted terseness – 'It was never my intention' – signs of what I had been reading and how, even in an agony which, however petty, was certainly unfeigned, I retreated from my experience to an account of it. By expressing it neatly, if with a certain incantatory (Hemingwayesque?) repetitiousness, I turned subjection into subject-matter. I do not need to be told that the letter is both artful and callow, self-pitying and accusing. I see myself pinned and catalogued like one of Preston's butterflies, and I almost acquiesce in my own helplessness by the relish of its description. Yet by describing it so clearly, I am already, literally, coming to terms with it. The clipped English phrases may be a touch Levantine in their lamentation but they put the case succinctly enough. Once a thing is said it is no longer the thing it was. I was being forced into being a writer.

If I appended a ritual apology for bothering my father, I hesitated very little before doing so. I was, in truth, not suicidal; I was not in danger; I was in a panic. Even if it had occurred to me to go to HAM, I should not have known what to say; nor had I any reason to expect his concern. My want of religious conviction did not, I now observe, exempt God from the plot. I quote my tearful eloquence without any illusion that it will earn retrospective sympathy. I realise now with what (deliberate?) cruelty I inflicted it on my father, who felt obliged both to do something about it and to conceal my wretchedness from my mother. Am I wrong in sensing that the letter, for all its curtness, very nearly gloats over the news it contains? Affecting only to want to 'talk to somebody', I cursed Cedric with the curse he laid on me by first fathering a Jew and then sending me to school among the Philistines.

Looking back, what interests me is less my own sorry role than the speed and accuracy with which those at the heart of the conspiracy knew how to wound me. How far did what had been happening, and was still happening, in Palestine prime their malice? Anti-Semitism was probably worse in Britain after the war, as a result of the terrorist war being waged by Irgun Svei Leumi and Menachem Beghin's 'Stern Gang', than it had been when Hitler was murdering European Jewry. Post-war British anti-Semitism was rarely violent, though a number of incidents came close to being riots; wisely perhaps, they were little publicised.

My long dread of what other Carthusians might see in the newspapers says little for my nerve, and less for my pride, but it was unceasing during the years before the state of Israel was established. I lacked even the furtive partisan-ship which gives duplicity a secret zest. I was not duplicitous at all: I simply wished that all that business had nothing to do with me, not least because, in my own mind, it did not.

In The Limits of Love, I described a dream (did Freud ever wonder if Jews, with their secret anxieties, dream more elab-orately than most people?) in which I saw myself alongside my father, on the way to the gas chambers. The confusion of my schoolboy misfortunes with the agony of Auschwitz was unworthy, to put it mildly. Is it indefensible? If the dream was indeed dreamed, the author cannot be blamed (except on aesthetic grounds) for reporting its scenario as it was pre-sented to him. If it was not, it can be defended only on the grounds that the novelist hinted that it was intentionally self-indulgent and melodramatic. Does not close reading suggest that even the dreamer – whether it was me the schoolboy or me the young novelist – recognised the gross implausibility of the analogy between school and concentration camp? The section ends:

> A man muttered to him: 'We should fight.' It was his father. Paul said: 'Fight the sky, fight the earth, fight the truth.' The dark foyer closed over the two of them. Paul said: 'Where's Mummy?' His father said: 'She's at home.' The darkness covered their heads. Paul said: 'It's no use now. Nothing's any use now.'

If there is self-pity in this paragraph, there is more self-mockery. The bathetic question 'Where's Mummy?' as good as concedes that the dreamer/author knows very well that he does not fit into the tragic role he has wished on himself. I did not, at the time, see the other Lockites as Nazis; nor did their persecution mean anything to me but the blighting of my social life and the need somehow to retrieve my social standing. I set about it badly by going to one of the conspirators with whom I had acted in the House Play and whom I thought something of an intellectual (he had a very fat volume of George Bernard Shaw on his study shelf).

When I asked him what I had done to deserve his enmity, he was embarrassed, and resentful, that I should have singled him out. He muttered that I spent too much time with people older than myself (Atkinson) and 'things like that basically'. If such a skimpy indictment suggested lack of conviction, it also showed how futile it was to hope for a reprieve. My ostracism was not a matter of just reproach but an opportunity for casual group fun. If my silly case had anything in common with the agonies of those in Europe, it was in the intoxicating vindictiveness of the malice and in the amusement, and sense of solidarity, which the hunt provided for the pack. The Jews may, or may not, have done this or that, but whether they were alleged to be Bolsheviks, plutocrats, white slavers, deicides, Zionists, intellectuals, profiteers, journalists or lawyers, what individual could claim exemption because he or she was none of those things? The anti-Semite will always find, or fabricate, a criminal category into which the Jew falls.

My embarrassing letter home said 'I am not a person', quite as if my relegation to pariahdom had deprived only me of being who I was, if anyone (the Nazis referred to their victims as 'pieces' or 'items'). The routines of denigration are sadly repetitive, whether in the tragedy of the camps or in the farce of public schoolboys having a little fun. What I missed was that those who were at the source of my annihilation as a specific person were themselves escaping from identities which were almost as obnoxious to them as Jewishness was to little Freddie (whom they nicknamed 'The Rose', because of my healthy cheeks, and because it rhymed with having a nose like a hose). Clever kids! Were those who competed in finding ways to hurt me all that interested in what victim they chose? The Yid was a natural for the part, but not only because of his behaviour, not only because he was clever or sharp-tongued: in the routine way of things, that was what he was for.

The Welshman, the Yorkshire thicky, the descendant of Disraeli's greatest rival (who, although always right, never quite got the better of Dizzy), the bed-wetter, the culturally deprived suburbanite, the tinted son of a unique sub-continental peer of the realm, all these soft conspirators needed no darker scheme than to get together at the Yid's expense. In my exaggerated fancy, I saw them in boots and swastika armbands, candidates for the Hitler youth, but their fathers – who had, no doubt, taught them many of their harmless jokes and jewy jibes – were likely to have fought in the war which saved England, and the Yid (who should have stayed in Jew York), from the Nazis. The Lockites who banded, briefly, to spoil my life were not Hitlerian youths; nor were their parents dedicated Mosleyites. Yet they put on the uniform of age-old malice and it fitted them perfectly. Its language spiced their dull wits with facile re-inventions: Berkeley, a good cricketer and our hockey goalkeeper – who was a perfectly nice chap most of the time – could not resist adding to the laughs by saying that I supported Yiddlesex, not surprisingly, since Yidrich played for them. When my small nightmare subsided, David resumed his former amiable attitude to me. Why not? What had he done that was so terrible? Graham Greene entitled one of his novels *England Made Me*; and me, and them.

The blather of abuse to which I was subject was never delivered to my face; it was as if I were not there; I was relegated to an idea. My enemies avoided the physical stuff. They may have feared that I had Buchan-Hepburn's left hook, which I did not, or they may – more probably and more interestingly – have had some instinct to remain somehow blameless, whatever I might do, by needling me only verbally and indirectly. In this way, they remained honestly innocent of any indictable offence; was it their fault if I chose to take things personally?

Apart from the merely autobiographical, the interest of my antique misfortune lies not only in recalling who participated in the Jew-bait (as Robin Gladstone quite specifically termed it, when proposing a resumption at a later date) but also in noticing those who stood idly, or curiously, by. There was, beside these, a class that hardly noticed what was taking place. If most of the Lockites who banded most eagerly against me were fairly bright, none was of the first intelligence. All had got School Certificate at the same time as I, though with fewer distinctions. It is a matter of record that the nub of the cabal was composed of envious peers. My degradation promoted them: to weaken me gave them a common strength. In Sinha's case, he may have been hoping less to prove that he was a white man than to establish the fluency with which he had become one. His badinage lacked the *accuracy* with which Gladstone and a few others pierced my armour. Among those who neglected to take any part in the Jew-bait were both the Scots, the sex-fiends (Tony Trafford *en tête*) and a boy called Garland, whom I used to see in Studio. For the rest, naive Fascism, like so many religions, was attractive not least because it armed individuals with the illusion of corporate muscle, and virtue: human unity is a conscienceless ambition.

Among those who watched, knowingly, but did 'nothing neither way' was Robin Jordan, to whose Hamlet I later played Osric. Robin had introduced me to W.H. Auden's *The Age of Anxiety* and wanted to be a writer. Years later, when he mentioned those few weeks in the spring of 1948, I said that I was silly to take something so transient so badly. 'Frankly,' he said, 'I was surprised you didn't kill yourself.' If he was saying that my passivity was less pathetic than I feared, he was also admitting that he had stood by, without a word or gesture of consolation while someone whom he had befriended was so mercilessly mocked that he thought that he might commit suicide. How often is Gentile sympathy a kind of gloating in drag?

After I wrote that letter to my father, he feared the same thing. Having an appointment with the Headmaster, George Turner, he took the train to Godalming. After 'Bags' had defected to Eton, the school had been uncertain whom to appoint. At first, Birley's deputy took over, a pleasant, red-faced man called 'Tommo' Thomson (not all our schoolboy nicknames were ingenious, though 'Oily' Malaher was a nice one, unless you were Mr Malaher, likewise 'Shag' Williams, the stinks beak who thought Klaus Fuchs had done nothing wrong to betray scientific secrets to the Russians). Tommo was succeeded by Turner, who had recently retired from running a school in Kenya. He spoke warmly of 'my Africans' who had enstooled him as a chief before he left. He was a short, dry, clerically spoken bachelor of small charisma who had been Headmaster of Marlborough before going on his mission to the Kikuyu. He had so obviously been appointed *faute de mieux* and was so unsuited to Charterhouse that neither we nor he quite knew why he had been pressed to take the job.

My father never told me much about what had gone on between them, but I do know that at one point Turner asked Cedric what he proposed that he should do. My father said something acidly tactful along the lines of 'It's your school', to which Turner replied that I had, after all, sought admission to a Christian foundation. Nevertheless, he would try to talk to my Housemaster.

Knowing nothing of Cedric's démarche (which would have more alarmed than consoled me), I remained isolated and hangdog. I continued to turn up to play soccer, although no one else on the team talked to me and no one passed me the ball. Sometime in the second half of a first 'tics match, the other side (Robinites?) had a goal kick, which was taken with some vigour by their goalie. I was so resigned to icy solitude that, though I faced the ball as it was lofted towards the centre circle, I misjudged its flight. Heavy and greased with mud, it hit me full in the face. I fell to the ground and stayed there. No one came near me. When I took bloody fingers from cut lip and bleeding nose, the game was going on, amid smirks.

Later, one of our side, whose name was Alan Morris, a dark, curly-headed, handsome boy a year younger than I, was taking a throw-in. I stood dutifully available, though I knew that I should not be given the ball. He threw it in and, as the others chased it down the field, he said, with a strange smile on his pretty, freckled face, 'Jew', before trotting away. Thirty years later, I gave the name Adam Morris to the Jewish hero of *The Glittering Prizes*. It is not only the mills of God that grind slowly. In fact, Morris was too young to have anything to do with the Jew-bait. It was my small good fortune that

241

class solidarity deterred the cabal from recruiting those below them in seniority, if only because it would have conceded a measure of social parity. The prejudices of elites are often jealously denied to their inferiors. What made Alan Morris's remark worth recording is that he was – and, I hope, is – a (half?) Jew. For a luxurious moment, he was able to be one of them and not one of us. How neatly ironic it would have been if I had had the guts to punch him in the nose! In that case, my only fight would have been with another Jew. The tragedy of Jewish factions in Europe, which so often attacked each other with less restraint than their persecutors, would have been repeated in a Surrey schoolboy farce.

The writer has the sad consolation of hoping, in the end, to have the last word. That bleak ambition, and intention, settled on me like a vocation during those woeful days. I had always had a certain facility when it came to entertaining, or sarcastic, story-telling, but my brief, limboesque purgatory, in the Long Quarter of 1948, determined my life. It did not give me talent; it gave me fuel. Isolation had been thrust upon me. Now I embraced it and rejected the common world: writing needed only paper and pen. Authorship depended (I imagined) on no machinery of promotion; genius was certified – so romantic myth promised – by rejection. Words were more reliable friends than Gladstone, R.E., or even Jordan, J.F.R.. The writer did not apply for jobs or seek company. He proved himself by his brilliance and was published – naive imagination had no bounds! – because talent can never be silenced. The novelist's life was a sort of perpetual examination, which suited me.

Having embraced what I could not avoid, I felt stronger. Did Spinoza not say that freedom lay in the recognition of necessity? If I could not kick against the pricks, at least 'the Rose' could describe them, when the moment came, as pricks. My only petty claim to have been slightly less than a coward is that eventually, when most of the cabal were in Hall, I dared – perhaps because I sensed that they were becoming bored – to challenge them to a series of fights, starting with the weakest. In that way, I told them, more people would have a chance to hit me. When I invited 'Tubby' Gladstone to be the first in the ring with me, I had, it was clear, gone too far, or at least far enough. Within a few days, I was restored to sociability. Was it a relief to the cabal that I allowed myself to be grateful for the truce? HAM may well have been told by George Turner that he had better do something; he may even have done it. My father had seemed quite incensed. You never knew with Jews.

However friendly anyone might be to me from that time on, I never trusted any of them. I smiled, I chatted, I argued, I even amused, but I never revealed anything of myself which might arm their malice in the future. Charterhouse made something very plausible out of me. I vested my anger only in my style, which was wilfully English. Years later, I had one of my characters say, 'I can be very grammatical if roused.' In that spirit, I became a fierce pseudo-Hazlittian critic of, for instance, Film Society's selection of Nightmail for Saturday night showing. Auden's famous verse commentary was, I declared wittily, no more than ordinary; the English cinematic vanity about their documentary tradition has always seemed evidence more of their visual lameness than of any wish to tell the unvarnished truth. Who is Grierson to me that I should fawn on him?

I worked with renewed energy in class because gaining an Oxford scholarship, and its consequent half-holiday, would rub the cabal's noses in their own mediocrity, without my doing anything directly to them, or even acknowledging their existence. If I had learned any lesson it was to bide my time.

I was lucky to perceive myself as persecuted rather than bullied. The distinction is not idle, though those who are persecuted can, of course, also be bullied. I do not claim to have suffered on behalf of the Jews, and I wish that I had not suffered at all, but it is less ruinous to the morale to be able to say, if only to oneself, that one was not simply picked on because one looked soft or had buck teeth. The man who is persecuted for what he believes, as I was not, or for his race, which I was, is forced into awareness of others who have been humiliated, or much worse, for the same reason: even in his loneliness, he is not entirely alone. His self-pity, if he feels it, is recruited to pity for others; likewise his indignation. I was not made more of a Jew than before – nor do I doubt that part of what the cabal disliked was specific to me – but I emerged disillusioned in a way that was finally fruitful rather than laming.

I have known people who were bullied, one in particular whose father removed him from the school (good old Winchester). What such boys endure, or fail to endure, damages them permanently. The bullied child is never reminded of his solidarity with anyone else. His isolation excites no wider allegiance and asks no larger question than 'Why me?'. He concludes only that he is worthless and, when assaulted, defiled. Such boys often proceed to persecute themselves: as adults, they elect to be the pariahs they have been made to feel: addiction and masochistic narcissism become their common features. The persecuted child may have been singled out, but he is also a type; for what it is worth, the Yid finds out how much his petty calvary resembles that of other Jews. He can persuade himself that his case belongs to history, not merely to psychology: it comes to mean something. Through it, he is made aware of politics and religion, of the tenuous relations between individuals and groups; he is forced to grow up. The bullied child is denied the confidence, or the competence, to do so. As an adult, he may bully others, especially women, and/or become a junkie; he never escapes being one of a pathetic kind. However badly he behaves to others, he thinks only of himself and how unfairly he is being treated. Unfortunately for such sad narcissists, life is a school which your father cannot take you away from.

I cannot claim that what happened has given me any appetite for exclusively Jewish company, nor any lifelong piety or sense of community. If anti-Semitism forces its victims into acknowledging their Jewishness, it does nothing to prove that Judaism is their required faith or Zion their divinely ordained destination. Anti-Semitism is given too much respect by seeking only to unearth its deep roots. Certainly, it has its savage and specific strains, but its milder forms can be a symptom merely of a lonely crowd's search for an anti-ism which will give fools a common cause and a common target, a common hate and a common exemption from it. Sartre's notion of the anti-Semite is of a man who wakes up each morning wondering who he is and then, blinking into addled wakefulness, remembers what defines him: he hates Jews. Shades of Pétain's pathetic question, 'Qui suis-je?'!

I played no Samsonian part during those days, but I did – albeit despite myself – endure. Thanks not least to my father's failure to remove me from Charterhouse, I was scarred but not broken. Where else was there to go? As Cavafy reminded his friend, 'Kainourious topous then tha vrees ... etsi pou tee zoee soo reemaxes etho ... s'oleen teen gee teen chalases' (You will not find new places ... now that you have wasted your life here ... you've wrecked it in the whole world). The Jew is going to be the Jew wherever he goes.

Soon after my unhappy episode, Israel was officially founded, thanks more to the Russians and the Americans than to the British, who had first endorsed, and later done their sighing best to abort, its birth. Hilary was much excited by the creation of a Jewish state – so much so that, to my annoyance, she preferred to talk about it than to let me kiss her a few thousand times more.

At the beginning of the next quarter, it was announced that there would be a painting competition. Since Charterhouse had a good deal in common with the Corporate State which Mr Drake had instituted, briefly, at Copthorne, the competition was organised by Houses: each House would have an official entry, selected by the House Man. I had started painting in oils during the holidays. Gladly alone in my room, I did a view over the back gardens towards the hazed skyline of London. I brought the picture back to Studio to finish. When the time came, the art master (he was too nice to me for his name to be memorable) included it in the work submitted to HAM for his official choice of three to represent Lockites. Garland, who did nice still-lifes of bottles and jugs, entered three pictures. HAM chose them all and thus, as if by chance, excluded mine.

The art master was more surprised than I. He decided nevertheless to hang my rejected suburban landscape in the exhibition. It was to be judged by Claud Rogers, a painter of the Camden Town school whose townscapes earned him a mild fame. He looked every inch a Bohemian, with his shaggy beard and his leather elbows, as he walked round the exhibits. When he came to mine, he stopped and made a note before moving on. When all the interested people assembled for his verdict, Rogers remarked courteously on the high standard and then, contrary to programmed expectation, announced that he had especially liked three paintings. He would begin with the one that he placed third. It was mine. He led the company to where my Putneyscape was hanging and indicated the significant forms with which I had so artfully shaped a banal scene into a comely whole. Of course, I had had no more notion that I had honoured Roger

Fry's aesthetic recipe than Monsieur Jourdain that he had spoken prose all his life. Yet I have never won any prize, or been the subject of any eulogy, which gave me greater pleasure. HAM's straight face might have been nailed to his thin, colourless lips. His choices did not win any prizes; nor did Lockites. Who came first? His name was Johnson; he later won a scholarship to the Slade.

Towards the end of that same summer, it was decided by 'Magger Mo' (Major Morris, the Irish commander of the JTC, who drove an MG) that there should be a promotions exam. This involved doing a written paper on military matters and also drawing a sketch map on which dangers and targets were designated for troops coming along the same road as one's own section. Still a private in the House Platoon, I had paraded on Tuesdays with listless regularity. When it came to the exam, however, the usual circumstances procured the usual response: I tried. The questions were not difficult and I was not stupid. When the results were posted I had leaped from inglorious privacy to being an acting corporal (surging up the ranks, I had skipped lance-corporaldom at a stroke). I was now entitled to wear two stripes on my khaki sleeve, which distinguished me from most of the House Platoon.

This promotion scarcely proved my leadership qualities, but it had remarkable house-political consequences. As usual, the end of the school year would leave gaps in the monitorial body. All the senior members would be going, leaving Jeremy Atkinson as Head Monitor elect. His father being a naval man, J.J.W.A. had no inclination to be a soldier boy, even though – since he was already a corporal – he should have become House Commander. He decided that he would have enough to do working for his Oxford scholarship, playing football for the school and running the House. The next in line for high command was, all of a sudden, Acting Corporal Raphael, F.M.. Jeremy therefore informed me that I was to be the House Commander in OQ 1948. I was less flattered than alarmed. My ostracism had been revoked, or lapsed, but I had small confidence in my ability to exercise authority. What if members of the cabal, or anyone else, openly spat, so to say, on my Jewish khaki or refused to obey my orders? I had no way of enforcing them unless – and here came the vital career move – I was made a Monitor. When I told Jeremy, nervously, that I would not be House Commander otherwise, he was unsurprised. He relayed my conditions to HAM who, for all I know, had already decided to make me a 'mo'. By a military fluke, I was translated to high civilian office.

Having attained a position of power, I impersonated authority by adopting the grand manner in which, during my first year, B.S.C.G. Randall had banged the door in order to procure silence when he took the banco hour in Long Room. Would Long Room hush and simmer for me, as it had for him? Here goes! To my prudently concealed surprise, I discovered how easy it was to instil respect. And how sweet to play the stern but interested guardian! I looked condescendingly over little Latinists' shoulders and, if in amiable mood, pointed out, with an instructive frown, where a mistake might be being made. 'Thanks, Raphael.' 'That's OK. Get on with your work, the rest of you.' How sweet is power when tasted raw!

My new eminence, as delicious as it had been unexpected, made House Commandership a Tuesday opportunity for combining rigour with originality. The Oration Quarter was marked by the Drill Competition, in which Lockites had never done better than second from bottom. My opening speech to the troops was, as Thucydides might have said, *gnomee xympasee*, roughly along these lines: 'Here we are again, obliged to spend Tuesday afternoons, whether we like it or not, practising marching about, sloping and presenting arms, doing turns on the march, saluting and minding our dressing. It's all a bore and a waste of time, but what can we do about it? Here's what I suggest. Since we have to do it anyway, we might as well amuse ourselves, and surprise Saunderites and corps-fiends of that kind, by doing it better than anyone could imagine. I'll do my best to play the sergeant-major and shout "Turn" on the right foot, or the left one, as the occasion requires, and you can all pretend to be taking it as seriously as I am, and that way, if we do well, we can be pleased with ourselves twice over: we shall have done well, and we shall have amused ourselves at the expense of those who take this nonsense seriously.'

This speech was made as the platoon fell in outside the foggy Fag Entrance and out of earshot, of course, of Magger Mo or any other member of Brooke Hall. It went down rather well. I had no trouble with discipline: when I yelled, the platoon responded quite as if I were a genuine martinet. My strutting and shouting became something that the rest of them recognised as a performance. I commanded the platoon as if I were directing a play, and my pseudo-squaddies reacted as if they were the cast.

When the officers from Southern Command arrived, with their guardee caps over their noses, and marked us up on their clipboards, they found me and my deputy (Corporal Cellan-Jones, who had one set of exercises to command on his own) to be in convincing voice; the platoon stamped and turned and saluted and presented arms – with simultaneous puffs of greenish blanco – like true troupers. Lockites was placed fifth, if I remember rightly, and I was commended for my keenness. In the post-competition Honours List, Jim Cellan-Jones became an acting-sergeant and I a full sergeant. One of the examining officers asked me if I had considered Sandhurst. I confessed that I had not.

In the middle of all our stamping and saluting, a single figure in lustreless boots wandered, for some reason, on to the parade ground. His forage cap was unbuttoned at the top, so that the usually vertical flaps dangled over his ears. He looked like some grounded Portuguese aviator. One of the regular officers called him over. He was a shambles and a disgrace and why did he not salute? He saluted. Seemingly unabashed by the derision with which he was regarded, he explained that his house platoon – Bodeites – had been dismissed and he was on his way back. Rigid with self-importance, I thought he was a disgrace to the school as he shambled off, after one more reluctant, perfunctory and almost insolent salute. His name was Brian Glanville. He is the only Carthusian with whom I have remained friends all my life, though we scarcely knew each other at C'house. Under entirely different circumstances and at entirely different hands, he had suffered from vicious anti-Semitism, not only in Bodeites but also at his prep school, Newlands. It did not break his spirit, though it may have liberated his wit. Disillusionment and isolation can be very eloquent. Since Simon Raven was scarcely our contemporary, we are the only Carthusian novelists of our day.

At some point during that winter, Field Marshal Sir Bernard Law Montgomery came down to explain to the school how he won the war. Since there were a number of manifest coughs and sneezes in the audience, he instructed us to take one minute in which to cough, blow noses and sneeze, after which he expected our full, silent attention. It was a minute of hacking and trumpeting.

Once we were properly purged, he began – with the aid of the usual maps and a pointer – to spell out his strategic philosophy. He was, after all, the hero of Alamein and Chief of what was still the Imperial General Staff. He spoke in a tone of command which bwooked no contwadiction (though no Oxonian, he did tend to the Oxford blurwing of 'r's into 'w's). Having earned and procured deference else-where, he may never have noticed how he began slowly to lose his grip on his Carthusian audience. The more he spoke, with staccato firmness, of 'deliverwing blow after blow', the more murmurs and exploded giggles came from the body of the hall. How could the Field Marshal know that 'blow' was chaste Charterhouse slang for 'fart'? The more blows he stwuck, and the Germans weceived, the more unsuppressed the laughter he provoked.

A few weeks later, in the same hall, the staff and their wives (not least the fanciable Mrs Polunin, the bilge beak's woman) put on a production of *The Importance of Being Earnest*. It was perhaps a bolder choice than they knew. Modern critics find endless camp jokes in the *double entendres* with which Wilde larded the text ('earnest' itself was Victorian slang for 'gay', which, in 1948, was not yet current slang, though Victorian female prostitutes had described themselves as such). The Brooke Hall version of the play was not only without the smallest indication that it might be a celebration of homosexuality in the form of a romantic comedy; it was also without comedy. Wilde might have emerged from the cloud under which he had been effaced during his last years, but he was not yet a figure of martyred sainthood: who today would dare to remark that the rent boys with whom he consorted were almost certainly under the present age of consent? Oscar might well be treated even more savagely now, and for longer, than he was in Reading Gaol. Though spared the treadmill, he would have to endure a more pitiless and much more explicit press than he did in his own day; and God help him once he was inside. However that may be, he would, I am sure, have derived sublime pleasure from the ponderousness with which his lightest epigrams were delivered and received at Charterhouse. What could have been more memorable – or more camp maybe – than *The Importance of Being Earnest* being performed, and greeted, as if it were Strindberg? It must have required directorial devotion of a heroic order to eliminate from Wilde the smallest indication that he had a shred of humour or one whit of wit.

The last four quarters of my Carthusian life were lived in the comfort of easy authority. I became the Hore-Belisha of a tiny empire, without the menace of an unruly War Office. I no longer slept in a cube (only the Junior Monitor had to do that, in order to supervise the grockles), but in the 'Mos' room', where the senior quartet could keep the light on as long as it suited us and maintained a relaxed, Christian-named familiarity.

The Classical Sixth was the only form in the school to enjoy wicker-seated armchairs at our individual desks. Our hauteur was as unconcealed as it must have been insufferable. Bryce Cottrell and James Rennie were good enough to try for, and win, Oxford scholarships in our second quarter in the Sixth. Simpson, D.A.J., and I fell just below their quality and would wait until the following autumn.

Since the Uncle's relegation upwards, to emeritus retirement, Ivor Gibson had become the Sixth Form master. He was widely rumoured to have a glass stomach, as a result of some unnamed, but very serious illness. His allegedly fragile anatomy kept him confined to his own home, to which the Sixth had to repair for the double periods which serious scholarship demanded. In order to maintain the myth of his enfeebled condition, I.F.G. received us in the conservatory/morning room, where he lay under a blue knitted rug, his rumpled face often badged with puffs of cotton wool. He was either a clumsy shaver or had a very tender skin; probably both. The mole on his jaw was sprigged with a miniature beard. He smoked a pipe and spoke in a voice which might have been whiny but for its catarrhal charm. The knitted rug concealed a variety of texts to which he might want to refer and also a number of biros (which had come down in price and were no longer luxuries). Since the pens were blue, and easily lost in the rug, he attached lengths of white string to them. In this way, he had only to find one of their tails and reel in what he needed.

Gibbo was not quite as immobile as his delicate reputation suggested. Whatever his stomach was made of, it did not prevent him taking the wheel of an rectilinear Morris 8, which he drove with enough panache to detach the front bumper, on more than one occasion, from the chassis.

Gibbo liked me, and I liked him. I fell into brief disfavour only on winter afternoons when, after playing soccer, we had double Latin. It was tempting to arrive early in order to get one of the two chintzy armchairs adjacent to where he was reclining. The trouble was that, having had a hot, monitorial 'tosh', it became very difficult to remain awake, once one was comfortably seated. I tried not to nod off, but when I did, I was wakened by 'Raphael, are you asleep?' 'No, sir.' 'Go home.'

I was obliged to pick up my books and walk, in humiliated solitude, back to Lockites. Shame alone impelled me to work even harder to recover his favour, which he was not unwilling to show. My work improved enough for me, and Gibbo, to believe in my Oxford chances. I.F.G. may not have been a great scholar (Peter Green rates 'the Uncle' way above him), but − a keen racing man − he was certainly a great trainer: he coaxed and nagged and gave us faith in our abilities. When the quality of my elegiacs sagged, he sighed and sucked his pipe. 'What's the matter, Raphael, are you in love or something?' I was in love, madly, and frustratedly, with Hilary, to whom I addressed letters full of passion and high-minded romantic humbug. She responded more measuredly, which impelled me into her arms, if I could get there, in the brief weeks of my holidays.

Although Ivor Gibson was the most inspiring master I knew at Charterhouse (you only need one), 'Sniffy' Russell, whose illegible handwriting made it difficult to profit from his copious comments in the margin, was a good scholar. If he lacked Gibbo's seductive astuteness, he had our respect, though he did once say, to an insolent boy (not me), 'I will

253

not be slapped in the face with a wet fish.' Sniffy, of course, came to the Sixth Form room to take his periods. So too did George Turner, who felt obliged to exercise his right to teach the elite.

Rights do not establish competence: Turner's Greek was risible, his Latin little better. We were incensed, and scornful, when he chose Caesar's *Gallic War* as a text. We had all done the story of Caesar and Vercingetorix at prep school and knew, with cruel accuracy, that Turner, alone of us, was not up to Tacitus or Livy. He did not even do us the honour of selecting Caesar's *De Bello Civili*, which had a more complicated style. Perhaps even that glib self-justifier Julius found it necessary to mask the iniquity of waging war on fellow Romans, rather than on barbarian Gauls, by a more elaborate vocabulary and more complicated syntax. Did Vladimir Nabokov not say, in *Lolita*, that you can always rely on a murderer to have a fancy prose style?

The Sixth contained not only those of us who had been promoted to it but also the residue from the previous year who had yet to take their Oxbridge exams. One of these was the Saunderite Tony Jordan, whom I suspected of being Jewish. He had school colours for cross-country running and a rare facility for Latin versification. He was said to be able to read an English poem one evening and wake up and write out the hexameter or elegiac version the next morning, and we believed it. He was well up to reading Caesar's *Gallic War* without using the *en regard* Loeb edition, which was not true of George Turner. However, Tony was both swift and lazy, which led him to take the Loeb out of Lib. and bring it into class. He opened it on his lap, in the dead ground below his desk, and hence out of Turner's eyeline, in case he was 'put on'. Perhaps he did it only in order to show up the HM's inadequacy. In the event, it enabled him to translate with dazzling acceleration. Poor Turner was not able to keep up and asked, at once plaintive and accusing, if anyone knew who had taken the Loeb from Library. We all did, but no one said so.

Turner said, 'Jordan, will you go to Library and see if it's been returned? I want to check something you just said.'

'I'm pretty sure I was right, sir,' Jordan said.

'Go and see, would you, please?'

Tony managed to secrete the Loeb under his coat as he strolled to the door. He returned a few minutes later, flourishing the missing volume. 'It was there, sir,' he said, 'on the shelf.'

'How could I have missed it?' Turner said.

Had the HM been had, or did he have us? No evidence will ever now establish the truth; evidence (I should be saying a few years later) of how blurred is the line between metaphysical and empirical questions.

As Head Monitor of Lockites, Jeremy Atkinson was, *ex officio*, a School Monitor and obliged to read the lesson in Chapel. Being a member of the Classical Sixth, I too was on the list of those who, in the usual way of things, would have to take their turn at the brassy, spreadeagled lectern. The memory of reading my bit to the Copthorne Sunday evening assembly came back with terrifying force. I had acted in plays, with eager audibility, but I so dreaded having to go down and read the lesson that I played the same card which my father had, all those years ago, after he had gagged on the greasy bacon in Officers' Training Camp: I declared to the Chaplain that I had a conscientious objection, as a Jew, to reading in a Christian chapel. Henry Bettenson, who had taken us for Homer in the Under Sixth, accepted this with becoming tolerance. Cowardice and scruple were, he allowed, indistinguishable.

Bettenson was a solemn cleric (and theologian), but an amusing teacher. Somewhat in the style of old Elam, who taught my father at St Paul's, he could react dramatically to schoolboy crassness. Affronted by a botched translation, he would threaten to hang himself. On one occasion, he affected to be so exasperated that he took off his gown and jacket, removed his braces and slung them over the brass light fitting above his desk. He then climbed on to the desk and looped the braces around his neck. As if in some implausible film, it was at that very moment that George Turner, accompanied by a visiting schools inspector, knocked and, without being invited, walked into the room.

'Ah, Mr Bettenson, not a bad moment, I hope.'

'Very bad, Headmaster. I was about to commit suicide.'

'This is Mr Foreman from the Ministry of Education.'

'How do you do?'

'How do you do? I'm sorry if — '

'Do you need a hand, Mr Bettenson?'

Bettenson climbed down, unaided, and explained that Waring's rendering of the meeting between Priam and Achilles had left him little alternative but to put a premature end to his days. Thanks to Mr Foreman, he would postpone it. The lesson resumed. If the Headmaster understood very little of it, he nodded approvingly. Many years later, I read in André Maurois's memoirs how the French philosopher Alain, who was also a *lycée professeur* in Rouen, was surprised in class by the *recteur* and a schools inspector. He was obliged to reveal that he was in the process of delivering a lecture to an all-male class in *terminale*, most of them eighteen-year-olds, on the duty they owed prostitutes. The inspector asked him to proceed, which he did, explaining to his charges that, whatever their *métier*, prostitutes deserved to be treated with courtesy and consideration. In the inspector's subsequent report, Alain received his highest endorsement. Would George Turner and his companion have taken so civilised a view?

My last year at Charterhouse was comfortable with privilege. Not only was I among the elite of the Classical Sixth; I could also send little boys with messages to the far corners of the school, stay up as late as I chose and attend the Thackeray Society, the intellectual club to which I (and, no doubt, the rest of the Sixth) had been elected. The crustless refreshments were very good. William Rees-Mogg OC addressed my first meeting. His subject was Communism. He had left the school only three years earlier, but he already had the air of precocious senility which allowed him to age so young that since then he has not aged at all. He read out accounts of plenary sessions of the CPSU in which Stalin was frequently interrupted by 'stormy applause in the hall'. The Mogg pronounced this phrase with such well-timed patrician distaste that the rigged enthusiasm of the delegates became horribly comic. I was reminded of *proskynesis*, the dog-like grovelling which the Persian Kings of Kings exacted from their courtiers. The Mogg's hatred of Communism was, however, delivered in so haughty a tone, and with so little recognition of the possibility that there could be anything in Socialism worthy of the smallest respect, that I was driven to a timid defence of the *possibility* that there *could* be more in some kinds of Communism than he, or Stalin, allowed. Although now a seventeen-year-old Sixth Former, a full sergeant *and* a holder of house colours for hockey (recently bestowed by David Berkeley, the House Captain and now first eleven goalkeeper), I spoke to the Mogg in the 'festive' tones of a small boy given a Saturnalian opportunity to cheek a senior. My impertinence was, nevertheless, tentative; his sonorous response put a fruity end to it.

When my turn came to read a paper to the society, moved maybe by memories of going with my mother to vote for him in 1936, I elected to write about Franklin Roosevelt. I had little idea of how to go about it and relied, far too much, on a biography by – can it have been? – Compton Mackenzie, which I found at home. If my source was not detected by 'Sniffy' Russell, he had a good enough nose for cribbed monotony to guess that I had composed little more than a précis of it. Being a mixture of coached cleverness and naive ignorance, I found it difficult to imagine that any printed text was not reliable, even though I believed it when the Arrow told me that Vellacott was a very unreliable Euripidean scholar (was he?). My version of Franklin Roosevelt was that of the hero of the New Deal, without whom Fascism might, as Sinclair Lewis warned, have happened *there*. F.D.R.'s adroit, not to say unscrupulous, manipulation of the Democratic Party, and his accommodations with the Dixiecrats – the Southern racists who might have upset his fat majority – passed unnoticed in my callow eulogy. When Sniffy challenged me, at question time, I told him, quite as if it were an epigram beyond challenge, that the end justified the means. He gasped politely.

I knew that I had not taken enough trouble over the paper, but I genuinely did not know what trouble to take: I have always been intimidated by libraries and even now, when the catalogues are computerised, I tend to rely on stumbling on what I need. No natural scholar, I had started to read a great deal of fiction; I was resolved to be a novelist. I got through *War and Peace* while walking between classes with the rest of the Sixth. Since we had regularly to parade right through the school grounds and across Bridge, on our way to Ivor Gibson's house, I could often manage several pages at a time. As a Classicist, I was markedly less diligent than Cottrell or Rennie; although my verses could be nicely turned, I relied too often on flair. One of my reports from Gibbo said, with puncturing accuracy, that I had arrived at the point where I disliked having put my name to bad work, but not yet at the point where I avoided handing it in. My chances of an Oxford scholarship depended on setting myself higher standards. George Turner appended the comment that he wished that I would criticise myself with half the zeal with which I reviewed films in *The Carthusian*. Fat chance.

In the summer, although never remotely considered

eligible for one of the school elevens, or even for Nomads, I played cricket regularly for Lockites. I even took a wicket or two, but my greatest utility to the team was my fielding in the slips. Since both Buchan-Hepburn and Nicol were among the fastest bowlers in the school, I had plenty of stinging chances to prove how safe my hands were. David Berkeley, a left-hander in the Maurice Leyland tradition, had difficulty in finding a pair of opening batsmen who would stay in long enough for him to sit down before coming in at number three. For the Housematch against Gownboys (the House which had once been composed only of gowned scholars) he asked me to go in first.

Their opening bowler (medium-fast, left arm) was Holt, who had played for the first eleven. The game was played at the edge of Green, in front of Verites. My job was to stay in. I did, for an hour and a quarter of forward defensive concentration. I bored, you might say, for Lockites. In snicked ones and twos, I compiled a mammoth seventeen runs (one more, it will be remembered, than the heroic Bill Edrich had scored against the Aussies, on a sticky dog, on the first disastrous post-war England tour). After the match, which I think we tied, I 'received Houseteams'. This entitled me to wear a black and apple-green striped silk neck-square, should the opportunity arise.

The success of the House Platoon in coming third in the annual Arthur Webber competition added to my lustre. I devised a daring plan for attacking the enemy machine-gun nest which the Southern Command referees located near the usual bushy-topped trees. Routine tactics called for an 'O' group to assess the situation, after which the platoon commander made his plan. Having sited the Bren (to give covering fire), my presumed choice was between left- and right-flanking moves. It was, I suppose, typical that I should seek to be different. I sent the Bren and a couple of chaps to the right, to give covering fire from the flank, and ordered a frontal attack. It was the kind of decision that earned Field Marshal Haig his murderous reputation, but there was dead ground before the slope up the hill, and cover on it. If my plan was reckless, it was at least exceptional.

Rather like Rousseau, who won a prestigious essay competition by choosing to say that science was the enemy of human happiness, because the judges were relieved to read an entry that denied the obvious (and probably right) views of the majority, I turned out to be alone in having decided on a frontal attack and received high marks for martial originality. As a result, I ended the quarter as Sergeant-Major Raphael. Ivor Gibson rigged the end-of-quarter prizes so that I received a book token for my Latin verses; educated to humbug, I spent it on a volume of Keats, whom I never much liked. Jeremy Atkinson and I won a few rounds in the inter-house tennis doubles. My cup did not run over, but it was certainly more than half-filled.

During that summer, Charterhouse JTC was conscripted to Aldershot for a prolonged field day, which involved sleeping under canvas on straw-filled palliasses. The highlight of the manoeuvres was a battle between ourselves and Eton. Since I was by now among the senior House Commanders, I was in command of an attacking force of three platoons. A clutch of regular officers, with armlets, were the solidly invisible neutral umpires who threw thunderflashes around to make the battle louder and more realistic and also told people whether they were dead or not.

I devised an insolent plan to attack the Etonians while they were having lunch. All was surely fair in war, though love was not yet sanctioned. Had not Napoleon won his first lightning campaign in Italy by passing unsportingly through neutral ground in order to outflank and surprise the Austrians? It might have shocked Corelli Barnett, who has reproached Napoleon for his lack of sportsmanship, but we caught the Etonians, flat-footed and unarmed, gorging on

Capuan luxuries: they had *hampers*, and *silver*. They were at once so startled and so uninterested by our oikish enterprise that they did not even consent to pay us the tiny compliment of trying, however belatedly, to jump to arms. They ate on, clearly intent on humbling us with their munching morgue. Outraged by their refusal to surrender, or even, it seemed, to hear my demand that they do so, I grabbed the pale blue beret from their commander's head and waved it, in empty triumph. He continued to chew at a chicken leg (God, it looked good!) and, wiping his lips, was heard to say, 'Give me back my cap,' wipe, wipe, 'you bloody bugger.' I did. No wonder Simon Raven always wanted to be an Etonian.

On the last night before the long summer holidays, there was a Bacchanalian atmosphere in Lockites. Someone offered round a box of chocolate fingers, which we smoked, after biting off the ends as if they were Havanas. Who could deny that we were growing up, even if David Berkeley, drunk on blackcurrant cordial, later sang a song beginning, 'Every-body's doing it, doing it/Picking his nose and chewing it, chewing it'?

Gibson's plan was that I should have a trial run at Cambridge in early December and then try for an Oxford scholarship in the spring of 1950. I had a long reading list for the summer and I had been sufficiently encouraged, and warned, to intend to get through it. I also wanted, very much, to caress Hilary's breasts before I was eighteen. The first ambition proved easier to achieve than the second. Hilary was keen that I assist her with her Livy (a set book for Higher School Certificate, which the Classical Sixth disdained even to take), and she seemed to like my kisses, when I could get them in, between Trasimene and Cannae, but caution trumped desire. We necked, we did Livy, we necked some more and then, almost invariably, her mother came into the room. Being schooled to stand up in such cases, I was obliged to hunched courtesy, with my hand in my pocket. To be young in those days was no enduring bliss.

My mother was not yet forty. It had been ten years since she had seen her parents or set foot in the US. We sailed from Southampton to New York soon after the summer holidays began. My father was going to New York, on business, a few weeks later. My mother and I would travel to Kansas City first and then join him in NYC.

I worked at Cicero's *Pro Milone* and Sophocles' *Antigone* on the boat, between movies and 'horse-races' and bingo sessions, and tried to decypher Theocritus without the aid of MacWilliam's oversized Liddell and Scott. That third prize in the House painting competition had stimulated my interest in the history of art; I was also reading Kenneth Clark and – can it have been? – André Malraux. Malraux, like T.E. Lawrence, was given to exaggerating the scale and precociousness of his reading and it may be that I was limited to less pretentious sources (I had a collection of floppy Penguin monographs, which included Victor Pasmore and John Piper and Fernand Léger). I owe it to Claud Rogers to say that, had I not received his improbable accolade, I should not have equipped myself with the secret weapon of a range of quotations from and about artists that was to have great influence on my future.

I have small memory either of the crossing to the US (can it again have been on the MV *Britannic*?) or of our few days in New York before we took the Superchief, from Grand Central (?) to Chicago. It was a sleek, stainless-steel train of a luxury which relegated the Southern Railway to the age of Stevenson. On the way north from New York, we passed row upon row of anchored 'Liberty ships' each of which had been built, in a process developed by an engineer called Henry Kayser, in a matter of weeks. At the height of the Battle of the Atlantic, they were turned out in their hundreds;

they were launched sideways, which speeded things up for some reason. Now the war was won, and they were rusting junk. America itself seemed never to have been in the war; there were no bombsites, nothing but the same wide and unblemished landscape we had left in 1938. The Depression had yielded to pulsing prosperity. America was now, and unquestionably, what my grandfather had always called it: 'God's own country'.

We sat in the Observation Car and marvelled at mile on mile of thick woods in the upper Hudson valley. I was oddly moved by the trim furniture of the American landscape, not least the white clapboard houses which so often featured in the paintings of Edward Hopper (he was in Penguin too). The journey lasted nine or ten hours, but the only incident I recall is of a young woman covered in sweat running through the dining car calling, 'Help me! Help me! My baby's having convulsions.' She had been feeding her baby and her blouse was more unbuttoned than blouses usually were in those days. Can that be why no one paid much attention to her?

I was reminded of a day when, after going to see my English grandmother, I was sitting on the top of a 74 bus, on the way down Cromwell Road, when we passed a woman in a white shirt walking along the pavement. The height from which I looked down on her enabled me to see down her blouse to where a naked, nippled breast bobbed under the white cotton. When the 74 reached the end of the line, at The Green Man on Putney Hill, I was still rigid with the privilege of what I had seen. Men in mackintoshes queued for hours at the Windmill and paid furtive money to see less. Imagine the shamelessness of a woman who did not – as John Steinbeck put it, in The Grapes of Wrath – 'hammock' her breasts in a brassière.

My mother and I had to change trains at Chicago. Irene was more moved than I to be in the city of my birth. We had time to drive by the Grant Hospital, which was a modest brick building in those days. Chicago might have been Irene's city; it was not mine. The South Side and the Near North Side meant something precise to her; to me they had a pleasing ring but conjured no answering images. We drove under the Loop and the El on our way, through the tenderloin district, with its burlesque houses, to Deerborn Street. The station was in such a tough neighbourhood that we did not venture outside. My mother was reminded of how she had once been crossing the street when some gangsters came out of a bank they had been holding up, cops shooting after them as they did so. She was so alarmed that she didn't notice where she was going and caught her heel in the streetcar track. The gangsters fired back at the cops and Irene was in the middle, trying to disengage her shoe. I daresay she still has it.

Kansas City MO (which its inhabitants regarded as wholly distinct from, and superior to, the adjacent Kansas City, Kansas) was wide and low, with no limit, it seemed, to its recently commissioned garden suburbs. My grandparents had an unassuming apartment in a largely Jewish district. I had left them as a little American boy and returned a (physically) mature almost-eighteen-year-old with an English accent and vocabulary. The first thing I said, as we went into the living room of the apartment, was, 'This is homely.' I intended, of course, to express how cosy and friendly it was. How could I know that, in American, 'homely' meant ugly?

My gaffe was laughed away, but it proved how far I was removed from the world in which I had been small. God help me, I had been translated into English; I was a tourist from a shattered world visiting one which was not only intact but infinitely enriched. What had impoverished Europe had brought a boom to America. Where were the bread lines now? Kansas City was opulent with ideally landscaped mini-Levittowns, all of which discriminated against black – and many against Jewish – tenants. The houses were sometimes duplexes but they contrasted grandly with the pre-fabs which were the Labour government's post-war answer to the housing shortage in England. I had never before seen picture windows, with their wide, clear views of the instant gardens and imported hills which had been trucked in to lend undulating variety to the great plain of the Midwest.

My Englishness was cute, and inextricable. I observed my mother's birthplace, and the many people she still knew there, with compassionate curiosity. How could anyone who had seen Denis Compton want to go and watch the Kansas City White Sox 'batters' slogging, or missing, the fat balls thrown at them by the Baltimore whatever-they-weres? The double-header night games were exciting only because they had a lurid vulgarity not to be found at Lord's, and because of the hot-dog men who climbed through the bleachers with their creaking baskets of cheap treats. America was a land of plenty of plenty: you could eat all the fried chicken you wanted for $2.19; and I wanted a lot.

I spent earnest mornings in the ancient world, conning dead languages. I must have been unique among all those living within five hundred miles of where I frowned over Tacitus and Thucydides. I was irremediably alien from the interests and culture of the kids with whom, in the evenings, I went on motorised treasure hunts or hung out in the innocent way of 1940s provincial Americans, all of whom were so normal, so white-toothed, so freckled, so nice-right-through that they might have been drawn by Norman Rockwell, whose down-home illustrations badged the covers of the *Saturday Evening Post*. Oh those pot-bellied stoves!

Everyone was real nice to me in Kansas City. Yet the weeks we stayed there were more dutiful than exhilarating. I saw what I should now never belong to, if I ever really had, and I was happy to leave for New York, where we were to spend several days before sailing back to England on the *Queen Mary*. The only change KC worked on me was in my appearance. Some distant cousin had a clothing store and I had been taken care of with new fawn pants which had a zipper instead of fly buttons. What Carthusian had ever heard of such a thing? I also had shirts with button-down collars, and loafers. The trousers were very similar, in colour and cut, to those of the first lootenant's uniform which Irvin, my mother's kid cousin, had worn when he last visited us in Manor Fields.

New York was the place. I had been with gangs of teenage kids in KC, but I never went on a solitary date with a girl. In New York, I once again met the little girl with whom I had played in Central Park. I was nearly eighteen; Mary Jane Lehman had to be about the same age. She was small and pretty, with fair curly hair and a freckled smile and a good figure. I could not believe my luck when she seemed free to see me pretty well when I wanted. Unlike Hilary, she did not even pretend to be busy. On our first night back, she took me to see the sights.

We went to the movies in an art house near 42nd Street. They were showing Ben Hecht and Charles MacArthur's *The Scoundrel*, with Noël Coward playing the wickedest, wittiest man in the world. The second feature was *The Invisible Man*, with Claud Rains. He appeared for only ten minutes, and then spent the rest of the movie with his face covered in bandages. I hardly noticed him, or the mackintoshed Noël, because I had no sooner put my arm, with infinite apprehension, around Mary Jane's shoulders than she turned her face to mine and expected to be kissed. While Coward behaved really badly, and then penitently, on the screen, I kissed a girl who was pretty and unreluctant and liked being kissed, a lot.

After the movie, we went to a deli and then we walked through a Times Square devoid of pimps or pushers. The 1940s were innocent years in the US. There was a big fun palace where you went downstairs and played pingpong. We did some of that and then we walked back up town towards Central Park West, where 'Jinx', as she now called herself, still lived. I could not walk very easily without declaring my desire, but if she noticed she was more amused than shocked. She did not seem shocked, or surprised, by anything. I could not swear that it was love, but I certainly fell into it. I could not believe my luck when we got back to her parents' apartment and resumed, on the couch in the living room, the long kisses which tasted like the fruit of paradise. What had I been doing in England? How could I have suffered so abjectly for the uncertain pleasure of Hilary's sporadic favours?

In the early hours of the morning, I heard a door open in the corridor and soft steps on their way to the living room. I wiped lipstick from my mouth and composed myself to look innocent as Jinx's mother, Teddy, came into the room in a floral wrapper.

'Hi, kids,' she said. 'Are you OK? Got everything you want?'

'Yes, thank you, Mrs Lehman.'

'We're fine,' Jinx said.

'You need anything to eat, fix yourself something, OK? Have a good time.'

She went back to bed. Is it possible that mothers of that kind existed in Mr Attlee's England? She had as good as encouraged us to neck the night away. I was almost as shocked as I was liberated. There was no humbug quite like a 1940s public-school humbug. Mary Jane was not only attractive, she was so *happy* to be attractive. When I said I loved her, she just grinned at me. I can now guess that she had never met anyone who more ridiculously combined anxiety and passion. My desire was as obvious as my attempts to avoid it embarrassing her. But it didn't embarrass her one bit. It pleased her, for God's sake.

We were going to sail for England in two or three days. How could I bear ever to be separated from this pretty, eager, laughing (but not silly) girl? The next night, I had a date with the daughter of another of my mother's friends. Her name was Lois. She was tall and dark and elegant, I guess. Her hair was pulled back in a ponytail (Jinx's was curly and short) and she had a drawling languor which she thought very sophisticated. Her mother was a judge and a Republican, but nice.

Lois was fine. We had been given tickets to the theatre: Henry Fonda in *Mr Roberts*, a realistic comedy set on a merchant ship in the war. I sat chastely with Lois in the stalls. People did not neck in the theatre, so I was spared any invitation to instant betrayal of Mary Jane. In the interval I flirted with Lois, somewhat in the style of Noël Coward's wickedest man in the world. I was, after all, an experienced New York roué.

As I was coming back to Lois with a couple of Cokes from the bar, a middle-aged man almost bumped into me.

I became rather English: 'Excuse me, sir.'

He looked at my flushed face and then at Lois and he said, 'I'll bet you're one hell of a ladies' man.'

Not 'will be' but 'are'! Why would anyone ever want to go back to England? Where was Thucydides now? To hell with Plato. Only Ovid scanned in New York.

After the show (of which I remember only the repeated call over the ship's PA system 'Now hear this ...'), Lois asked me back to her parents' apartment. I had told Jinx, with anguished apology, that I was not able to spend the early part of the evening with her but that I might be free around ten. 'Fine,' she said, 'call me at home. I'll be there.'

Lois's parents were out. The apartment was comfortable. The opportunity could not have been more sweetly offered. I kissed Lois for a while, because I did not want to hurt her feelings, but I felt like a traitor. In my heart, I was true to

268

Jinx. I thought only of when I should be able, without giving offence, to look at my watch.

'I really have to go,' I said.

'It's only just ten.'

'That's the thing. I wish I didn't, but I do. My folks...'

Oh the sweet uses of false sincerity! All the ruses which modern kids have used and discarded, I daresay, by the time they are twelve were new and thrilling. 'Si la jeunesse savait...' It was never more true – at least in the milieu that I, alas, was in the middle of – than when I was almost eighteen. I kissed Lois once more, waved, hurried to the elevator – wiping her too-dark lipstick from my mouth, and teeth – and ran to the nearest telephone booth.

'I'm sorry. It's a bit late, but...'

'Come on over,' Jinx said. 'I'll be here.'

She was; she was. By some miracle, I was able to return to exactly the same dream I had enjoyed the previous night. I had never been as happy as I was in those few days with Jinx since I left Manhattan in 1938. What the hell was I having to go back to school for? What did I care about Oxford? I wanted to stay in New York and make love with Mary Jane. As I kissed and kissed her, and she let me caress her pretty breasts, she told me that there were all kinds of things we had not yet done that we could, and would. She told me that. Was there a girl in England, no matter how wicked, who would tell you that she wanted to do the same things you wanted to do? If there were, you did not meet them at the Liberal Jewish Synagogue. Hilary was pretty, and at some times less wary than others, but making love to her was Sisyphean: you always started again at the bottom of the hill, so to speak, and never reached the peak. Jinx and I gave each other a thousand kisses and then a thousand more. We did not make love in the full sense, anything like, but we were happy. I was more than happy. How should I ever bear to be away from her? Did she have other dates, a regular boyfriend? My suddenly licensed vanity had no doubt that she was now entirely devoted to me. She wanted me! America was the most wonderful place in the world. There was nowhere else.

On our last date, on the morning when my parents and I were due to board the Queen Mary, Jinx wore a light cotton suit, with a little bolero jacket and a very low-cut blouse. She combined boldness with sweetness. She showed me her breasts like a promise of what was to come. I swore that I would write to her as soon as I could; and she would write right back. I had been given love and now it was taken from me. Could I have refused to go? Reality produced its chilly handcuffs and led me away, a moral Crippen fated to repatriation.

I waved and waved as my best girl grew smaller and smaller on the pier. Did she have a date that night? I was sure that she would be as faithful to me as I meant to be to her. There was nothing like an American girl, nothing like that American girl. Jinx, Jinx, Jinx; I could think, and probably talk, of nothing else. What had happened to my life that I should care who was going to be Head Monitor the following quarter? Jeremy Atkinson had won the Holford Hewitt scholarship and departed to Christ Church, Oxford; I should now be even more pettily important than before. What was Carthusian importance compared to Jinx's mischievous passion?

My mother was not sympathetic. She had regrets of her own. She too was sailing back to a glum, bankrupt country where shortages had made joylessness an ingredient of patriotism. Irene grew increasingly impatient with my lover's sighs. Did I have the time, or the wit, to consider whether my advertised longing for Mary Jane excited my mother's jealousy? She and I had not truly been friends, and we both knew it, since the day that I went to boarding school. The reasons for sending me were unarguable, but she felt that she had betrayed me. She could never quite forgive me for making her do it. We had talked a lot, in my adolescence, and laughed at many of the same things (not least Leo Rosten's *The Education of Hyman Kaplan*) and I admired her appearance and style, but we were not, as the cant has it, *close*. She never played the conniving American mother as Teddy Lehman did: she never seemed to want me to be happy, least of all with a girl.

My father was quicker to warn me, again and again, against the dangers of that sort of thing than to encourage me to take pleasure in it. Sex was a trap and could be an embarrassment: he found it easier to tell me about what to do after having wet dreams (wash) and of the necessity of using French letters than to suggest that I should enjoy what lay ahead. Who would have guessed that he had been a lounge lizard and, when the music was right, a dago? Though he might be in his underpants, with his face half-lathered, as he lectured me, he was never more bowler-hatted, metaphorically, than when 'having a word' about the pitfalls in the road ahead of me. It did not occur to me to wonder why he was at once so reticent and so anxious. His attitude echoed the advertisements about VD in the underground which announced, in grim print, 'Clean Living is the Only Real Safeguard.' English youth was advised to resign itself to abstinence, if it could manage it, or (though this was not expressly recommended) to masturbation, if it could not. Even then, some specialists insisted that tossing yourself off led, if not to blindness or hairy palms (a dead giveaway), at least to bags under your eyes. Marriage was the only cure.

Shipboard life was very much as it had been before the war. The menus were just as copious (since the Cunarders could stock up in New York) and the wooden cut-out horses still raced; bingo was still called; pingpong was still played. Joan Crawford was big-eyed at the movies, and Jimmy Cagney was a Yankee-Doodle-Dandy. The dance bands pandered to foxtrotters in all classes except steerage. Why not have a good time? I wanted to be with Mary Jane. I thought of her breasts under that skimpy bolero. My zippered trousers resisted the thrust of my imagination.

My mother's patience was exhausted one evening as we stood by the rail and I was still sighing as if no one had ever known such woe before. The bad loser had lost what could never be found in surly, careful London. When would I ever be happy again? Easy: never, unless I could return to New York which, in my hot fancy, stood only for Jinx Lehman.

Suddenly, my mother was telling me of her troubles. She did not specify what exactly they were, though the death of Irvin Weintraub, to which I gave no thought, was recent enough to make my small pains indeed ignominious. Europe was thick with corpses, but death had no reality to me; it had happened to others and never touched me. It was that night, on the long, empty Cabin-Class promenade deck, with its brown rows of half-folded deckchairs, that Irene told me the family secret: Cedric had fathered a child before he was married and, somewhere in the world, I probably had a sister. Molly, my father's mistress, had promised him that she could not have children. She was a broker on the Baltic Exchange (of how many women was that true in the 1920s?) and she was not Jewish. When she told Cedric that she was pregnant, his parents paid her to 'go away'. Not long after that, he went to India. That way, there was no chance for Molly to exert pressure on him. The rest I knew, didn't I? Yes, I did, but I saw it in a different light.

Why did Irene choose that moment to tell me all this? My half-sister's existence had not come as a recent, disillusioning shock to her; Cedric had very properly confessed before asking her to marry him. Perhaps she was tired of my wishing all the virtues on my father; perhaps she used the scandal, such as it was, to cover some grief of her own about which she did not care, or dare, to be explicit. In mid-

Atlantic she informed me that my father was not the man I assumed him to be; and implied, without saying so, that she might not be the woman I thought she was. Not yet forty, was she simply jealous of my unconcealed passion for a young girl? Whatever her motive, I was, in those few moments, divorced from her. I did not despise or dislike her for it, but her announcement insisted that there was an unsuspected distance between how I thought things were, within the family, and how they really were. The effect was less to shame than to drive me away. As in a dream, I felt no particular emotion; my reaction was intensely visual. What I saw, in those few seconds, is there for ever, as often as I care to summon it. I can see the long, caulked planks of the deck stretching to the saloon door and then my father's face coming out, on a neck which is, on this sole occasion, elongated and almost scrawny (in anatomical truth, Cedric had a very short, thick neck). He does not step over the high, steel threshold but leans out to look along the deck to where Irene and I, like shipboard lovers, are standing, apparently together and, in spirit, apart. The light glints on his rimless glasses and he smiles in a way that touches me; it is so marked by hope and by uncertainty.

It would be untrue to say that I came to dislike my mother from that moment. She remained, and remains, someone of whom I am proud, in many ways: she is elegant, clever and amusing, and she has been a loving grandmother and great-grandmother. No one who meets her fails to like her. Why what happened that night, for whatever reason, on the Queen Mary had the effect it did on my feelings for my parents, I cannot say, any more than I can why Irene ever told me what she did, when she did. There it was. The spoilt boy resented her presumption that my longing for Mary Jane was nothing compared to the things that had happened to her.

Quite soon, I began to regret, and resent, that my father (a

Casanova!) had posed for so long as the vessel of morality. Why had he given the impression that sex was a visitation, less painful than boils, but – unless you were careful – with much more serious consequences? He could more honourably, and so liberatingly, have told me the truth and encouraged me to have as good a time as he had, though not before taking precautions. If only he had said, 'Go thou and do more or less likewise!', as he did when he had driven the ball straight down the Wimbledon Park fairway.

Games had a clearer claim on my father than life itself; in some respects he preferred them. In a game, you did your best; within the rules, your conduct, allegiance and purpose were simplified beyond doubt. Life was more complicated; its ends never gathered into a single point. Though 'philosophy' meant little more to him than a kind of stoicism, tinged with what he remembered of Socrates, it retained its dark blue dignity for my father, but he never went much further, during his adult life, than listening to C.E.M. Joad on *The Brains Trust*. He did much reading, but little of any seriousness; he spoke with suburban artlessness of 'long-haired poets'. He respected brains more than learning, wit more than Lit.

Books were a diversion, not an inspiration, to Cedric. The only one he ever recommended to me with any force, in my adolescence, was Dale Carnegie's *How To Win Friends and Influence People*. He feared, with some justice, that my sullen air, whenever I was baulked, would stand in the way of my success. He did not want anyone to call me 'that sulky young man' as they had him. Nothing alarms a father more than a son who takes all too evidently after him.

What I was successful *at* mattered less to him than succeeding, with a smile, at something. He begged me to take Carnegie to heart; Dale Carnegie's text was, and is, a bible for Babbittry; it instructed America in the uses of insincerity. Recommending flattery – what Carthusians called 'groising' – in order to ingratiate oneself with those from whose good opinion one hoped to profit, Carnegie codified the marketable perversion of civilised values. Honour, truth, friendship, perhaps love itself, were to be recruited to the interest of material self-advancement. *How To Win Friends* is probably among the dozen most blandly wicked books ever written. Carnegie was a Machiavelli who advised the mediocre on how to become merchant-princes. To recommend his nastily plausible manual, as if it were by some up-to-date Lord Chesterfield, revealed sorry ambitions for my gentlemanly future. Cedric might as well have encouraged me to remain an American Jew. I took my revenge on Carnegie, and paid a sort of tribute to him, when – in 1960, and under a pseudonym – I wrote a precociously cynical, and briefly notorious, little volume called *The S-Man, A Grammar of Success*.

On the way home on the *Queen Mary*, I had my eighteenth birthday, and the pound was devalued. One day it was worth $4.00 and the next it was worth $2.80. We had been among the last visitors from England to the US for whom a pound was really a pound. The dollar had always been a function of sterling, at least in British eyes; now the pound was, and would remain, a function of the dollar. The US had first won the war, and now the peace.

Did Hilary Phillips sense that I had had a small adventure in New York? She was much nicer to me. I took her on the Round Pond in Regent's Park. She borrowed her sister's flat one evening and told me about a man she had met and the things he had wanted to do. We kissed less innocently, though we never did more than kiss. I remained an overgrown schoolboy, even if I did have zippered pants.

I did not wear them when the time came to return to Charterhouse. Once back, I might as well never have been away. In the new House Seniority, Howard Aplin, an impeccable mediocrity, had been made Head Monitor. I did and did not resent being passed over; I rather expected it. HAM was not my friend. I was, however, wryly amazed to discover that Robin Jordan, who had always denied any appetite for office, and officiousness, had not only been made a Monitor (which his seniority and all round 'spoeyness' merited), but also a School Monitor. By virtue of this, he not I became Second Monitor. The twinge of jealousy, and loathing of HAM for having contrived this humiliation, proved that, even after Mary Jane, and zippered trousers, less had changed in me than I might have wished. Something had, however: the English world still had a certain authority over me, and I still wanted to shine in it, but at the same time I saw it to be prim, dated and absurdly smug.

It was now sweetly amusing to give the impression of taking C'house seriously. Resuming my weekly role as a sergeant-major, I once again yelled the House Platoon into readiness for the drill competition, quite as if it mattered a damn. This time, I told them, we might as well win the bloody thing.

The main thing, however, was to get a scholarship to Oxford. Ivor Gibson had already told me that I should have a trial run at Cambridge, where he had half a dozen candidates from the Sixth whom he distributed through the various groups of colleges, so that we should not baulk each other. My group included St John's (Gibbo's first choice for me), Queens', Christ's, Emmanuel and Sidney Sussex (imagine having to go there!). Still determined to emulate my father and go up to Oxford, it occurred to me that the Holford Hewitt, which Jeremy Atkinson had won the year before, and was open only to Carthusians, would be an easy way in. Robin Jordan had said that he too was thinking of applying for it, but he should not be a formidable a rival. The award was open to specialists in all the Sixth Forms, including history, science, modern languages and so on, but a Classical senior scholar could expect to prevail.

I was now an elderly child, happy to parade through the house with senatorial *gravitas*, correcting the plebs with a sigh and, at last, addressing my peers by their first names. I was much younger when I wrote to Mary Jane. She responded as ardently as I might hope. Her letters came in small mauve envelopes and they were lightly scented. She promised that we should one day enjoy lying together, sated, 'flesh on flesh and bone on bone'. Sated! I wrote back that I could not wait. But I did. I wrote to Hilary too, and she to me, but without Mary Jane's explicit ardour. Both dear charmers were absent, but how sweet it was to know that one had them both, sort of! And how cruel to have neither in truth! It was enough to make one want to cycle to Guildford with Tony Trafford.

Tony's father was a doctor. He had assured his son that sex was a pleasure, not a crime, still less a sin. Tony was a fairly bright and entirely shameless boy. He showed small interest in House politics, though he 'turned up' (played games) willingly, and ably, enough. His main exercise was cycling to places where girls could be found.

I am not sure at what precise stage in our parallel adolescences a girl called Elaine came to Lockites as housekeeper. One of her duties was to help Mr Lockhart, the butler, with serving both breakfast and 'home bill', the Carthusian word for high tea. The bill for ordering extras, such as eggs and bacon, had originally been sent to parents; the name persisted when the practice was abandoned. Breakfast and home bill were served from the butler's hatch; juniors lined up one side and seniors on the other, with the right to 'brick in', of course.

Elaine must have stayed at least as long as a summer term because, as the weather warmed, she took to serving the morning porridge, and the evening baked beans, in a shortish white coat with, so our hot gazes perceived, very little if anything under it. She had a pallid Slavic face, with sloping cheekbones and clear, grey eyes. As she leaned forward to serve us, her breasts were thrust prettily, and provocatively, before us. Did she know what havoc her unguarded cleavage caused? Did she not? Seconds were never more popular, no matter what the menu, than when she was at the hatch. She did not flirt; she did not smile; but oh that V-necked white coat of hers!

I cannot be sure whether what Tony told me, sometime later, is wholly true. Is scepticism or envy a more likely reason to doubt that he did indeed make love to Elaine? He was very specific about their arrangements. She slept on the Private Side, of course, but her attic room could be reached through a door beyond Music Room. This had, I suppose, to be left unlocked in case of fire. Tony would get up in the middle of the night and walk, as uncreakingly as possible, along senior cubes, through the forbidden door and along to Elaine's bedroom.

Jealousy and a sense of moral obligation, if they could be distinguished, must have impelled some virtuous Lockite to 'show up' Elaine's lucky lover. Tony was hardly reticent about his amorous triumph and, since there was a House Purity Society (indeed there was), whose members disapproved of filth, and a long tradition of self-righteous delation, it was not difficult to imagine who was likely to have betrayed him. The founder of the House Purity Society was fond of singing the song, 'She'll be wearing pink pyjamas when she *comes* ...'.

Tony told me later that HAM asked him if he had indeed been doing what, um-er, had been reported to him. One can imagine the nervous tongue between the grey lips. Tony did not deny it. HAM said that he would have to call Dr Trafford forthwith and have him come and collect his son. Such conduct was unendurable. Meanwhile, Tony should pack his trunk.

Dr Trafford was not only a medical man, he had also been an amateur middleweight boxing champion. He drove up from Epsom (I sometimes visited the Trafford house during the holidays) and, to HAM's amazement, failed to share the Housemaster's view of his son's delinquency. He did not accept that Tony had been delinquent at all, unless he had forced himself on the girl. Had he? HAM admitted that there was no suggestion of that. Well, then, since Tony was a normal, sexually ripe adolescent, what did HAM think he should do about his perfectly natural, and very demanding, sexual desires? That was not, in point of fact, at issue. Dr Trafford's son had broken school and House rules and there was only one penalty for that kind of thing.

Dr Trafford asked whether HAM intended to be a Housemaster all his life. No, in point of fact, he couldn't be; after fifteen years there was always a change. Did he then hope to become a Headmaster somewhere? HAM did not see the relevance. Dr Trafford did. If, he said, HAM persisted in the absurd course of blighting his son's life, and so put a black mark on his school record, he would bring a law suit against him for defamation of character.

'You will lose,' HAM said.

'Possibly,' Dr Trafford said, 'but not before counsel puts you and your cowardly prudery in a very bad light indeed. If you persist in wrecking my son's future, I shall do my best to do the same to yours.'

'This kind of behaviour is against the rules. It must be punished.'

'Then punish it,' Dr Trafford said. 'I should never have been brought into this. Proceed as if I hadn't.'

Tony was gated for the rest of the quarter. Elaine was, of course, expelled. I doubt if her subsequent career was greatly blighted.

I had noticed that all the Cambridge essay papers in my group had one question every year concerning art or the arts. Since my third prize in the painting competition, I had begun to think that I might be a writer *and* a painter. I had always been interested in the subject, but Claud Rogers had licensed its becoming a small obsession. I prepared myself, with quotations and a plethora of names, to answer that regular question, in whatever form it was posed. Art became my banker. If there was no question on it, I should have to waffle effectively on something else, but with luck I should not have to rely on my Latin and Greek alone to impress the examiners. If I had drawn the right conclusion, and my bet came off, I should have no one to thank but myself. It was revenge of a kind against a school which I had never wanted to attend and with which, despite Gibbo, I always felt at odds.

Whether from cowardice or indifference, I still went to Chapel on Sunday evenings. Had I wanted to make a conscientious objection, I might have succeeded, but I liked the hymns well enough. I was, however, less punctilious in getting to Chapel on weekday mornings, either because I was lazy or because I was still trying to improve my Greek verses. I would wander up Lockite steps in time for school and, though I still did not (and never would) have the right to walk down the middle of the road, amble into the Sixth Form room as the others came out of Chapel. The Sixth now contained the previous year's Under Sixth, which included a few reputed hot-shots, not least Lloyd, G.E.R., who is now Professor Sir Geoffrey Lloyd, the expert on Greek science and a fellow of King's College, Cambridge. I was wise to leave before he had the chance, which he would certainly have taken, to move ahead of me.

On Sunday nights, there was a sermon, nearly always from a visiting preacher. I did not listen with much interest to what the Provost of Guildford had to say on a dark autumn evening 1949, but – even as a senior member of the school – I was still wary of any mention of Jews. The old man (he must have been sixty, for God's sake) was talking about

Jesus's life when he was a young boy and apprenticed to his father as a carpenter. 'We can imagine how hard he worked, and how good a craftsman he became. He and his father would make all kinds of things and then, at the end of the week, Jesus would take them to the village storekeeper to sell them.' The preacher cleared his throat. 'And the storekeeper – *being a Jew* – would give him as little for them as he could.'

The Provost got his laugh, and smiled slightly, before making his moral point, whatever it was. He had scarcely called for a pogrom, or been greeted with *Ziegheil*, but I was raw, and angry. If the Head of the school, or even George Turner, had let slip such a remark, I might have pretended not to hear it, but I was incensed that a preacher (I retained a naive belief in the good faith of the Anglican clergy) should display prejudice, and play for laughs, so smugly. The fact that he was supposed to be good added scandal to malice. Was the preacher an opportune scapegoat for Gladstone's cabal whom I had confronted, not long before, with such sorry want of panache? It is always easier to attack a single elderly hypocrite, who has to pretend to be good, than a gang of young louts who are out for blood. The Provost was practically a bishop – and hence could be shamed.

Not unlike my father when infuriated by his uncle Jessel, I hurried back to my study, sat down and wrote the Provost an unguarded letter. Cicero sharpened my irony and inflated my style. Less abusive than unrestrained, I told the old bastard that he had repeated the same kinds of things which the Nazis had said (as if they had ever been so moderate!) and that his remarks were a particular disgrace when uttered in the War Memorial Chapel, since so many – some of them Jews – had died (I liked to think) fighting just the kind of prejudice he had displayed. Prompt with righteousness, I posted the letter on my way to the *Aeneid*, book four, in R.C. Fletcher's edition, the next morning (the letter box was by the Porter's Lodge).

A few days later, I was summoned to see the Headmaster. I walked up to Saunderites that evening dry with apprehension, but I failed to guess why George Turner might want to see me.

G.C.T. was sitting at his desk, with a green-shaded lamp shining on a piece of blue writing paper with an embossed address at the top. He removed it to reveal the letter I had written to the Provost of Guildford.

'Did you write this letter?'

'It looks very like it.' My tone was nervous, but cold. How could one respect a man who could not do Caesar's *De Bello Gallico* without using a crib?

'To a guest of the school.'

'I'm sorry?'

'The Provost was a guest of the school and you have seen fit to insult him.'

'I have seen fit to point out that he said something he shouldn't have said. Or do you think he should? Sir.'

I was trying to remain as calm – and as smoothly spoken – as righteousness and tactics warranted, but I was already choked.

'I am not going to be drawn into that. It's a question of manners.'

'Were the gas chambers a matter of manners? Sir.'

'I advise you to be very careful, Raphael.'

I stood there. I looked at him. Silence too can be eloquent. I had learned as much from Sir Patrick Hastings, whose forensic skills were advertised in *Sixty Famous Trials*, one of my favourite books. A good advocate knew when to sit down, and shut up.

Turner said: 'The Provost has authorised me to tell you that he would not have said the things he did say if he had known that there were any Jews in the chapel.'

I could feel tears in my throat. The ones I could not swallow bubbled out of my eyes and ran down my cheeks. Blast it.

'And ... how does that ... sound to you? Sir.'

'I consider it very generous of him. He also asks me not to punish you for writing as you did.'

'He's too generous, sir.'

'I want you to write and thank him.'

'Thank him.'

'And apologise.'

'For—?'

'Writing this impudent letter to a guest.'

'He wasn't my guest, sir.'

'I am trying to be tolerant, Raphael.'

'I can't do as you ask, sir. I can't apologise. Sorry.'

'What are your plans for university entrance, Raphael?'

'I want to go to Oxford, sir, obviously.'

'I see. And which college do you have in mind?'

'I was thinking of trying for the Holford Hewitt, sir, to Christ Church, next quarter. After my trial run at Cambridge.'

'Are you are aware that it is for me to recommend who shall be eligible to sit for the Holford Hewitt?'

'Do you think I'm ineligible, sir? That's not Mr Gibson's view, I don't think.'

'Eligibility is not a matter merely of being clever enough.'

'Don't Christ Church want clever people, sir? I didn't realise.'

'It's also a matter of character. And the decision lies wholly in my hands. I want you to write to the Provost and I want you to come and tell me that you have done so.'

'I shan't be able to do that, sir.'

I wish that my tone had been as resolute as the truish words which, in Thucydidean style, I have attributed to myself. They are not false to what I said, but they were pronounced in a strangled voice. I was once again the little boy who, out of breath and with solid lungs, tried to read his 'bit' to the Copthorne assembly. How could George Turner not have the grace even to be embarrassed? I was, I realised, incurably alien. Despite all my schooled efforts at conformity of accent and culture, as far as the Headmaster was concerned I was the embarrassment.

I should not be surprised to have to report that, in the end, I did sit down and write an apology to the Provost of Guildford, so close were duty and servility in the public-school ethos. In fact, however, I did not write. Had I done so, would I have been allowed to sit for the Holford Hewitt? Even if I had, I have little doubt that the Headmaster's confidential report would have sunk my chances, just as I still believe that that interview with Dr Spencer Leeson resulted in my being relegated from Winchester. Who knows?

The Drill Competition took place in the middle of the quarter. The Lockites House Platoon was shit-hot. They stamped together; sloped arms together, saluted together; turned on the march together, dis-missed together with a snap and steadiness worthy of the Buffs (my father's old regiment). When the results were posted, we were equal first with Robinites, who were commanded by a total corps-fiend called David Vansittart, who later, I believe, became a Guards officer. My reaction was childishly triumphant. I went into outside 'bogs' in Lockites with one of the platoon's .303s and fired a blank round. In most eyes, I had won brief glory for the House; in my own, it had been a triumph against it.

As a result of our success, I was promoted to Under Officer. There was no giddier eminence for a boy soldier. I was entitled to wear officer's uniform, including a Sam Browne, but with light blue ribbon instead of pips. I could wear brown shoes, if I wanted to, on Corps days. Only straight-nosed, fair-haired, blue-eyed Vansittart and I bore so high a rank; we were chalk and cheese in the same martial wrapping. I carried my leather-covered swagger stick with a new, casual aplomb. Quite often Magger Mo took me on tours of inspection in his open MG with the bulbous horn. When I first arrived at Lockites, I could have imagined no less likely distinction for myself, but there I was: the Napoleon of Godalming Hill.

Cambridge in early December 1949 was damp and glumly cold. A trio of Carthusians was given a room in the Wedding Cake in St John's. None of the others was a Classicist. The room had no fire that I can remember (though it did have a fireplace) and there was, of course, no bathroom. You had to go down the stairs to wash or pee. I cannot remember doing much of either. Cambridge was not a place where I had any intention of staying for long. Ivor Gibson had chosen to enter me for St John's because, he told me, it was the kind of college where I might achieve something. Simpson, D.A.J., had gone to King's, which was, Gibbo thought, a little fancy for me.

I walked each morning, through gritty snow, to Emmanuel, where my group was being examined. There was a sweet irony in having to go to Emmanuel to take my papers. It was widely known (though I cannot say how I came to hear of it) that the Master was an evangelical anti-Semite. Perhaps Gibson had known of this when he made Emmanuel my penultimate choice; I should certainly be its last. There were six hundred candidates for the two Classical major scholarships which St John's was offering. Since that college was my number one choice, it was unlikely that any other would want me, if it did not.

The first paper was Latin prose, my favourite composition. I was keen, but not nervous: this was not, to my mind, the real thing. That would be Oxford. I worked fast and then I checked and, remembering Gibson's reports, checked again. Did all the adjectives agree? Were the genders right? Had I observed the sequence of tenses and used the subjunctive everywhere that I should? Had I finished each sentence with one of the accepted Ciceronian clausulae, of which 'esse *videatur*' was the most obvious example (not to be used more than once)?

I came out of my first three hours with high, almost smug, confidence. A conviction that I had got off to a good start sustained me through the week. I was like a decathlete who had scored well in his best event. When it came to the Greek unseen, I consoled myself that no one could translate Pindar without making a few wild guesses. The only paper I approached in a state of armed anxiety was the general paper: if there was no question about art (it hardly mattered how it was phrased), I should lose my inside track.

We filed into Emmanuel's big hall and turned over our papers. You had to write an essay on just one of a number of curt subjects. I scanned the list and there it was: 'Art and its relation to Life'. While others dithered, I began to write. As soon as I had written the epigraph, '"Art is one of the four things that unite men" – Turgenev', I was certain that I was saved. Had I been asked who Turgenev was, or where he said this, I should have been unable to answer, but who was to know that? My essay was long and bristled with names, from Hokusai to Picasso, from Malraux to Willenski (an aesthetician, famous in those days, who claimed that architecture was central to the visual arts). I did not omit to hazard the view that the fluting on Greek columns was a formalisation of the skirts on archaic statues and I cited the caryatids on the Erechtheum as corroboration, though not 'the Uncle' as the source of my opinion. I remarked fluently on the collaboration between art and commerce in Renaissance Italy and, beside the Medicis and Venice, I dwelt idiosyncratically on the harmonious contention of the tower-builders of San Gimignano. Pretentiousness and genuine interest, bluff and a degree of knowledge filled page after page with the proof of a precociousness which was all the sweeter since, except for the bits I lifted from A.L. Irvine's art lectures, it owed nothing to Charterhouse. As for my Latin and Greek, I had learned a good deal from the Arrow and from Ivor Gibson, but I had not risen all that much higher than the foundations laid by Ernest 'Skete' Workman.

Since St John's was my first choice of college, my only interview was with the Senior Tutor, R.L. 'Bede' Howland. He was a renowned sportsman, who had played soccer for Shrewsbury and put the weight, I think, for the university. He was cheerful and intellectually incurious. If he had seen my quotation from Turgenev, he showed no interest in its provenance. We got on very well. He did not ask me if I went to chapel.

I left Cambridge in the snow. Standing on the famous long platform, waiting for the London train, I assumed that, with any luck, I should never return. The Oxford scholarships took place in the spring. Was I good enough for bloody Balliol?

I went home to Manor Fields before catching a train back to Godalming. A couple of weeks of school had still to be served. I had no certainty that I had done well, but I had the nerve to put on my zippered American trousers, and a colourful Fair Isle sweater, before heading for Waterloo. My bold wardrobe announced that I no longer cared what Charterhouse, or Carthusians, thought of me. Flash? You bet.

Did HAM wish me well when I shook hands with him for what was to be, in point of fact, the last time? I was not yet sure that I should not be returning for the Long Quarter 1950. If it turned out that I had not achieved anything at Cambridge, I still had Oxford in prospect; and even if I had, Oxford was still an alluring destination. The fact that Robin Jordan had been made a School Monitor meant that, however high my military standing, I was unlikely to achieve equivalent civil distinction. I took it to be beyond question that HAM had deliberately advanced Robin above me, out of malice. Years later, I discovered, from Jeremy Atkinson I think, that HAM had in fact recommended me for that distinction but that George Turner, either out of spite or because of misreading, had preferred Jordan, J.F.R.. Since my departure was only provisionally final, I left Charterhouse by what Harry Iredale would have called 'la petite porte'. No one wished me well, and I wished no one well.

My results were due from Cambridge soon after the beginning of the holidays. Only those who had received awards would be notified, by telegram. I waited and I waited. As evening darkened the Manor Fields windows, so did it my mood. A day passed, and another. If I did not want to go to Cambridge, why was I so full of hope, and dread? To fail was to lose, and I did not like to lose.

One evening, when I had again waited anxiously all day, the front doorbell rang. There were still telegraph boys in those days, in blue uniforms and little caps. The telegram was in a yellow envelope. I told the boy to wait a minute and opened it, alone, in the kitchen. 'ELECTED MAJOR SCHOLARSHIP CONGRATULATIONS TUTOR ST JOHN'S COLLEGE CAMBRIDGE.'

I ran to find half-a-crack to tip the good messenger, obliged him, to his amazement, to down a tot of whisky, told him it was the best news I had ever had and allowed him to go. I then ran to telephone Ivor Gibson.

'I'm not *entirely* surprised,' he said.

'How do you think I'll do at Oxford, sir? In view of this.' Gibson was a racing man. He had disposed his horses on their various courses and his reward had been no less than five major Classical scholarships in our year (plus an Exhibition or two). He said, 'Are you sure you shouldn't take what you've been offered? You've been lucky this time. I can't promise you will be again.'

He spoke in his usual pipesmoker's way, with puffs between phrases. His words did not offend me. Nothing would have offended me that night. I agreed at once, and perhaps with relief (who knew if Turgenev would be any use to me at Oxford?). I said that I had decided not to return to school the following quarter. I wanted to do something else, more real, before I went up to Cambridge the following October. Part of that reality, though I did not declare it, was to find a way of lying, flesh on flesh and bone on bone, with Jinx Lehman.

Unable to resist a vindictive adieu to George Turner, I wrote him a letter saying, as dryly as triumphalism could manage, that since I had now won an open major scholarship to Cambridge, it was of no importance to me whether or not he considered me eligible for a (mere) closed scholarship to Oxford. My colours had turned pale blue in an instant. Robin Jordan was without a serious rival for the Holford Hewitt, which he won the following spring. Turner had the last word, however: alone of all the winners of major awards in my year, I was not given a 'leaving scholarship' with which to buy books for my university career. On the other hand, my name was inscribed on one of the boards in Lockites, which was preserved and transferred, when the old buildings were pulled down, and a new Lockites constructed, not far from where I did those twenty hours of penitential digging for HAM's baize-aproned gardener.*

A few weeks into 1950, I received a letter from Mr Howland, who would be my tutor, and director of studies, the following academic year. He informed me that my papers were fair to good, but that I needed to do a great deal of reading in the months to come. My Latin prose had been particularly disappointing. Had I known that at the time, should I have been able to approach the remaining papers with the same confidence?

---

*No frequent visitor to Goldaming, I saw the new Lockites (which even houses a few sixth-form girls!) when on a recce for a 1980s television film entitled *School Play*. My unnamed school was a metaphor for England itself: the boys never left their Alma Mater, but stayed on, emulous for 'haberdashery' all the way to senility. Denholm Elliott was masterly. The BBC has never repeated it.

In the event, I saw Jinx again only briefly, some months later, when she came on a cultural visit to England. She was in bed, with flu. I never even kissed her, except hello. As for Hilary Phillips, she was less excited than alarmed by my success. She was nineteen. Soon, she told me, she would be on the shelf. How could she possibly wait three years before she got married? I understood, sulkily, even though I swore that I should never get over it. She was engaged less than a year later.

Before Christmas, at a meeting of an amateur dramatic society, a tall, slim girl came in wearing a green mackintosh, with shining black hair and long legs and flat black shoes and a smile that made me ask her name. I cannot pretend that it was her intelligence which first attracted me, but I had at last got truly lucky: she was not only beautiful, but also a scholar in history at Westfield College, London. She was modest, and confident, enough not to think that scholarships mattered all that much, though she allowed mine to.

I am an American who sounds English, a New Yorker who has lived in London, off and on, for over sixty years, a Jew who has never read the Torah (though he owns a copy). I root for the US in the Olympics and for England at football and cricket. I wanted to go to Winchester and was sent to Charterhouse; I dreamed of Oxford, and was proud to go Cambridge. I thought I loved at least one of two girls, and fell in love with a third, who has made me as happy as a man can well be. Does life have an ordained pattern? I am at once the things I am and, under the skin, some of the things I turned out not to be. Byron once listed all the people (and objects, including 'alabaster lit from within') to whom he had been compared. He revelled in his multiplicity. I have no Byronic pretensions, but a writer of fiction is lucky to be the vessel of diversity; he must enjoy what he cannot avoid. Jew or (pseudo-) Gentile, Turk or Greek, American or English, Wykhamist or Carthusian, Cantab. or the other thing, what am I really? How different would I have been, if I had been different? Cavafy warned 'kainourious topous then tha vrees': there are no new places to be found, in which to remake your life. The small blessing for a writer is that he can come to a fork in the road and take it. In fiction we can be falsely true to all our possibilities. God bless America, God save the Queen, Shema Yisroel – what percentage of me says which, with how much innate passion?

Pascal once wrote of man, 'Whichever side he takes, I shall not leave him at rest. Does he exalt himself? I lay him low; does he humble himself? I exalt him and continue to contradict him until he comprehends that he is an incomprehensible monstrosity.' Or, as the Americans sometimes say, when you serve first an unreturnable ace and then a double fault, 'Same guy!'